THE SAMARITAN PENTATEUCH

Society of Biblical Literature

Resources for Biblical Study

Tom Thatcher, New Testament Editor

Number 72

THE SAMARITAN PENTATEUCH
An Introduction to Its Origin, History,
and Significance for Biblical Studies

THE SAMARITAN PENTATEUCH

AN INTRODUCTION TO ITS ORIGIN, HISTORY, AND SIGNIFICANCE FOR BIBLICAL STUDIES

by
Robert T. Anderson
and
Terry Giles

Society of Biblical Literature
Atlanta

THE SAMARITAN PENTATEUCH
An Introduction to Its Origin, History,
and Significance for Biblical Studies

Library of Congress Control Number: 2012951581

Printed on acid-free, recycled paper conforming to
ANSI/NISO Z39.48-1992 (R1997) and ISO 9706:1994
standards for paper permanence.

Contents

Abbreviations

AB	Anchor Bible
ABD	*The Anchor Bible Dictionary*. Edited by David Noel Freedman. 6 vols. New York: Doubleday, 1992.
AnBib	Analecta biblica
ANYAS	Annals of the New York Academy of Sciences
BA	*Biblical Archeologist*
BASOR	*Bulletin of the American Schools of Oriental Research*
BCH	*Bulletin de Correspondance Hellénique*
BHS	*Biblia Hebraica Stuttgartensia*
BJRL	*Bulletin of the John Rylands University Library of Manchester*
BZAW	Beihefte zur Zeitschrift für die alttestamentliche Wissenschaft
CBQ	*Catholic Biblical Quarterly*
CSBS	Canadian Society of Biblical Studies
DJD	Discoveries in the Judean Desert
DSD	*Dead Sea Discoveries*
EncJud	*Encyclopaedia Judaica*. 2nd ed. 22 vols. New York: Macmillan, 2006.
FRLANT	Forschungen zur Religion und Literatur des Alten und Neuen Testaments
GAT	Grundrisse zum Alten Testament
Hen	*Henoch*
HSM	Harvard Semitic Monographs
HTR	*Harvard Theological Review*
HUCA	*Hebrew Union College Annual*
IEJ	*Israel Exploration Journal*
JAOS	*Journal of the American Oriental Society*
JBL	*Journal of Biblical Literature*
JJS	*Journal of Jewish Studies*
JQR	*Jewish Quarterly Review*
JSOT	*Journal for the Study of the Old Testament*
JSOTSup	Journal for the Study of the Old Testament Supplement Series
LUOSMS	Leeds University Oriental Society Monograph Series

MdB	Le Monde de la Bible
MGWJ	*Monatschrift für Geschichte und Wissenschaft des Judenthums*
NIDNTT	*New International Dictionary of New Testament Theology.* Edited by Colin Brown. 4 vols. Grand Rapids, 1975–1985.
NovT	*Novum Testamentum*
NTS	*New Testament Studies*
POTTS	Pittsburgh Original Texts and Translations Series
RB	*Revue Biblique*
RBL	*Review of Biblical Literature*
RevQ	*Revue de Qumran*
RTL	*Revue théologique de Louvain*
SAC	Spiro-Albright Correspondence
SBFCM	Studium Biblicum Franciscanum Collectio Maior
SBLSCS	Society of Biblical Literature Septuagint and Cognate Studies
SES	Sociétè d'Études Samaritaines
SHR	Studies in the History of Religions
SJLA	Studies in Judaism in Late Antiquity
SNTSMS	Society for New Testament Studies Monograph Series
StPB	Studia post-biblica
TSAJ	Texts and Studies in Ancient Judaism
TSK	*Theologische Studien und Kritiken*
VTSup	Supplements to Vetus Testamentum
WTJ	*Westminster Theological Journal*
WUNT	Wissenschaftliche Untersuchungen zum Neuen Testament
ZAW	*Zeitschrift für die Alttestamentliche Wissenschaft*

Credits

This book includes material incorporated from:

Benyamin Tsedaka and Sharon Sullivan, *The Israelite Version of the Torah: First English Translation Compared with the Masoretic Version*. Grand Rapids: Eerdmans, 2012.

Robert T. Anderson and Terry Giles, *Tradition Kept: An Introduction to the Literature of the Samaritans*. Grand Rapids: Baker, 2005.

Included material is used by permission.

Photographs courtesy of Special Collections, Michigan State University Libraries.

The authors would like to express appreciation to the college of Humanities, Education, and Social Sciences and especially the Department of Theology at Gannon University for a partial release from teaching duties extended to Terry Giles.

Introduction

The Samaritan Pentateuch (SP) is the sacred text of the Samaritan community. That community, made famous to the West in the New Testament stories of the "good Samaritan" and the "woman at the well," is of ancient origin, yet it persists to this day. Throughout its long history, the Samaritan community has always recognized as sacred only the first five books of the Hebrew Bible, the Pentateuch, but in a version quite distinct from the other two better known ancient versions of the Hebrew Bible: the Masoretic Text (MT) and the Septuagint (LXX). The SP shows its distinctiveness most noticeably through a number of scattered readings supporting the Samaritan insistence that worship be conducted on Mount Gerizim, recognized as God's chosen site instead of Mount Zion in Jerusalem. Mount Gerizim is also venerated in the SP by means of a unique rendition of the Decalogue, giving validation to worship on this sacred mount no less authority than God's own words. Less noticeably, the SP is differentiated from the MT and LXX by resisting an anthropomorphic representation of God, emphasizing the role of Moses, and preserving harmonistic editorial practices that, thanks to the witness from the scrolls recovered near the Dead Sea, are now known to be commonplace in the Second Temple period.

Like the Samaritan community itself, the SP has experienced all the vagaries of a troubled history. At times respected and fought over by those who sought to own its influence, at times dismissed and forced to wander in exile from its homeland, and at times all but ignored, the SP has persevered as the Samaritans themselves have. Since the seventeenth century, the majority of Western biblical scholarship has assigned the SP to a supportive and often minor role in the text-critical investigation of the Hebrew Bible. That role is changing.

Today the SP is assuming a central role in the critical examination of the textual history of the Bible. We now know that the SP and its predecessors played a vibrant part in the stream of textual witnesses to the Pentateuch prior to the turn of the eras. Recently, a growing appreciation for the pluriformity of the sacred text tradition in the Second Temple period, an appreciation that has shifted entire paradigms of scholarly investigation, has placed the SP at the heart of text criticism and canon studies. At the beginning of the twenty-first century, the SP has been published parallel to the MT, critical editions have been reprinted, early manuscripts have been digitized, and an English translation has made the SP far more accessible than ever before. The time is right for a reintroduction.

The purpose of this volume is to synthesize current scholarship on the SP, and to present that synthesis in a fashion useful for nonspecialists. As a synthesis, this volume is deeply indebted to the work of many experts in the field. Especially over the last decade, Samaritan scholarship has burgeoned far beyond what can be summarized in the pages of this book. In crafting this survey, we have attempted to be accurate, fair, and inclusive, mindful that we are representing the work of our colleagues to a wider audience. Any exclusions or misrepresentations are unintentional. Further, given the recent accessibility to new archaeological and textual data, it is not surprising that scholarly opinions concerning the SP, its character, and its place in the text history of the biblical tradition have changed during the last decades of the twentieth and first decades of the twenty-first century. It isn't uncommon to find that a given researcher's earlier published conclusions have been modified or abandoned in later writings. In creating this volume, we have attempted to be mindful of the fluidity currently expressing itself in Samaritan studies.

The Samaritans canonized only the Pentateuch, the first five books of what most Jews and Christians accept from Hebrew tradition. These books (Genesis, Exodus, Leviticus, Numbers, and Deuteronomy), known to both Samaritans and Jews by the first Hebrew word of each book, are second only to God in the basic affirmations of the Samaritan creed. The words of these books defined the location of the Samaritan holy place and the services performed there, and established the qualifications for the priesthood and its hierarchy. The task of their interpretation is the major source of priestly status. The SP is read and revered in all services of Samaritan worship. Its words are carved in stone to decorate and protect synagogues, and are carefully copied by hand on parchment or quality paper to be passed down from one generation to the next.

The SP has been in meaningful, sometimes accidental and sometimes deliberate, dialogue with the MT and LXX texts of the Pentateuch. The reintroduction of the SP to Europe in the seventeenth century immediately placed the SP in the midst of a religious controversy that would last nearly two hundred years. This controversy cast the SP into a support role, propping up either the LXX or the MT reading. As that controversy waned, so did interest in the SP—at least for a time. All that is now changing and the SP is once again moving toward center stage in text-critical discussions of both the Hebrew Bible and the Christian New Testament. The last several decades have witnessed the publication of new materials from Qumran, extensive archaeological excavations at Gerizim, and historical enquiry into the Hasmonean and Herodian periods, all vectoring together to shine a spotlight on the formative influence exerted by the SP textual tradition and the Samaritan religious community on the text history of the Hebrew Bible and the early history of the Jesus movement. The present volume is focused on the origin, history, and significance of the revered text of the SP within both the Samaritan community and the communities it has touched: early Christianity, Judaism, Islam, and the community of scholars who have been attracted to it.

Plan of This Book

This book follows a primarily chronological outline, tracing the history of the SP from its origins to its most recent translations. Chapter 1 surveys three stories of the origins of Samaritanism, establishing what can be known of the early Samaritan community and the common pentateuchal traditions of the Second Temple period. The SP textual tradition is placed within the context of origins reaching back to the late Second Temple period.

In chapter 2, we turn our attention to the Qumran scrolls. The materials from Qumran give us a window into the literary milieu of late Second Temple period Palestine. The Qumran scrolls point us toward the recognition of a pluriform Hebrew Bible, revealing scribal practices that blur the modern boundary between composition and exegesis. This pluriform scriptural tradition provides the seedbed from which the SP would grow.

Chapter 3 considers the specific Qumran materials that are most closely linked to the SP. We look at these materials for what they may tell us about the prehistory of the SP. Labeled "pre-Samaritan," this collection of Qumran materials shares certain harmonizations and interpolations that will come to characterize the SP.

Chapter 4 examines the movement from the pre-Samaritan text to the SP by the addition of a sectarian editorial layer. The pre-Samaritan text participated in a common literary milieu with the proto-MT, LXX, and various unaligned texts also evident at Qumran. The sectarian adoption of the pre-Samaritan text parallels similar textual preferences by other religious groups between the first century B.C.E. and the first century C.E.

Chapter 5 examines the textual characteristics of the SP. There are several significant differences between the SP, MT, and LXX and many minor differences. This begs the question of the extent to which the SP is an independent source and whether, and how, it is related to either the proto-MT or the LXX (or its Hebrew *Vorlage*). Evidence from the DSS has contributed to this conversation and has enabled a more nuanced approach to the comparison of text families, including a sectarian recension of the pre-Samaritan text. Particular attention is given to a number of interpolations characteristic of the SP, especially in the Decalogue of Exod 20.

The presence of the SP and its advocates is felt in emerging sectarianism among Jews, Samaritans, and Christians. It is quite noticeable in the text and narrative of the New Testament, a phenomena that is explored in chapter 6. More enthusiastic scholars have sometimes overstated the case, finding a Samaritan behind every olive tree in the New Testament.[1] Most New Testament research, however, falls on the opposite end of the spectrum so that, despite decades of significant scholarship, the likely influence and presence of Samaritan interests in the New Testament still have very low visibility. As will be seen, Samaritan culture was in the midst of the northern Palestinian milieu that produced the Q source and the Gospels of Mark and John. The religious ideas that flowed between the various sects of Gnosticism, Judaism, and Christianity moved with the Jews who travelled the roads of Samaria and the Samaritans who travelled the roads of Judea. Samaritans were an intentional target of sectarian missions, including those of both Hellenistic and Apostolic Christians. Samaritans make important appearances in the New Testament stories. New Testament writers had Samaritans in their field of vision as they composed their works and may have made use of readings from the SP.

Chapter 7 highlights the most revered copy of the SP currently in existence, the Abisha Scroll. Evidence from this scroll, additional significant artifacts (scroll cases, amulets, and stone inscriptions) bearing pentateuchal inscriptions, and scribal traditions are used to trace the history

1. Most notable is Heinrich Hammer's *Traktat vom Samaritanermessianias: Studien zur Frage der Existenz und Abstammung Jesu* (Bonn: Georgi, 1913). In Hammer's view, Jesus himself was a Samaritan.

of the SP through the first millennium, in many ways a hidden era in SP studies. This chapter describes centers of scribal production as well as the prominent scribal families responsible for the continuation of the SP tradition into the second millennium.

Chapter 8 describes the impact of the SP when it first became available to Western scholars. M. H. Goshen-Gottstein has said that the mid-seventeenth century was the first watershed in the history of textual criticism.[2] This flurry of interest, reflecting larger Catholic/Protestant theological tensions, was fueled by the arrival of the SP in Europe. Each side hoped that the SP would prove whether the LXX (preferred by Roman Catholics) or the MT (preferred by Protestants) offered the more original text of the Old Testament. As we will see, scholars in subsequent centuries have developed less heated and more sophisticated ways of considering the evidence.

Chapter 9 follows the SP as it survived through the centuries by adopting and adapting the common language of its various places of residence, both at Mount Gerizim and in the Samaritan diaspora. When Aramaic replaced Hebrew as the spoken language among Jews and Samaritans, each developed an Aramaic paraphrase of their Scriptures. The Samaritan Aramaic Targum was adapted differently in different chronological periods, influenced by factors like the sophistication of individual scribes, the influence of Arabic, and theological currents. A Greek translation, the *Samareitikon*, referenced by several of the church fathers (particularly Origen), may have been a translation of the Targum. It raises the issue of the existence of a Greek translation of the SP. In the Middle Ages an Arabic SP evolved. More recently, interest in the SP has grown, and it has been published in various editions, at times parallel to the MT and most recently in parallel English translations.

An appendix with a survey of modern tools and translations that may assist the interested SP student, followed by a bibliography, concludes the book.

---

2. Moshe H. Goshen-Gottstein, "The Textual Criticism of the Old Testament: Rise, Decline, and Rebirth," *JBL* 102 (1983): 372.

1
Stories of Samaritan Origins

The SP is the sacred text and ideological core of the Samaritan religious community. That community and this text are so intertwined that it is almost impossible to think of one apart from the other.[1] Consequently, our investigation into the origins of the SP will necessarily find its context in the origins of the Samaritan religious community. Historical inquiry, archaeological excavation, and detailed textual investigation of the Qumran materials during the last decades of the twentieth century and the first decade of the twenty-first century call for a reassessment of presumed conclusions about the origin of the Samaritans and their sacred text. In broad strokes, there are three competing narratives concerning the origin of the Samaritan religious community: that of the Samaritan community itself; that of the ancient Judean community, now encoded in the Hebrew Bible particularly interpreted through the writings of Josephus; and that advanced by modern critical scholars.

The Samaritan Story

The Samaritan version of the community's origin, and of the origin of the SP, is recorded in several chronicles produced by the community and, with

1. See Reinhard Pummer, "Samaritanism—A Jewish Sect or an Independent Form of Yahwism?" in *Samaritans: Past and Present* (ed. Menachem Mor and Friedrich Reiterer in collaboration with Waltraud Winkler; Studia Samaritana 5; Berlin: de Gruyter, 2010), 1–24. Also see József Zsengellér, "Origin or Originality of the Torah? The Historical and Textcritical Value of the Samaritan Pentateuch," in *From Qumran to Aleppo: A Discussion with Emanuel Tov about the Textual History of Jewish Scriptures in Honor of His 65th Birthday* (ed. Armin Lange et al.; FRLANT 230; Göttingen: Vandenhoeck & Ruprecht, 2009), 189–202.

some modifications, recounted by K. Lincke.[2] According to the Samaritan version, the Samaritan community represents the pure Israel, from which other factions later broke off.[3] In like fashion, the Mosaic Torah preserved by the Samaritans is considered the genuine version, while the text favored by the majority of Judaism is viewed as a product of the heresy of Eli, Samuel's mentor and guardian, promoted by the false cult centered in Jerusalem, and later extended further by the deceptive work of Ezra. The story can be found in *Kitab Al-Tarikh*.

> Now, he (Eli) had two sons, Hophne and Phinehas, who rounded up young women of attractive appearance and brought them into the Tabernacle that had been built up by their father. They let them savor the food of the sacrifices, and had intercourse with them inside the Tabernacle. At the same time the children of Israel became three factions: a (loyal) faction on Mount Gerizim; a heretical faction that followed false gods; and the faction that followed Eli son of Yahni in Shilo.[4]

> Samuel went down to Shilo, he and his disciples with him, and continued sacrificing and making offerings wherever he saw fit. He changed the name of God Powerful and Glorious, went to Sufin, and built an altar for himself there, and offered sacrifices upon it. When he grew older, his disciples said to him, "Put a king over us!" So he took Saul son of Kish from the tribe of Benjamin and made him (their) king.[5]

> The book of the Torah was the same for both groups, and they did not disagree over the Hebrew script.[6]

The Samaritan Chronicle II is aware of the השמרנים (Samarians) label and explains its application to the Samaritans:

2. Karl F. Lincke, *Samaria und seine Propheten* (Tübingen: Mohr Siebeck, 1903). See also Moses Gaster, *The Samaritans, Their History, Doctrines, and Literature* (London: Oxford University Press, 1925).

3. Israel Tsedaka, "Mount Gerizim and Jerusalem," *Proceedings of the Fifth International Congress of the Sociétè d'Études Samaritaines, Helsinki, August 1–4,* 2000 (ed. Haseeb Shehadeh and Habib Tawa with the collaboration of Reinhard Pummer; Paris: Geuthner, 2005), 21–26.

4. Robert Anderson and Terry Giles, *Tradition Kept: The Literature of the Samaritans* (Peabody, Mass.: Hendrickson, 2005), 154.

5. Ibid., 156.

6. Ibid., 157.

> In the days of Omri a man of the community of the Samaritan Israelites, of the tribe of Ephraim the son of Joseph, went and bought Samaria from Shemer for two talents of silver; and he fortified the city and called its name after the name of Shemer; the owner of the hill of Samaria. It had previously been a fortress belonging to the community of Jeroboam the son of Nebat, which the Ammonites had disposed them of and had demolished.
>
> Now this noble man went and bought it and afterwards he began rebuilding it. So he and his people, the descendants of Ephraim the son of Joseph, inhabited it and all the cities which lay round about it. They called its name and the name of the cities which lay round about it Har Shomron. The Israelites who dwell in these cities were named Shomronim after the name Shomron and its cities.[7]

Etienne Nodet represents a segment of historical-critical scholarship lending support to the central thesis of ancient Samaritan origins favored by the traditional Samaritan community. While he does not appeal to events concerning Eli or Shemer or some of the other ancient details filling the Samaritan version of origins, Nodet does suggest that the community has its roots in the distant past among northerners who were not exiled by the Babylonians and who constitute the original Israelites.[8] He concludes, "If anything, the returnees [those coming from Babylon represented by Ezra and Nehemiah] created the split or the separation by not cooperating with the people of the land. The former developed into the Jews of Jerusalem and elements of the latter eventually became the Jews of Samaria, better known as the Samaritans."[9] Nodet finds the early Samaritans related

---

7. Ibid., 247.

8. Etienne Nodet (*A Search for the Origins of Judaism: From Joshua to the Mishnah* [trans. Ed Cowley; JSOTSup 248; Sheffield: Sheffield Academic Press, 1997], 200) maintains that the Samaritan Chronicles, although certainly layered with late additions, "call for a careful examination, since they should contain elements to counterbalance the bias of Judaean historiography."

9. Ibid., 370. Nodet likewise maintains that "because of its content, the most likely possibility is that the book of Joshua came from the Samaritans to the Jews, and not vice versa" (195). More recently Nodet has argued that "the Samaritans of Shechem are the heirs of the early Israelites, and not a downgraded Jewish sect as old Judean traditions and many modern scholars claim" ("Israelites, Samaritans, Temples, Jews," in *Samaria, Samarians, Samaritans: Studies on Bible, History and Linguistics* [ed. József Zsengellér; Berlin: de Gruyter, 2011], 121).

to a Yahweh cult centered in Shechem (at times referred to as "Bethel"), strongly tied to Jacob and Aaron traditions, and eventually, but no later than the mid-fourth century B.C.E., transferred to nearby Gerizim.[10]

Nodet claims support for his reconstruction from a Qumran fragment of Deut 27:4b–6 published by James Charlesworth.[11] The fragment, dated to the late Hasmonean period, identifies "Mount Gerizim" (הרגרזים) as the site on which to build an altar. It is considered by Charlesworth to have preserved the original reading of Deut 27:4. Consequently, the tradition represented in the MT, which locates the altar on Mount Ebal, is considered the variant tradition. Charlesworth suggests that the fragment is earlier than the SP and that "most likely the Samaritans followed an old reading that originated in the north and is Samarian (not Samaritan)."[12]

Similarly, Nodet maintains that the "law of Moses," minus the weekly Sabbath commandment, first appeared in Samaria "at Shechem, in connection with Gerizim and its priesthood," and was committed to writing sometime between 250 and 200 B.C.E.[13] Interaction with the returning Babylonian exiles resulted in some shared customs (such as the weekly Sabbath) and considerable literary activity between the Shechemites and the Jerusalemites, including a shared Pentateuch.[14] Inevitably, tensions arose between the two groups over the Jerusalemites' insistence that they and they alone were heirs of "all Israel." These tensions were expressed in competing claims to a legitimate priesthood and a gradual marginalization of the Shechemites concurrent with the ascendency of Jerusalemite Judaism.[15]

---

10. Lawrence Schiffman (*Qumran and Jerusalem: Studies in the Dead Sea Scrolls and the History of Judaism* [Grand Rapids: Eerdmans, 2010], 193) seems to be in general agreement with Nodet's early dating for the Samaritans. He says, "We see Samaritanism as beginning in the biblical period, before the canonization of the Prophets and Writings," and "we can expect that some rules derived in Ezra and Nehemiah from earlier Prophetic writings, for example, those pertaining to Sabbath observance, may not have been accepted by the Samaritans for whom the Prophets were not part of the canon."

11. James Charlesworth, "What Is a Variant? Announcing a Dead Sea Scrolls Fragment of Deuteronomy"; online: www.IJCO.org/?category ID=46960.

12. Ibid.

13. Nodet, *Search for the Origins of Judaism*, 191.

14. Ibid., 191–95.

15. Nodet's thesis, while generating a fair amount of discussion, has not won broad scholarly support. See Jean-Claude Haelewyck, "Les origins du Judaisme: A

The Judean Story

It has become common for interested readers to turn to 2 Kgs 17 for an account of Samaritan origins. This version of the story traces the community back to forced immigrants from Mesopotamia, who eventually adopted a heretical form of Yahwism. Many English translations identify the "Samaritans" as the subject of the story in verse 29, and it is not uncommon to find this identification reinforced in textbooks for Old Testament survey courses.[16] Closer inspection, however, reveals that the שמרנים of 2 Kgs 17:29 are not the "Samaritans" at all but rather the "people of Samaria," whose relationship to the Samaritan religious group (שמרים) is not clear.[17] In fact, as Louis Feldman notes, "Even in Josephus, we cannot always be sure that the word translated 'Samaritans' may not refer to Samarians, that is, the inhabitants, not necessarily Samaritans, of Samaria."[18] Feldman's observation is significant simply because Josephus's

---

propos de l'essai de E. Nodet," *RTL* 23 (1992): 472–81; and Reinhard Pummer, "The Samaritans and Their Pentateuch," in *The Pentateuch as Torah: New Models for Understanding Its Promulgation and Acceptance* (ed. Gary Knoppers and Bernard Levinson; Winona Lake, Ind.: Eisenbrauns, 2007), 248–49.

16. For example: John Bright, *A History of Israel* (3rd ed.; Philadelphia: Westminster, 1981), 276; Roger Beckwith, *The Old Testament Canon of the New Testament Church* (Grand Rapids: Eerdmans, 1985), 129; John Collins, *An Introduction to the Hebrew Bible* (Minneapolis: Fortress, 2004), 272; John Walton and Andrew Hill, *Old Testament Today* (Grand Rapids: Zondervan, 2004), 242; Michael Coogan, *The Old Testament: A Historical and Literary Introduction to the Hebrew Scriptures* (New York: Oxford University Press, 2006), 450; Steven Harris, *Understanding the Bible* (Mountain View, Calif.: Mayfield, 2000), 179–80; Lee Martin McDonald, *Forgotten Scriptures: The Selection and Rejection of Early Religious Writings* (Louisville: Westminster John Knox, 2009), 75–76; and even the footnotes of English Bible translations: *New Revised Standard Version* (Oxford: Oxford University Press, 1991), 489; *New International Version, Study Bible* (Grand Rapids: Zondervan, 1995), 552. More recently, Karel van der Toorn (*Scribal Culture and the Making of the Hebrew Bible* [Cambridge: Harvard University Press, 2007], 361–62 n. 60) seems to posit the mid-fourth century B.C.E. for a "definitive schism" between the Jews and Samaritans.

17. Regarding the structure of 2 Kgs 17:24–40, see Gary Knoppers, "Cutheans or Children of Jacob?" in *Reflection and Refraction: Studies in Biblical Historiography in Honour of A. Graeme Auld* (ed. Robert Rezetko et al.; Leiden: Brill, 2007), 223–39. See also J. A. Montgomery, *The Samaritans, the Earliest Jewish Sect: Their History, Theology, and Literature* (Philadelphia: John C. Winston, 1907; repr., New York: Ktav, 1968); and Louis Feldman, *Studies in Hellenistic Judaism* (Leiden: Brill, 1996), 115.

18. Ibid., 116.

paraphrase of 2 Kgs 17 (*A.J.* 9.288–291) has influenced the widespread perception that the Kings author is referring to the Samaritans. In describing the plight of deportees in the region of Samaria, Josephus says that they are "called in the Hebrew tongue Cutheans; but in the Greek Samaritans." Josephus goes on to describe this group in overtly negative terms:

> And when they see the Jews in prosperity, they pretend that they are changed, and allied with them, and they call them kinsmen, as though they were derived from Joseph, and had by that means an original alliance with them: but when they see them falling into a low condition, they say they are no way related to them, and that the Jews have no right to expect any kindness or marks of kindred from them, but they declare that they are sojourners that come from other countries. (*A.J.* 9.291)

Having posited a connection between the "Cutheans" and the Samaritans,[19] Josephus describes, in a somewhat inconsistent manner, conflict between the Jews and the Samaritans, who are "evil and enviously disposed to the Jews," during the time of Darius (*A.J.* 11.84–119) and a reaffirmation of the schism during the reign of Antiochus IV "Ephiphanes":

> When the Samaritans saw the Jews under these sufferings, they no longer confessed they were of their kindred, nor that the temple on Mount Gerizim belonged to Almighty God.... And they now said that they were a colony of Medes and Persians: and indeed they were a colony of theirs. (*A.J.* 12.257)

Josephus also acknowledges the existence of a Samaritan temple on Mount Gerizim, placing its construction in the Hellenistic Period (*A.J.* 11.340–347).[20] Not surprisingly, Josephus does not include the Samaritans in his various listings of the Jewish "sects," thus indicating that he viewed the Samaritans as a separate nation and not as a branch of Judaism.[21]

---

19. József Zsengellér, "Kutim or Samarites: A History of the Designation of the Samaritans," in Shehadeh and Tawa, *Proceedings of the Fifth International Congress*, 87–104. See also Knoppers, "Cutheans or Children of Jacob," 226–27.

20. As Joseph Blenkinsopp notes, Josephus's claim here "is justifiably considered suspect" ("The Development of Jewish Sectarianism from Nehemiah to the Hasidim," in *Judah and the Judeans in the Fourth Century B.C.E.* [ed. Oded Lipschits et al.; Winona Lake, Ind.: Eisenbrauns, 2007], 385).

21. Feldman, *Studies in Hellenistic Judaism*, 117.

The obviously polemical character of Josephus's narrative, giving vent to social realities of the late first century C.E., warns against accepting his account of Samaritan origins as historically accurate in all its detail.[22] Feldman, summarizing his assessment of Josephus's presentation, concludes that "the separation of the Jews and the Samaritans, like that of the Jews and the Christians, was not sudden but took place over a considerable period of time."[23] Likewise, recent observations concerning the redactional history of 2 Kgs 17 remind us that this text too has a point to make beyond simple historical reporting, and therefore cannot simply be taken at face value in attempting to pinpoint the origin of the Samaritan community.[24] Knoppers, commenting on 2 Kgs 17:34b–40, concludes that "the text assumes ethnic continuity, rather than discontinuity, in the postexilic population of Samaria." József Zsengellér similarly asserts that the Assyrian deportations "did not produce defined effects on the formation of the religion and society of this [Samaritan] community."[25]

The Scholars' Story

Recognizing the tendentious and inconsistent nature of the accounts provided by Josephus and the problems associated with 2 Kgs 17, modern Samaritan scholarship has struggled to reconstruct a narrative of origins that fairly considers all the evidence (and lack of evidence).[26] As Rein-

---

22. See Lester Grabbe, "Pinholes or Pinheads in the Camera Obscura? The Task of Writing a History of Persian Period Yahud," in *Recenti tendenze nella ricostruzione della storia antica d'Israele: convegno internazionale; Rome, 6–7 marzo 2003* (Rome: Accademia nazionale dei Lincei, 2005), 157–82; Ingrid Hjelm, "Samaria, Samaritans and the Composition of the Hebrew Bible," in Mor and Reiterer, *Samaritans: Past and Present*, 94; Magnar Kartveit, "Josephus on the Samaritans—His *Tendenz* and Purpose," in Zsengellér, *Samaria, Samarians, Samaritans*, 109–20.

23. Feldman, *Studies in Hellenistic Judaism*, 136.

24. Knoppers, "Cutheans or Children of Jacob," 223–39.

25. Ibid., 226; József Zsengellér, "Canon and the Samaritans," in *Canonization and Decanonization: Papers Presented to the International Conference of the Leiden Institute for the Study of Religions (LISOR), Held at Leiden, 9–10 January 1997* (ed. H. Kippenberg and E. Lawson; SHR 82; Leiden: Brill, 1998), 161.

26. See, e.g., Harold Henry Rowley, "The Samaritan Schism in Legend and History," in *Israel's Prophetic Heritage* (ed. B. W. Anderson and W. Harrelson; New York: Harper, 1962), 208–22. Rowley states emphatically, "It is time the Samaritan legend [Samaritan origins presented from 2 Kgs 17] disappeared from any factual account of the origin of the Samaritan schism" (222). See also Frederic Raurell, "The Notion

hard Pummer notes, modern scholars have concluded that "there was no schism between Samaritans and Jews in the fifth century B.C.E."[27] As recently as 2007, Bob Becking could lament, "The origins of Samaritanism are still hidden under the dust of the past."[28] Efforts to shake off the dust and uncover those origins have produced a number of proposed historical reconstructions, debated and refined throughout the twentieth century.

The following reconstruction of Samaritan origins has enjoyed broad scholarly support.[29]

> (1) The city of Shechem was rebuilt by nobles from Samaria after a failed rebellion against their Greek overlords. This group, transplanted by the Assyrians (2 Kgs 17), had a long history of antagonism toward Jerusalem, as reflected in Ezra-Nehemiah, and were viewed suspiciously by the Judeans in Jerusalem because of their

---

of History in the Hebrew Bible," in *Deuterocanonical and Cognate Literature Yearbook 2006: History and Identity: How Israel's Later Authors Viewed Its Earlier History* (ed. Nuria Calduch-Benages and Jan Liesen; Berlin: de Gruyter, 2006), 1–20; Ingrid Hjelm, *Jerusalem's Rise to Sovereignty: Zion and Gerizim in Competition* (JSOTSup 404; London: T&T Clark, 2004), 37–41.

27. Pummer, "Samaritans and Their Pentateuch," 257.

28. Bob Becking, "Do the Earliest Samaritan Inscriptions Already Indicate a Parting of the Ways?" in Lipschits et al., *Judah and the Judeans in the Fourth Century B.C.E.*, 213.

29. James Purvis, "The Samaritans and Judaism," in *Early Judaism and Its Modern Interpreters* (ed. Robert Kraft and George Nickelsburg; Atlanta: Scholars Press, 1986), 81–98; Frank Moore Cross, "Aspects of Samaritan and Jewish History in the Late Persian and Hellenistic Times," *HTR* 59 (1966): 201–11; Frank Moore Cross, *From Epic to Canon: History and Literature in Ancient Israel* (Baltimore: Johns Hopkins University Press, 1998), 174–75; G. Ernest Wright, *Shechem: Biography of a Biblical City* (New York: McGraw-Hill, 1965), 172–81. See also Hans Gerhard Kippenberg, *Garizim und Synagoge: Traditionsgeschichtliche Untersuchungen zur samaritanischen Religion der aramaischen Periode* (Berlin: de Gruyter, 1971), 74–81; Rainer Albertz, *Religionsgeschichte Israels in alttestamentlicher Zeit* (GAT 8; Göttingen: Vandenhoeck & Ruprecht, 1992), 580–81; Pieter van der Horst, *De Samaritanen: Geschiedenis en godsdienst van een vergeten groepering* (Serie Wegwijs; Kampen: Kok, 2004), 11–45; Jean-Daniel Macchi, *Les Samaritans: Histoire d'une legend: Israël et la province de Samarie* (MdB 30; Geneva: Labor et Fides, 1994), 27–29; Etienne Nodet, *Search for the Origins of Judaism*, 154–94; Nathan Schur, *History of the Samaritans* (Frankfurt: Lang, 1992), 35–43; József Zsengellér, *Gerizim as Israel: Northern Tradition of the Old Testament and the Early History of the Samaritans* (Utrechtse Theologische Reeks 38; Utrecht: Faculteit der Godgeleerdheid, 1998), 180–81.

mixed ethnic and religious origins. "The Samaritans [nomenclature now assigned to the immigrants at Shechem] who rebuilt Shechem were nevertheless attached to the Hebrew God, even if their ancestors had worshiped other gods."[30]

(2) While rebuilding Shechem, the Samaritans erected a sanctuary to YHWH on Gerizim, attaching themselves to ancient YHWH traditions much as Jeroboam had in establishing cult sites at Dan and Bethel (1 Kgs 12:26–29).

(3) The priesthood established by the Samaritans at Gerizim was independent of the Jerusalemite priesthood.

(4) Because the priesthood at Shechem was independent of Jerusalem, the temple at Gerizim should not be viewed initially as a schism from, rival to, or protest against the Jerusalem cult, but simply as a second site of worship within Judaism.

(5) Only when relationships deteriorated between the Seleucids and Ptolemies in the second century B.C.E. did a schism take place between the Jews and Samaritans, the Jews objecting to the Samaritans' submission to Antiochus IV. Tensions came to a boil under the Hasmonean king John Hyrcanus, resulting in the destruction of the temple on Gerizim in 128 B.C.E. and of Shechem in 107.[31]

(6) No later than the second century B.C.E., the Samaritans edited a version of the Pentateuch, claiming it to be the legitimate Pentateuch and rejecting the Judean literature (prophets and writings).[32]

---

30. Nodet, *Search for the Origins of Judaism*, 125.

31. Jarl Fossum ("Social and Institutional Conditions for Early Jewish and Christian Interpretation of the Hebrew Bible with Special Regard to Religious Groups and Sects," in *Hebrew Bible/Old Testament: The History of Its Interpretation* [ed. Magne Saebø; 2 vols.; Göttingen: Vandenhoeck & Ruprecht, 1996–2008], 1.1:244) considers the destruction of the Gerizim temple, which he dates to 129 B.C.E., as the critical moment of division: "From that time onwards we can talk about Samaritans and Jews."

32. Esther Eshel and Hanan Eshel ("Dating the Samaritan Pentateuch's Compilation in Light of the Qumran Biblical Scrolls," in *Emanuel: Studies in Hebrew Bible, Septuagint, and Dead Sea Scrolls in Honor of Emanuel Tov* [ed. Shalom Paul et al.; VTSup 94; Leiden: Brill, 2003], 240) support this conclusion by stating, "During the

> The competing textual versions finalized the schism between Jews and Samaritans.[33]

The above reconstruction locates the production of the SP in the second century B.C.E., making the text a culminating witness to the long-developing religious schism between Judaism and the Samaritans.[34] A second-century B.C.E. date for the final editing of the SP is supported by Esther and Hanan Eshel, who assert that "these sectarian additions were carried out prior to the destruction of the Samaritan temple on Mount Gerizim in 111 B.C.E."[35]

The historical reconstruction outlined above, while shared by many Samaritan scholars at the end of the twentieth century, must now be reexamined in light of new data, both archaeological and textual. Yitzhak Magen, director of the most recent archaeological excavations on Mount Gerizim, is convinced that "numerous discoveries from the sacred precinct substantiate the existence of a Temple to the Lord" on Mount Gerizim, the first phase of which dates to the Persian period.[36] The temple

---

second century B.C.E., Jewish harmonistic scrolls probably reached the Samaritans and the sectarian additions were made to the SP." Philip Davies (*Scribes and Schools: The Canonization of the Hebrew Scriptures* [Louisville: Westminster John Knox, 1998], 67) assumes the presence of the Samaritan Pentateuch in the Persian period.

33. Purvis, "Samaritans and Judaism," 87–89.

34. Magnar Kartveit (*The Origin of the Samaritans* [VTSup 128; Leiden: Brill, 2009], 351) is of the opinion that the cult site on Gerizim provides the distinguishing mark for the origin of the Samaritan community: "The moment of birth of the Samaritans was the construction of the temple on Mount Gerizim." He goes on to say, "A Samaritan identity must have developed long enough before the early second century B.C.E. to have spread into the diaspora." Therefore, "we may confidently assume that the temple was erected in the Persian age" (ibid., 353). The manner by which Kartveit identifies the beginning of the Samaritan community with the construction of a cult site on Gerizim only may not be sufficient. While it is certainly true that Samaritans worshiped at Gerizim, particularly in and following the Hellenistic age, all who worshiped at Gerizim may not have been Samaritan, particularly earlier than the Hellenistic age. If, as now appears probable, Deut 27:4 originally read "Gerizim" instead of "Ebal" in the pre-Samaritan texts, Gerizim is likely to have been visited by more than the Samaritan religious faithful.

35. Eshel and Eshel, "Dating the Samaritan Pentateuch's Compilation," 239.

36. Yitzhak Magen, "The Dating of the First Phase of the Samaritan Temple on Mount Gerizim in Light of the Archaeological Evidence," in Lipschits et al., *Judah and the Judeans in the Fourth Century B.C.E.*, 166. Bob Becking ("Earliest Samaritan

is evidenced by finely dressed ashlars, proto-Ionic and Aeolic capitals, a small gold bell, perhaps from the hem of a priestly garment, and numerous inscriptions (nearly four hundred dated from the fifth and fourth century B.C.E. through the medieval period), some referencing the "house of sacrifice," "the house of the Lord," [reconstructed] and "that which Joseph offered for his wife and his sons before the Lord in the temple."[37] Magen is convinced that the "long-standing debate concerning the beginnings of the Samaritan temple" on Mount Gerizim can be concluded with archaeological evidence, including carbon-14 examinations of bones and ashes, that "securely dates the construction of the first phase of the temple to the mid-fifth century B.C.E. and not to the late fourth century B.C.E.—the time of Alexander the Great—as was claimed by Josephus (and subsequently by later scholars)."[38]

Building on these data, Magen suggests the following historical outline for the temple on Mount Gerizim, from its construction in the fifth century B.C.E. to the destruction of the site in the late second century B.C.E.

> (1) Construction of the temple in the mid-fifth century B.C.E., perhaps by Sanballat the Horonite, who also established a priestly lineage at Mount Gerizim.[39]

Inscriptions," 215) is equally convinced that "archaeological excavations on Mount Gerizim have brought to light various structures that can only be interpreted as the remains of a temple to YHWH."

37. Magen, "Dating of the First Phase," 166–68. See also Ephraim Stern and Yitzhak Magen, "Archaeological Evidence for the First Stage of the Samaritan Temple on Mount Gerizim," *IEJ* 52 (2002): 49–57; and Yitzhak Magen, Haggai Misgav, and Levana Tsfania, *The Aramaic, Hebrew, and Samaritan Inscriptions* (vol. 1 of *Mount Gerizim Excavations*; Judea and Samaria Publications 2; Jerusalem: Israel Exploration Society, 2004).

38. Magen, "Dating of the First Phase," 176. Hanan Eshel has written in support of the fourth century date ("The Samaritan Temple at Mount Gerizim and Historical Research," *Beit Mikra* 39 [1994]: 141–55). Menahem Mor ("The Building of the Samaritan Temple and the Samaritan Governors—Again," in Zsengellér, *Samaria, Samarians, Samaritans*, 103) is of the opinion that the Samaritan temple, "whose founding is described by Josephus, was built in the interim between the fall of the Persian kingdom and the conquest of Eretz Israel by Alexander the Great."

39. Magen notes that there is no Iron Age settlement evidenced on Mount Gerizim ("Dating of the First Phase," 178). Kartveit agrees with Magen's assessment. He writes, "The moment of birth of the Samaritans was the construction of the temple

(2) The temple at Mount Gerizim grew in political and religious importance following the destruction of Samaria by Alexander the Great and the migration of Samarian leadership to Mount Gerizim. Mount Gerizim then became the "religious, national, economic, and political center of the Samaritans during the Ptolemaic period."[40]

(3) Continued use of the first phase of the temple until the late third century B.C.E., during the reign of Antiochus III.

(4) The second phase of the temple began with new construction during the reign of Antiochus III (ca. 200 B.C.E.). During this second phase, the temple was joined by a Hellenistic city to the south and west of the summit.[41]

(5) Both the city and temple were destroyed by John Hyrcanus I (111–110 B.C.E.).

Magen's findings suggest that there was an alternative worship site to Jerusalem on Mount Gerizim throughout the Second Temple period, and that this Gerizim temple, its officiates and devotees, and the residents of the nearby city were "Samaritan." Magen hints at the rationale for his use of the label "Samaritan" by noting an assumed correlation between the construction of the temple on Mount Gerizim and the split between Samaritans and Jews.[42]

Yet while the evidence for the existence of a temple on Mount Gerizim as early as the fifth century B.C.E. seems conclusive, it is not yet clear when a *Samarian* temple on Mount Gerizim (i.e., an Israelite temple in Samaria) became the *Samaritan* temple on Mount Gerizim (i.e., a temple

---

on Mount Gerizim," and "we may confidently assume the temple was erected in the Persian age" (*Origin of the Samaritans*, 351, 353).

40. Magen, "Dating of the First Phase," 182.

41. Ibid., 171–72. Mor ("Putting the Puzzle Together: Papyri, Inscriptions, Coins, and Josephus in Relation to Samaritan History in the Persian Period," in Shehadeh and Tawa, *Proceedings of the Fifth International Congress*, 54) is also convinced that the Samaritan temple was built "in the Interim between the fall of the Persian Empire and the conquest of Israel by Alexander the Great."

42. Magen, "Dating of the First Phase," 191. See also Becking, "Earliest Samaritan Inscriptions," 215.

frequented by and devoted to a specific Israelite religious sect).[43] While it is beyond doubt that Samaritans worshiped on Mount Gerizim in later centuries, it is not at all clear that, in the fifth and fourth centuries B.C.E., only Samaritans worshiped there.[44] Noting this problem, Bob Becking has suggested several possibilities for the religious use of the building: continuation of the northern Israelite rituals; proto-Jewish rituals comparable to contemporary cults in Jerusalem or Elephantine; or a proto-Samaritan cult.[45] These three alternatives are not mutually exclusive, and may have been indiscernible from one another at various time periods.

Like Magen, Knoppers has also suggested that newer evidence may necessitate a revision of the assumed north/south tensions that undergirded the previous scholarly consensus. "The archaeological and epigraphic remains suggest that major contacts between Yehud [Judea] and Samaria preceded the time of Nehemiah and continued after his term(s) of office ended. The Persian Period was an era of cultures in contact. For many residents of Yehud and Samaria, close relations between their two communities were a fact, not an issue."[46] Consequently, "viewing the Samaritans

---

43. The identification of a fifth-century temple as "Samaritan" is also followed by Lester Grabbe, "'Many Nations will be Joined to YHWH in That Day': The Question of YHWH Outside Judah," in *Religious Diversity in Ancient Israel and Judah* (ed. Francesca Stavrakopoulou and John Barton; London: T&T Clark, 2010), 182.

44. Hjelm ("Mount Gerizim and Samaritans in Recent Research," in Mor and Reiterer, *Samaritans: Past and Present,* 26) acknowledges the Samaritan occupation of a "very large temple in this place in the Hellenistic period" that "rested on foundations that had been enlarged to the east and the south in the early second century B.C.E. from a temple built no later than the mid-fifth century B.C.E." In a 2011 publication ("Samaritans: History and Tradition in Relationship to Jews, Christians and Muslims: Problems in Writing a Monograph," in Zsengellér, *Samaria, Samarians, Samaritans,* 179), Hjelm gives expression to the tendency to identify the Samarian temple on Gerizim as Samaritan. She writes, "The Samarian/Samaritan temple on Gerizim was in place from early in the 5th century." Later in the same paragraph, she continues, "Thus the Samaritan temple and community did not arise in the late 4th century as claimed by Josephus, but was in existence more than a century earlier."

45. Becking, "Earliest Samaritan Inscriptions," 216. Robert T. Anderson ("The Elusive Samaritan Temple," *BA* 54 [June 1991]: 104–7) has expressed doubts that the Samaritans had a temple on Mount Gerizim, rather than a more modest tabernacle. The issue is not the existence of a building on Mount Gerizim, but the relation of the building and or the Gerizim site to the Jerusalem site: alternative, competitor, supplement, or equivalent.

46. Gary Knoppers, "Revisiting the Samarian Question in the Persian Period," in

as a breakaway Jewish sect is too simplistic. The Yahwistic Samarian community must be granted its own historical integrity."[47] In support of this argument, Knoppers points to the presentation of the northern Israelite tribes in Chronicles:

> [The Chronicler] acknowledges, even promotes, features shared by all Israelites over the centuries. He openly affirms a common identity for all people who see themselves as the descendants of Jacob (almost always called 'Israel' in Chronicles). He does not stigmatize the residents of the former northern kingdom as the descendants of foreign settlers or even as a mixed race. The northern remnant addressed by Hezekiah is as Israelite as the southern remnant is."[48]

Significantly, he says, "members of both communities could conceivably achieve complete unanimity on the principles of one God, one people, and one sanctuary, but still encounter deep division about where such unity was supposed to be centered."[49]

To illustrate his point, Knoppers imagines a hypothetical conversation between the author of Chronicles and the Samaritan "woman at the well" whom Jesus meets in John 4.

> She [the Samaritan Woman] might discuss the divisions caused by the existence of different worship centers at Mount Gerizim and Jerusalem. On this issue, the two could agree. In this respect, the fourth century B.C.E. was not so different from the first century C.E. But the Chronicler

---

Judah and the Judeans in the Persian Period (ed. Oded Lipschits and Manfred Oeming; Winona Lake, Ind.: Eisenbrauns, 2006), 280.

47. Gary Knoppers, "Mount Gerizim and Mount Zion: A Study in the Early History of the Samaritans and Jews," CSBS *Bulletin* 64 (2004): 11.

48. Ibid., 29. Magen makes the same point in "Dating of the First Phase," 187. See also Pummer, "Samaritans and Their Pentateuch," 258–60; Pancratius Beentjes, "Israel's Earlier History as Presented in the Book of Chronicles," in Calduch-Benages and Liesen, *Deuterocanonical and Cognate Literature Yearbook 2006*, 57–75; Ehud Ben Zvi, *History, Literature, and Theology in the Book of Chronicles* (London: Equinox, 2006); Ben Zvi, "Who Knew What? The Construction of the Monarchic Past in Chronicles and Implications for the Intellectual Setting of Chronicles," in Lipschits et al., *Judah and the Judeans in the Fourth Century B.C.E.*, 359–60.

49. Knoppers, "Mount Gerizim and Mount Zion," 29. See also Knoppers, "Did Jacob Become Judah? The Configuration of Israel's Restoration in Deutero-Isaiah," in Zsengellér, *Samaria, Samarians, Samaritans*, 39–67.

> would probably dispute the assertion made by the narrator of John and declare that "Jews do share things in common with Samaritans." In fact, the writer might go further and insist that "Jews share many things in common with Samaritans." It was precisely because there was so much overlap between the two groups that an appeal could be made from one to another.[50]

Overall, new data have forced a reevaluation of past reconstructions of Samaritan origins, to such an extent that the consensus view outlined above has gradually eroded. As early as 1975, R. J. Coggins argued that the split between the Samaritans and rabbinic Judaism did not occur until well after the turn of the eras following a very gradual separation between the groups.[51] Alan Crown suggested an even later date, the third century C.E., for Samaritan origins.[52] The conversation about Samaritan origins has necessarily included reflection on the nature of a religious "sect";[53] definitions of "Samaritanism," postexilic Israelite religion, and prerabbinic and rabbinic Judaism; enquiry into the relationship between Samaritans and Sadducees; and consideration of the various political, religious, and economic forces that led to the formation of a Samaritan community and the SP. As might be expected, the scholarly conversation has become quite nuanced, with new data forcing new conclusions.

Conclusion

Progressively detailed excavations on Mount Gerizim,[54] better understandings of Second Temple period relationships between Samaria and

---

50. Knoppers, "Mount Gerizim and Mount Zion," 31.

51. R. J. Coggins, *Samaritans and Jews: The Origins of Samaritanism Reconsidered* (Oxford: Basil Blackwell, 1975), 161. See also Kippenberg, *Garizim und Synagoge*, 60–93.

52. Alan David Crown, "Redating the Schism between the Judeans and the Samaritans," *JQR* 82 (1991): 17–50. In "Samaritan Scribal Habits with Reference to the Masorah and the Dead Sea Scrolls," in Paul et al., *Emanuel*, 169, Crown states that the Samaritan system of paragraph divisions found in the SP "developed between the first century B.C.E. and the third century C.E."

53. It is perhaps telling that Blenkinsopp ("Development of Jewish Sectarianism," 385–404), although referencing the temple on Gerizim, does not even mention the Samaritans.

54. Yitzhak Magen, "Mount Gerizim—A Temple City," *Qadmoniot* 23 (1990): 70–96; Magen, "Mount Gerizim and the Samaritans," in *Early Christianity in Con-*

Judea, and examinations of the materials recovered at Qumran[55] have all shed new light on the development of the SP and, in turn, on the origins of the Samaritan religious sect. Significant doubt is now cast on the former consensus view that Samaritans and Jews split in the fifth century B.C.E., with a pre-second-century B.C.E. date for the formation of the SP.[56]

Gradually, from this renewed conversation, two general conclusions are emerging. First, most scholars accept that there was no split between the Samaritans and the Jews in the fifth century B.C.E. In fact, the split between the two groups was gradual, uneven, and prolonged.[57] Second, it appears likely that the SP, with the specific sectarian readings characteristic of the text today, emerged sometime between the late second century B.C.E. and the early first century C.E.[58] If the standardization of the proto-MT began

---

text: Monuments and Documents (ed. Fréderic Manns and Eugenio Alliata; SBFCM 38; Jerusalem: Franciscan Printing, 1993), 91–148; Knoppers, "Mount Gerizim and Mount Zion," 5–32.

55. Ingrid Hjelm (*The Samaritans and Early Judaism: A Literary Analysis* [JSOT-Sup 303; Sheffield: Sheffield Academic Press, 2000], 45) offers an insightful and concise assessment of the impact made on Samaritan studies by materials from Qumran: "Those anchors [the destruction of a temple on Gerizim and the appearance of a Samaritan text type and script] began to give way in the course of DSS studies, and have left the scholarly world even more confused about the origins of the Samaritan Pentateuch, giving rise to renewed discussions about 'who changed what' and when."

56. McDonald (*Forgotten Scriptures*, 76) places the SP even earlier, contextualizing the Samaritan choice of the Pentateuch as the sacred text in the fifth or fourth century B.C.E.

57. Pummer ("Samaritanism," 17–18) writes, "Clearly, Samaritanism, like Judaism, is based on the Israelite biblical tradition, and the Samaritans' self-understanding as Israelites is a central tenet of their faith. Already in two second-century B.C.E. dedicatory inscriptions, found on Delos, they call themselves "*Israelites in Delos*." The authors of these inscriptions were undoubtedly Samaritans." But in greater detail than this, Pummer believes, we cannot go. He advises, "We may have to learn to live with ambiguity about the origins of the Samaritans in the hope that new evidence may come to light which will enable us to be more definite." Yet in referencing the same inscriptions from Delos, Gary Knoppers ("Nehemiah and Sanballat: The Enemy Without or Within?," in Lipschits et al., *Judah and the Judeans in the Fourth Century B.C.E.*, 326) writes, "It is clear that the *Samarian* worshipers at this sanctuary considered themselves to be Israelites" [emphasis added]. Becking ("Earliest Samaritan Inscriptions," 213) writes with a note of caution, "By the time of Jesus, Judaism and Samaritanism had developed into two separate religions. When this separation took place, however, is unclear."

58. Pummer ("The Samaritans and Their Pentateuch," 257) notes these two conclusions, but places the emergence of the SP in the second to first century B.C.E.

in the second half of the first century B.C.E. (see Letter of Aristeas[59]), and if the first Jewish revolt (66–72 C.E.) catapulted the emergence of the proto-MT as a standard text type in the prerabbinic movement,[60] perhaps the same sequence of events had an equally formative influence on the sectarian editing of the SP. That sectarian editing will bear the hallmarks of central and distinctive Samaritan beliefs: an insistence that Mount Gerizim is the divinely chosen place for worship; prominence given to Moses as the standard and measure for all presumptive prophets to follow; sacred status recognized for only the books of Moses, the Pentateuch; an emphasis on the transcendence of God that resists any anthropomorphic descriptions of the divine; and perhaps less noticeably but nonetheless importantly, a philosophy of history that places Gerizim at the center of the divine economy. A preferred state of blessing succumbed to an era of divine disfavor when Gerizim lost its central function among the factitious Israelites, only to be restored in an anticipated era of divine favor when a prophet like Moses, the Taheb, restores pure worship. Chapters 2 and 3 will turn attention to the relevant manuscript evidence, offering a proposed reconstruction for the origin and early history of the SP grounded in textual traditions predating the application of sectarian distinctives.

59. The date for the letter is debated, some placing it in the second century B.C.E. and others in the first. See Armin Lange, "'They Confirmed the Reading' (y. Ta'an. 4.68a): The Textual Standardization of Jewish Scriptures in the Second Temple Period," in Lange et al., *From Qumran to Aleppo*, 68–69.

60. Ibid., 79–80.

2
Textual Pluriformity in the Late Second Temple Period

The SP is a connected text. The SP is connected to a religious community for whom it is life and vitality. The SP is connected to the broader biblical tradition, providing a unique witness to that tradition. And the SP is connected to a Second Temple literary milieu, apart from which our understanding of the biblical tradition itself can only be partial and incomplete. In this chapter we will consider important editorial practices and literary characteristics that helped shape the various biblical versions and traditions. In chapter 3 we will examine specific Qumran texts that have immediate bearing on the SP and its development.

Since the last quarter of the twentieth century, the scrolls from Qumran have significantly impacted scholarly discussion on the development and history of the biblical texts, as well as the scribal practices behind their production.[1] Eugene Ulrich, noting that the Dead Sea Scrolls have "revolutionized our understanding of the text of the Bible in antiquity," suggests that the materials from Qumran should be viewed as representative rather than idiosyncratic.[2] This seems to be a safe assumption, for the general consensus is that the Qumran texts represent a collection of literary materials gathered from throughout Palestine, and so reflect more broadly than just on the Qumran literati.[3] Ulrich contends that Qumran has clarified

---

1. See the survey provided in Lange, "They Confirmed the Reading," 29–80.

2. Eugene Ulrich, "The Qumran Scrolls and the Biblical Text," in *The Dead Sea Scrolls Fifty Years after Their Discovery (1947–1997)* (ed. Lawrence A. Schiffman et al.; Jerusalem: Israel Exploration Society, 2000), 51.

3. "The manuscripts of Jewish scriptures in the Qumran library reflect the way these scriptures were copied and transmitted everywhere in ancient Judaism; i.e., Second Temple Judaism is characterized by textual plurality and not by textual standardization" (Lange, "They Confirmed the Reading," 48). This generalization of course

our understanding in two ways: first, by confirming the basic accuracy of the preservation of the Hebrew Bible in the two millennia since the scrolls were produced; second, by showing that "the biblical text we have inherited—the textus receptus—is only one form of the biblical text as it existed in antiquity."[4]

Both of Ulrich's observations have immediate application to the investigation of the origin and early history of the SP. The textual tradition that eventually became the SP was one "form of the biblical text as it existed in antiquity," a form that was shaped by at least some of the scribal practices that contributed to the early formation of the "textus receptus." In Ulrich's words, "4QpaleoExod^{m} and 4QNum^{b} [two of the widely recognized "pre-SP" or more commonly called, "pre-Samaritan"[5] texts representing a textual tradition from which the SP derived] have demonstrated that the text adopted by the Samaritans was simply one of the available forms of the Pentateuch circulating in broader Judaism in the Second Temple period."[6] If our exploration into the origin and development of the SP is to be successful, we must first consider the impact of the Qumran scrolls on our understanding of the wider scriptural literary milieu of the late Second Temple period. Only then will we be able to appreciate the place occupied by the SP in the stream of scriptural text. Not only have the scrolls added a wealth of new data by which to understand the scriptural texts and their history in the late Second Temple period, they have also forced a reconsideration of the categories and labels used to frame the scholarly discussion. In our journey, we will make use of recently developed paradigms, such as concentric circles, pointing us to an ever more focused understanding of the SP at the turn of the eras.

---

accounts for the fact that some manuscripts were copied at Qumran, as evidenced not least by the many inkwells discovered at the site, and that a recognized "Qumran scribal practice" is displayed in the textual characteristics of some of the scrolls. Ian Young ("The Stabilization of the Biblical Text in the Light of Qumran and Masada: A Challenge for Conventional Qumran Chronology?" *DSD* 9 [2002]: 364–90) contends that the Qumran texts are an aberration of the Jerusalem-centered standard textual form established by 164 B.C.E.

4. Ulrich, "Qumran Scrolls and the Biblical Text," 51.

5. The term "pre-Samaritan" in this context does not refer to the Samaritan religious community, but identifies a textual tradition prior to a Samaritan sectarian editing.

6. Ulrich, "Qumran Scrolls and the Biblical Text," 53.

Exegesis and the Formation of Canon

One of the fascinating (and at times frustrating) aspects of the evidence for the origin and early history of the SP is the compositional variety among the Qumran manuscripts. This variety has given rise to debate over appropriate nomenclature. The scrolls from Qumran are variously labeled "biblical," "rewritten Bible," "para-biblical," and "commentary."[7] All such labels reflect answers to common questions: How much can multiple versions of a text vary and still be considered the same composition? How much variety is allowed before "Bible" becomes "rewritten Bible" or "para-Bible"? Can two renditions both be "biblical"? The textual tradition that would eventually become the MT is only one tradition evidenced at Qumran, and the line between canonical constraint and exegetical ingenuity is a fluid boundary, with one process not always easily distinguished from the other. Bernard Levinson has advanced four theses that must be kept in mind as we attempt to understand the Qumran evidence:

> (1) Exegesis provides a strategy for religious renewal.
>
> (2) Renewal and innovation are almost always covert rather than explicit in ancient Israel.
>
> (3) In many cases, exegesis involves not the passive explication but the radical subversion of prior authoritative texts.
>
> (4) These phenomena are found in the literature of ancient Israel before the closure of the canon.[8]

Exegesis, the explanation and renewal of a sacred text, occurs during canon formation, not just after the establishment of an authoritative collection.

7. The debate has been far ranging and has necessarily considered the appropriate use of modern descriptions for ancient materials as well as the religious history of groups using those materials. See for instance Kristin De Troyer, "When did the Pentateuch Come into Existence?" in *Die Septuaginta—Texte, Kontexte, Lebenswelten* (ed. Martin Karrer and Wolfgang Kraus; WUNT 219; Tübingen: Mohr Siebeck, 2008), 269–86; Blenkinsopp, "Development of Jewish Sectarianism," 385–404.

8. Bernard Levinson, *Legal Revision and Religious Renewal in Ancient Israel* (Cambridge: Cambridge University Press, 2008), 20–21.

What one person may view as a creative departure from the authoritative text, another may view as a faithful rendering. Alexander Rofé has noted that a variety of editorial practices (including supplementing, adding to, deleting from, and reorganizing the received text) "started with the composition of the biblical literature and lasted until the revolt of the Maccabees in 167 B.C.E."[9] Eugene Ulrich is also convinced that the "compositional" period and the period of "transmission" of the biblical texts overlap and are "genetically linked as one development, not discretely separate."[10] Using Levinson's theses as provisional guides, we will dive into the stream of scriptural tradition expecting to find eddies and currents in the flow of text rather than abrupt changes and separation.

Qumran and the Textual History of the Hebrew Bible

The literary material recovered from Qumran has provided invaluable information for the reconstruction of the early history of the biblical texts, impacting theories of textual transmission at fundamental levels. A paradigm shift has taken place, with the quest for the "original version" of the biblical texts falling before the recognition of a "pluriform text" in the late Second Temple period.[11] As Timothy Lim notes, "it is no longer possible

---

9. Alexander Rofé, "Historico-Literary Aspects of the Qumran Biblical Scrolls," in Schiffman et al., *Dead Sea Scrolls Fifty Years after Their Discovery*, 38.

10. Eugene Ulrich, "The Dead Sea Scrolls and the Hebrew Scriptural Texts," in *Scripture and the Scrolls* (vol. 1 of *The Bible and the Dead Sea Scrolls*; ed. James Charlesworth; Waco, Tex.: Baylor University Press, 2006), 96–97.

11. "The question which [now] dominates the discussion of the history of the biblical text is how to explain the pluriformity observable in the MSS from Qumran, the MT and the versions" (Eugene Ulrich, "Pluriformity in the Biblical Text, Text Groups, and Questions of Canon," in *The Madrid Qumran Congress: Proceedings of the International Congress on the Dead Sea Scrolls, Madrid 18–21 March, 1991* [ed. Julio Trebolle Barrera and Luis Vegas Montaner; Leiden: Brill, 1992], 1:24). Ian Young (review of Hanne von Weissenberg, Juha Pakkala, and Marko Marttila, eds., *Changes in Scripture: Rewriting and Interpreting Authoritative Traditions in the Second Temple Period*, *RBL* [June 2012]: 4; online: http://www.bookreviews.org/pdf/8251_9022.pdf) is unequivocal in the matter. He writes: "The fluidity of the biblical texts, even quite late in the Second Temple period, has become widely accepted, and this model for how the biblical texts were composed is causing scholars to rethink many of the settled assumptions of previous scholarship. It is true that there are still scholars who seem not to have realized that the world has changed, but the studies in volumes such as this are a warning that such scholarly endeavors are in grave danger of becoming irrelevant."

to posit the proto-MT as the standard from which all others varied. In the context of textual diversity, the proto-MT text is one text type, albeit an important and well-attested witness among many."[12] In the centuries surrounding the turn of the eras, a variety of scriptural texts were used throughout Jerusalem and Palestine. The text type that would eventually become the SP was one of those textual traditions.

In Search of the *Urtext*

Paul de Lagarde (1827–1891) is famously associated with the theory that a single, primitive text (*Urtext*) lies behind the various recensions and textual families represented by the MT, LXX, and SP.[13] This notion of "the original text" has since gone through different iterations, probably the most influential by William Foxwell Albright (1891–1971). In a short article published in 1955, Albright set forth a paradigm of local text traditions that would dominate text-critical discussions for the remainder of the twentieth century.[14] Albright thought that many of the older books of the Hebrew Bible were composed or edited in Babylon and returned with the exiles to Palestine in the sixth and fifth centuries B.C.E. There, this proto-MT became diluted and morphed into the other extant versions, while the proto-MT itself, preserved in Jerusalem, in time and with few modifications, became the standard rabbinic version of the Bible known today.

Frank Moore Cross, building on Albright's theory, posited a restoration era "arch-type" that developed into three distinct text types during the Second Temple period, each associated with a geographical region: the Masoretic Text (Babylonia), the Samaritan Pentateuch (Palestine), and the Septuagint (Egypt).[15] Cross suggested that the pre-Samaritan text (i.e., a

---

12. Timothy Lim, "The Qumran Scrolls, Multilingualism, and Biblical Interpretation,"in *Religion in the Dead Sea Scrolls* (ed. John Collins and Robert Kugler; Grand Rapids: Eerdmans, 2000), 66.

13. Paul de Lagarde, *Anmerkungen zur Griechischen Übersetzung: Der Proverbien* (Leipzig: Brockhaus, 1863).

14. William F. Albright, "New Light on the Early Recensions of the Hebrew Bible," *BASOR* 140 (1955): 27–33.

15. Frank Moore Cross, "The Contribution of the Qumran Discoveries to the Study of the Biblical Text," in *Qumran and the History of the Biblical Text* (ed. Frank Moore Cross and Shemaryahu Talmon; Cambridge: Harvard University Press, 1975), 290; Cross, "The History of the Biblical Text in Light of Discoveries in the Judean Desert," in Cross and Talmon, *Qumran and the History of the Biblical Text*, 194–95;

textual tradition as it existed prior to a Samaritan sectarian editing) was an intermediary between the Egyptian recension now evident in the LXX and the proto-MT. The Egyptian text, Cross suggested, separated from the proto-MT as early as the fifth century B.C.E., and the pre-Samaritan not earlier than the Hasmonean era. Cross dated the emergence of a standard recension "sometime near the mid-first century A.D."[16]

While Cross's theory assumes that the various biblical text types all stemmed from a common arch-type, Shemaryahu Talmon considers the plurality of the major biblical text types to be a function of their use by various groups. Thus, Talmon associates the MT with the rabbis, the SP with the Samaritans, and the LXX with Christians.[17] Association of text types with the communities that used them assumes that multiple textual versions were available to those groups, and that specific text types prospered or declined with the fortunes of the factions within those social groups who used them.[18]

While the observations of Cross and Talmon have been important steps in the investigation of the history of biblical text types, vital questions remain. The focus on either regional or official texts "hides a more serious problem, namely the extreme difficulty in proposing a simple com-

---

Cross, *From Epic to Canon: History and Literature in Ancient Israel* (Baltimore: Johns Hopkins University Press, 1998), 209. See also Albright, "New Light on Early Recensions," 27–33.

16. Cross, "Contribution of the Qumran Discoveries," 291–92. The Jewish War and resulting destruction of Jerusalem are often seen as a catalyst for the emergence of the proto-MT as the standard scriptural text of rabbinic Judaism. See Ernst Würthwein, *Der Text des Alten Testaments* (Stuttgart: Deutsche Bibelgesellschaft, 1988), 18; Eugene Ulrich, "The Qumran Biblical Scrolls: The Scriptures of Late Second Temple Judaism," in *The Dead Sea Scrolls in Their Historical Context* (ed. Timothy Lim; Edinburgh: T&T Clark, 2000), 87; Emanuel Tov, "The Status of the Masoretic Text in Modern Text Editions of the Hebrew Bible: The Relevance of Canon," in *The Canon Debate* (ed. Lee M. McDonald and James A. Sanders; Peabody, Mass.: Hendrickson, 2002), 234–63; Moshe Greenberg, "The Stabilization of the Hebrew Bible, Reviewed in the Light of the Biblical Materials from the Judean Desert," *JAOS* 76 (1956): 157–67.

17. Shemaryahu Talmon, "The Textual Study of the Bible—A New Outlook," in Cross and Talmon, *Qumran and the History of the Biblical Text*, 321–400.

18. Eugene Ulrich, "The Canonical Process, Textual Criticism, and Latter Stages in the Composition of the Bible," in *Sha'arei Talmon: Studies in the Bible, Qumran, and the Ancient Near East Presented to Shemaryahu Talmon* (ed. Michael Fishbane and Emanuel Tov with Weston W. Fields; Winona Lake, Ind.: Eisenbrauns, 1992), 267–91. See also Fossum, "Social and Institutional Conditions," 239–55.

prehensive view which would maintain unequivocally that the Samaritans were a sect derived from Judaism, and therefore that the Jewish Pentateuch is clearly prior to the Samaritan, although it has been demonstrated that the Samaritan texts have not borrowed substantially from the Jews."[19] The evidence suggests, in other words, that the biblical texts may have been pluriform from the beginning.

A Pluriform Text

In contrast to the theory of a single *Urtext* behind the extant variants, Paul Kahle (1875–1964) suggested that the SP preserves a popular version of the Torah that existed alongside the other versions. These versions were not based on a common standard text; rather, a standard text eventually emerged from their plurality. This standard text or *textus receptus* is simply that version of the Torah which became, in due course, normative for translations and authoritative in the believing community.[20]

In recent years, the earlier focus on the specific geographical regions from which text types were thought to have emerged has given way to a focus on the characteristics of the text types themselves.[21] The very notion of an *Urtext* or "arch-type" from which three major recensions developed has been tempered by most[22] and abandoned altogether by some, the latter group of scholars emphasizing instead the pluriform nature of the biblical text.[23] Cross's work illustrates this evolving understanding in light of

---

19. Nodet, *Search for the Origins of Judaism*, 190.

20. Paul Kahle, "Untersuchungen zur Geschichte des Pentateuchtextes," *TSK* 88 (1915): 399–439; *The Cairo Geniza* (Schweich Lectures, 1941; London: Milford, 1947), 142–49. See also Lawrence A. Schiffman, *Reclaiming the Dead Sea Scrolls* (New York: Doubleday, 1994), 162.

21. See, e.g., Geza Vermes, "Biblical Studies and the Dead Sea Scrolls," *JSOT* 39 (1987): 122–25; Emanuel Tov, *Textual Criticism of the Hebrew Bible* (Minneapolis: Fortress, 1992), 180–97.

22. Talmon, "Textual Study of the Bible," 321–400; Bertil Albrektson, "Masoretic or Mixed: On Choosing a Textual Basis for Translation of the Hebrew Bible," *Textus* 23 (2007): 33–49.

23. Shemaryahu Talmon, "The Old Testament Text," in *From the Beginnings to Jerome* (vol. 1 of *The Cambridge History of the Bible*; ed. Peter Ackroyd and Craig F. Evans; 3 vols.; Cambridge: Cambridge University Press, 1970), 1:159–99; repr. in Cross and Talmon, *Qumran and the History of the Biblical Text*, 1–41; Shemaryahu Talmon, "The Transmission History of the Text of the Hebrew Bible in the Light of Biblical

research on the Qumran scrolls, which "force us to grapple in a wholly new way with problems of the canonical text. It is obvious that there never was an 'original text' at any one moment of time. Biblical books, those with authors or editors, were revised, rewritten, expanded, and truncated."[24] Similarly, Shemaryahu Talmon, building on the work of Kahle, notes:

> The textus receptus represents the post-divide biblical tradition of normative Judaism; the vulgar, that is, the variational texts, stem from an earlier, pre-divide period, and were preserved by a dissident faction (or factions) in the Jewish community at the height of the Second Temple period, that identified itself as "biblical Israel."[25]

Eugene Ulrich offers a succinct conclusion consequent to the examination of the Qumran materials: "the biblical text we have inherited is, alas, only one form of the pluriform biblical text as it existed in the Second Temple period, prior to the stage of the uniform Masoretic Text."[26]

The pluriformity of the biblical text in the Second Temple period has important implications for understanding the nature of the Qumran scrolls. As Ulrich notes, scholars have tended to label texts that resemble the MT as "biblical," while calling texts that vary significantly from the

Manuscripts from Qumran and Other Sites in the Judean Desert," in Schiffman et al., *Dead Sea Scrolls Fifty Years after Their Discovery*, 40–50; Ulrich, "Pluriformity in the Biblical Text," 23–41; Bruno Chiesa, "Textual History and Textual Criticism of the Hebrew Old Testament," in Trebolle Barrera and Vegas Montaner, *Madrid Qumran Congress*, 1:257–72. A brief overview is provided by Ronald Hendel, "The Text of the Torah after Qumran: Prospects and Retrospects," in Schiffman et al., *Dead Sea Scrolls Fifty Years after Their Discovery*, 8–11; James Bowley and John Reeves, "Rethinking the Concept of 'Bible': Some Theses and Proposals," *Hen* 25 (2003): 3–18.

24. Frank Moore Cross, "The Biblical Scrolls from Qumran and the Canonical Text," in Charlesworth, *Scripture and the Scrolls*, 73. Cross goes on to observe, concerning a religious implication of recent investigations: "Historical criticism has broken the back of doctrines of inerrancy and produced a massive retreat from and debate concerning doctrines of inspiration" (ibid., 73).

25. Talmon, "Transmission History," 50. See also Bertil Albrektson, "Reflections on the Emergence of a Standard Text of the Hebrew Bible," in *Congress Volume: Göttingen 1977* (ed. J. A. Emerton; VTSup 29; Leiden: Brill, 1978), 64.

26. Ulrich, "Qumran Scrolls and the Biblical Text," 58. See also Eugene Ulrich, "The Bible in the Making: The Scriptures at Qumran," in *The Community of the Renewed Covenant* (ed. Eugene Ulrich and James VanderKam; Notre Dame: Notre Dame University Press, 1994), 92.

MT: "non-biblical," "para-biblical," or "reworked biblical."[27] This model, however, is no longer viable, and "the nature of the biblical text in the Second Temple period shows us that the biblical text was pluriform and dynamically growing—the Qumran Scrolls, the Samaritan Pentateuch, the Septuagint, the New Testament, and Josephus all show that there were variant literary editions of many of the biblical books."[28] Exactly when, how, and by whom the proto-MT was granted preference among rabbinic Judaism are all points of debate. Many scholars point to the first Jewish revolt as the catalyst for the rise of the proto-MT among the forming rabbinic community. Despite many lingering questions, most scholars today would recognize that the documents that would eventually come to represent the scriptural tradition were in a state of dynamic flux during the late Second Temple period.

The Classification of Qumran Manuscripts

Recognition of textual variety at Qumran is reflected in a number of attempts to categorize the Qumran scrolls on the basis of textual traditions common to us today.[29] Of the several descriptive schemes offered in the late twentieth century, the five groupings presented by Emanuel Tov have been widely received.[30]

---

27. Ulrich, "Qumran Scrolls and the Biblical Text," 54.

28. Ibid., 54; citing Emanuel Tov, "Hebrew Biblical Manuscripts from the Judaean Desert: Their Contribution to Textual Criticism," *JJS* 39 (1988): 5–37.

29. Emanuel Tov (*Hebrew Bible, Greek Bible, and Qumran: Collected Essays* [TSAJ 121; Tübingen: Mohr Siebeck, 2008], 435–37) numbers the independent compositions from Qumran at no more than three hundred and possibly as few as two hundred and fifty, each of which averages two copies, some considerably more copies. Of this three hundred, Tov considers fifty-one as biblical compositions (in which Tov includes: biblical books, translations, and semi-biblical compositions). Of these fifty-one, forty-six are Torah texts extensive enough for analysis: twenty-four reflect the MT (or MT and SP equally); seventeen are nonaligned; three are exclusively SP; and two exclusively reflect the LXX (ibid., 145). The number of texts counted in each group varies from researcher to researcher. Schiffman (*Reclaiming the Dead Sea Scrolls*, 172) presents a similar percentage distribution, although the total number of texts is different. Ulrich ("Dead Sea Scrolls and the Hebrew Scriptural Texts," 77) numbers "about 230 manuscripts of the books of the Hebrew Scriptures" from Qumran and neighboring Judean desert sites.

30. Tov, *Textual Criticism of the Hebrew Bible*, 114–17. See also Bruce Waltke, "How We Got the Hebrew Bible: The Text and Canon of the Old Testament," in *The*

(1) Texts written in the Qumran practice: A large group of the Qumran texts display a similar and distinctive "orthography, morphology and scribal practices," suggesting that they were produced at Qumran. These documents reflect different textual backgrounds, having been copied from a proto-Masoretic text, pre-Samaritan texts, and other nonaligned texts.[31] The group evidences a "free approach to the biblical text which is reflected in adaptations of unusual forms to the context, in frequent errors, in numerous corrections, and sometimes, also, in negligent script."[32] Tov identifies twenty-five texts (seventeen of them biblical) from Qumran written in the Qumran practice.[33]

(2) Proto-Masoretic Texts: The proto-Masoretic texts, labeled "proto-rabbinic" by Frank Moore Cross, display the consonantal text of the MT, "one thousand years or more before the time of the Masorah codices."[34] Tov includes fifty-seven Qumran texts in this group, of which twenty-four are biblical texts, making it the largest grouping of biblical texts at Qumran.[35]

(3) Pre-Samaritan Texts: This group of texts, earlier referred to as "proto-Samaritan," reflect characteristic features of the later SP but without the typical SP sectarian qualities.[36] They are also

---

Bible at Qumran: Text, Shape and Interpretation (ed. Peter Flint; Grand Rapids: Eerdmans, 2001); Schiffman, *Reclaiming the Dead Sea Scrolls*, 172. Lange ("They Confirmed the Reading," 54–55) has expanded Tov's categorization scheme into six groupings: semi-MT, proto-MT, semi-MT/pre-SP (differing more than 2 percent from the consonantal text of the MT), pre-SP, *Vorlage* of LXX, nonaligned. Lange's categorization makes clear the fluid nature of the scriptural text at Qumran.

31. Tov, *Hebrew Bible, Greek Bible, and Qumran*, 146.

32. Tov, *Textual Criticism of the Hebrew Bible*, 114.

33. Tov, *Hebrew Bible, Greek Bible, and Qumran*, 146.

34. See Frank Moore Cross, "The History of the Biblical Text in the Light of the Discoveries in the Judeaen Desert," *HTR* 57 (1964): 287–92; Tov, *Textual Criticism of the Hebrew Bible*, 115.

35. Tov, *Hebrew Bible, Greek Bible, and Qumran*, 147.

36. Tov, *Textual Criticism of the Hebrew Bible*, 115. The label "proto-Samaritan" has fallen into disuse because none of these texts share the specifically sectarian readings now found in the SP. See James Purvis, *The Samaritan Pentateuch and the Origin of the Samaritan Sect* (HSM 2; Cambridge: Harvard University Press, 1968), 80; Emanuel Tov, "The Proto-Samaritan Texts and the Samaritan Pentateuch," in *The Samaritans*

sometimes referred to as "harmonistic" texts because they tend to interpolate material from other portions of the Pentateuch, resulting in a smoothing out of details and a greater narrative consistency. Samaritan scholars disagree on the exact number of Qumran scrolls that should be considered "pre-Samaritan," with some including only two or three texts (4QPaleoExod^{m}, 4QNum^{b}, 4QExod-Lev^{f}) under this heading and others as many as nine.[37]

(4) Texts Close to the Presumed Hebrew Source of LXX: Although no scroll from Qumran is identical or almost identical to the presumed Hebrew source of the LXX, at least four texts (4QJer$^{b,\ d}$, 4QLev^{d}, 4QDeut^{q}, 4QSam^{b}) closely resemble the LXX.[38]

(5) Nonaligned Texts: As Tov notes, "Many texts are not exclusively close to any one of the texts mentioned above and are therefore considered non-aligned."[39] Texts in this grouping may at times agree with the proto-Masoretic texts and at other times with the pre-Samaritan or LXX readings, without displaying a consistent tendency toward one or the other. This group of texts clearly demonstrates the fluidity of scriptural texts in the late Second Temple period. Tov includes fifty-seven independent texts from Qumran in this grouping, of which seventeen are "biblical texts in the Torah."[40]

It is important to note that scriptural texts from all five groupings existed side by side at Qumran. This fact suggests that the SP emerged out of a

---

(ed. Alan D. Crown; Tübingen: Mohr Siebeck, 1989), 397–407; Tov, *Textual Criticism of the Hebrew Bible*, 97; Pummer, "Samaritans and Their Pentateuch," 243–44.

37. Cf. Lange, "They Confirmed the Reading," 55; Tov, *Hebrew Bible, Greek Bible, and Qumran*, 147; Magnar Kartveit, "The Major Expansions in the Samaritan Pentateuch—The Evidence from the 4Q Texts," in Shehadeh and Tawa, *Proceedings of the Fifth International Congress*, 117; Eshel and Eshel, "Dating the Samaritan Pentateuch's Compilation," 220.

38. Tov, *Textual Criticism of the Hebrew Bible*, 115; Lange, "They Confirmed the Reading," 55. Lange (ibid., 46) contends that 4QLXXLev$^{a,\ b}$ "attests to the Old Greek translation of the Pentateuch."

39. Tov, *Textual Criticism of the Hebrew Bible*, 116–17.

40. Tov, *Hebrew Bible, Greek Bible, and Qumran*, 149.

literary milieu in which the biblical texts were not fixed, not in opposition to any one other version of the Scriptures.

Parallel Versions

Parallel versions of what would later become biblical books existed side by side within the Qumran library. In the Second Temple period, the biblical books themselves were considered sacred (or at least authoritative), not their specific textual forms.[41] This variety has led to considerable debate on the extent to which one text can differ from another version before it should be considered a new composition. This debate is more than a squabble over preferred labels, but rather an attempt to understand how the pluriformity of the various biblical texts was understood by the communities that used them. Citing the different versions of the book of Jeremiah, Michael Segal suggests that "the active intervention of scribes in these texts [biblical] was accepted in this period [late Second Temple] and was not viewed as an affront to the sanctity of the text. The text was of secondary importance to the composition itself, and thus scribes allowed themselves the freedom to 'improve' these works."[42] Similarly, Eugene Ulrich notes that "the use by both Jews and Christians of diverse forms of texts in the first century shows that neither community thought that a fixed text was necessary for an authoritative book; evidently differing forms of the text were acceptable."[43]

But at what point did a parallel version become a new composition? Sidnie White Crawford suggests that we think of ancient manuscripts as a spectrum, with open boundaries between the categories.[44]

---

41. Eugene Ulrich, *The Dead Sea Scrolls and the Origins of the Bible* (Grand Rapids: Eerdmans, 1999), 93.

42. Michael Segal, "Between Bible and Rewritten Bible," in *Biblical Interpretation at Qumran* (ed. Matthias Henze; Grand Rapids: Eerdmans, 2005), 16.

43. Ulrich, "Pluriformity in the Biblical Text," 36.

44. Sidnie White Crawford, *Rewriting Scripture in Second Temple Times* (Grand Rapids: Eerdmans, 2008), 12–13. See also George Brooke, "The Rewritten Law, Prophets, and Psalms: Issues for Understanding the Text of the Bible," in *The Bible as Book: The Hebrew Bible and the Judaean Desert Discoveries* (ed. Edward Herbert and Emanuel Tov; London: British Library, 2002), 32; Casey Elledge, "Rewriting the Sacred: Some Problems of Textual Authority in Light of the Rewritten Scriptures from Qumran," in *Jewish and Christian Scriptures: The Function of "Canonical" and "Non-*

Biblical texts expanded only by inner-biblical interpolation:	Reworked biblical texts, including extrabiblical insertions	New compositions in which biblical texts are freely altered:	New composition functioning as commentary, not limited to biblical base text:
proto-MT	4QRP	Jubilees	Habakkuk commentary (1QpHab)
pre-Samaritan		Temple Scroll	
		Chronicles	

←————————————————————————————→

At the left end of the spectrum are the proto-rabbinic texts and the pre-Samaritan texts. Even though the pre-Samaritan text is clearly exegetically enhanced when compared to the proto-MT, both were considered authoritative.[45] This group of manuscripts is characterized by inner-scriptural exegesis that sought to "clarify and interpret the scriptural text from within."[46] Differences in parallel biblical accounts were smoothed over by harmonizing them with a view to eliminating contradictions.[47]

Next on the spectrum are "texts whose scribal intervention does utilize material from outside the existing base text, but without the intention thereby of creating a new composition."[48] At times, these texts make the same claims to authority as the base texts they utilized, but these claims were, most likely, not as widely accepted as texts not enhanced by the insertion of external material. This group includes the so called "reworked pentateuchal texts" (4QRP) that incorporate nonpentateuchal material in the process of harmonization.

The third position on the spectrum is occupied by texts that manipulate their base text so extensively that "a recognizably new work is created."[49]

canonical" Religious Texts (ed. James Charlesworth and Lee M. McDonald; London: T&T Clark, 2010), 87–103.

45. Julio Trebolle Barrera ("The Authoritative Functions of Scriptural Works at Qumran," in Ulrich and VanderKam, *Community of the Renewed Covenant*, 107) seems to confirm this way of thinking about the ancient textual traditions: "The old tripartite scheme—Septuagint, MT and Samaritan Pentateuch—seems now to have been replaced with a scheme of shorter texts, intermediate texts, and longer texts."

46. Crawford, *Rewriting Scripture*, 144.

47. Ibid., 13.

48. Ibid.

49. Ibid., 14.

The relationship to the base text is easily detectable, but the new work has a purpose quite distinct from the base text. Chronicles, Jubilees, and the Temple Scroll fit this category.

Finally, on the far end of the spectrum are works that extensively rework the base text but make no claims to authority relative to that base text, and thus are not recognized as authoritative by any community.[50] These texts are best considered commentary or *pesher* on an authoritative text and are generally so labeled within the Qumran corpus of materials.

Combining the categories of Tov with the conceptual spectrum developed by Crawford, we now recognize at least three sets of pentateuchal traditions at Qumran: proto-rabbinic (MT), pre-Samaritan (SP), and nonaligned.[51] All three traditions are characterized by inner-biblical exegesis, practiced to a greater or lesser degree. The pre-Samaritan text group is marked by the interpolation of pentateuchal material that has an overall harmonizing effect, with the result that this group is sometimes labeled "harmonistic." The Samaritan scribes and their predecessors, those actively engaged with the pre-Samaritan texts, operated in many important ways within the larger stream of Jewish scriptural tradition, and the text that eventually became the SP is only one example of a common exegetical practice not bound by sectarian sensitivities. Chronicles, for example, reworks parts of Samuel and Kings, and in so doing becomes an independent composition.[52] Similarly, the LXX preserves in 1 Esdras a reworking of material taken from Ezra/Nehemiah. If some amount of "reworking" and fluidity was the norm in the late Second Temple period, caution should be exercised in labeling some texts "pre-Samaritan" and others "Samaritan." For, although the term "pre-Samaritan" is designed to indicate textual affinities with the later SP, there is nothing particularly sectarian about the pre-Samaritan texts. After the first century B.C.E., this technique of inner-scriptural exegesis began to die out, concomitant with the stabilization of the scriptural text. The acceptance of a fixed, unchanging text and the growing authority of the proto-rabbinic text type caused exegesis to become separated from the base text itself during the first century C.E. and later.[53]

---

50. Ibid.

51. A Hebrew source of the LXX may also be present.

52. Isaac Kalimi, *The Reshaping of Ancient Israelite History in Chronicles* (Winona Lake, Ind.: Eisenbrauns, 2005).

53. Crawford, *Rewriting Scripture*, 144.

At what point, then, should a "copy" of Scripture be considered "rewritten Bible," distinct from and independent of its source text? Michael Segal offers the following six literary criteria to distinguish between variations on a source text and new compositions:[54]

> (1) The *scope* of a rewritten text does not correspond to that of its source. By way of example, it can easily be noted that although Chronicles makes extensive use of Kings, the scope of the story, the beginning and ending, and the characters included in the Kings narrative is different from the rendition presented in Chronicles.
>
> (2) A rewritten text composes a *new narrative frame* that places the "composition as a whole into a new setting and thus offers a new ideological framework by which to understand the text."[55] Sometimes the reframing is extensive, providing an expanded expression of a second point of view (presumably the case when the writer of Kings refers the reader to the *Book of the Chronicles of the Kings of Judah* in order to learn more of Jehoshaphat's military exploits: 1 Kg 22:39). Or, the reframing can be accomplished by small but not so subtle changes. Once again a comparison between Samuel and Chronicles illustrates this narrative frame. The infamous census conducted by David is incited by God in 2 Sam 24 but by Satan in 1 Chr 21. This simple change in characters "reframes" an otherwise almost duplicate story.
>
> (3) A rewritten text may differ in *voice* from that presented in the source text. This difference in voice is evident in the Mosaic recounting of events in Deut 1–3 when compared to the rendition of the same stories in Numbers. In Deuteronomy, the story is "voiced" by a reminiscing Moses while in Numbers the story is told by an omniscient narrator.

54. Segal, "Between Bible and Rewritten Bible," 20–27.

55. Ibid, 21. This is seen clearly in the divergences between the SP and the MT in the famous יבחר/בחר (has chosen/will choose) variants.

> (4) A rewritten biblical text *expands and abridges* the source text. A scribe producing an abridged text makes "no pretense of producing a text identified with or equal to [the original]."[56]
>
> (5) Rewritten biblical compositions include editorial layers that *express "fundamental beliefs and concepts" different from those of the biblical source.*[57]
>
> (6) Rewritten biblical compositions *make explicit reference to the source*, thereby identifying themselves as different from, and thus independent of, the original text. The repeated references to the *Chronicles of the Kings of Judah* or the *Chronicles of the Kings of Israel* (1 Kgs 22:39, 45) illustrate this sourcing, as do the inclusion of embedded songs in biblical narrative (Josh 10:13; 2 Sam 1:18).[58]

Segal's fifth characteristic, differing beliefs and concepts, is most significant when attempting to identify the SP and proto-MT as distinct traditions. As Eugene Ulrich notes, it is the "specifically Samaritan features (namely, the addition of an eleventh commandment to build an altar on Mount Gerizim, and the systematic use of the past, and not the future, of the verb in the formula 'the place that the Lord has chosen' [not 'will choose']" that are missing in the Qumran Exodus scrolls.[59] A similar assessment is offered concerning Numbers (4QNum^{b}).[60] Identifying when and how the sectarian layer was added to the biblical source provides a point of reference for marking the beginning of the SP tradition. We will examine this sectarian layer at greater length in the next chapter.

Bible, Commentary, and the Question of Authority

Observations on the harmonizing tendencies of specific texts or the presence of interpolated material from either within or without the develop-

56. Ibid., 24.

57. Ibid., 25.

58. Terry Giles and William J. Doan, *Twice Used Songs: Performance Criticism of the Songs of Ancient Israel* (Peabody, Mass.: Hendrickson, 2009), 34–43.

59. Ulrich, "Bible in the Making," 86.

60. Ibid. Genesis is assessed to be a stable text type (except for variants in the chronological system) and Leviticus gives evidence of only one textual tradition.

ing biblical corpus focus on only one current within the stream of biblical tradition in the late Second Temple period. A second current within that stream of tradition concerns the authority of a textual tradition within the life of a particular religious community. An effort to understand the function of a scroll in the life of the community must necessarily consider scribal practices in the late Second Temple period and the gradual development of a sacred canon of texts. Eugene Ulrich has made the timely reminder that "we should probably not think of 'Bible' in the first century B.C.E. or the first century C.E., at Qumran or elsewhere. There were collections of Sacred Scripture, of course, but no Bible in our developed sense of the term."[61] The terms "Bible" and "biblical" are somewhat anachronistic; the evidence from Qumran suggests that "in the Second Temple period there was no 'canon' of sacred Scripture."[62] At most, one may say that in this period a body of sacred literature was in the process of being recognized as "uniquely authoritative, ancient in origin, and binding on the community for doctrine and practice."[63] The qualities of authority, antiquity, and directive for faith and practice bind a sacred text to the community of faithful. It is that bond between text and community that helps guide our search for the origin of the SP amid the versions from Qumran.

---

61. Ibid., 77. See also Hanne von Weissenberg, "Canon and Identity at Qumran: An Overview and Challenges for Future Research," in *Scripture in Transition: Essays on Septuagint, Hebrew Bible, and Dead Sea Scrolls in Honour of Raija Sollamo* (ed. Anssi Voitila and Jutta Jokiranta; Leiden: Brill, 2008), 629–40. John Barton ("The Significance of a Fixed Canon of the Hebrew Bible," in Saebø, *Hebrew Bible/Old Testamant*, 1.1:72) writes, "By the end of the Second Temple period, it was not a serious option to read one of the 'core' holy books of Judaism as meaningless or incoherent."

62. Crawford, *Rewriting Scripture*, 6. See also Bowley and Reeves, "Rethinking the Concept of 'Bible,'" 3–18.

63. Crawford, *Rewriting Scripture*, 6. See also Brent Strawn, "Authority: Textual, Traditional, or Functional? A Response to C. D. Elledge," in Charlesworth and McDonald, *Jewish and Christian Scriptures*, 104–12.

3
Qumran and the "Pre-Samaritan" Text

As was discussed in chapter 2, scriptural texts were fluid during the late Second Temple period, with various readings of the same text accepted side by side, at times accompanied by commentaries on the authoritative text. The SP is based upon one of these text types, generally referred to as "pre-Samaritan" and characterized as a harmonistic text type in use during the second and first centuries B.C.E.[1] This harmonistic text type was further modified by the Samaritans, probably sometime between the first century B.C.E. and the first century C.E., to make it conform to established Samaritan beliefs and practices. Sidnie White Crawford has provided a very clear and concise description of the pre-Samaritan text type:

> The Samaritan Pentateuch in fact contains an ancient edition of the Pentateuch, current in Palestine in the Second Temple period. The Samaritans adopted this Palestinian text as their canonical text and in the process added to it a thin veneer of sectarian editing, bringing the text into lines with their theology. This sectarian editing is easy to isolate. First, where Jerusalem is alluded to as the central place of worship for the Israelites, the Samaritans inserted a reference to Mount Gerizim (הרגרזים; one word) as God's actual chosen place. Second, to emphasize the notion that God has already chosen Mount Gerizim as the appropriate place of worship before entrance into Canaan, the Samaritan Pentateuch consistently changes the Deuteronomy formula "the place which the Lord will choose (יבחר)," an oblique reference to Jerusalem, to "the place which the Lord has chosen (בחר)," a reference to Mount Gerizim. However, once this thin veneer of sectarian changes is removed (a fairly easy task), what

1. See Stefan Schorch, "The Reading(s) of the Tora in Qumran," in Shehadeh and Tawa, *Proceedings of the Fifth International Congress*, 113–14.

> remains is an expanded text of the Pentateuch, characterized by massive and deliberate harmonizations and content editing.[2]

Reflecting this consensus view, Magnar Kartveit notes that "the SP originated in at least two stages: the first stage of the development resulted in a text that we have witnesses to in the biblical manuscripts 4Qpaleo-Ex^{m} [4QpaleoExod^{m}] and 4QNum^{b}.... These texts have been termed pre-Samaritan."[3] The "pre-Samaritan" texts include all of the major expansions found in the SP except the Samaritan tenth commandment. In addition to these major expansions, numerous minor variations (when compared to the MT) are found in the pre-Samaritan Qumran texts that are also shared with the LXX. This observation leads Kartveit to conclude that the major variants were inserted into the text following the LXX but prior to the 4Q texts—that is, sometime in the second to first centuries B.C.E.[4] This expanded text type (again when compared to the MT) is generally called the "pre-Samaritan" text because of its relationship to the later sectarian SP. However, the term "pre-Samaritan" is not intended to associate the text type with the Samaritan religious sect. Building on these observations, Reinhard Pummer notes that "there is now a consensus among scholars that the SP is an adaptation of a pre-Samaritan or harmonistic text known from Qumran that was produced in the second or first century B.C.E."[5] In this chapter we will survey those Qumran manuscripts and fragments generally identified by scholars as pre-Samaritan or harmonistic.

Paleo-Hebrew at Qumran

Prior to examination of the pre-Samaritan Qumran materials, there is one question of Qumran scribal practice that must be addressed because of its unique application to the SP. Examination of the Qumran scrolls must eventually consider the question of peculiar scribal habits that may have been practiced at Qumran. If the manuscripts from Qumran are idiosyncratic and originated at Qumran, then it is important to identify Qumran scribal practices, differentiating those practices and texts produced from a wider Judean and Samarian literary activity. This question has largely been

2. Crawford, *Rewriting Scripture*, 22.
3. Kartveit, "Major Expansions," 117.
4. Ibid., 18.
5. Pummer, "Samaritans and Their Pentateuch," 247.

put to rest by the growing appreciation of the true variety (pluriformity) among scriptural texts produced between the second century B.C.E. and the first century C.E. As Ulrich notes, "there is generally no detectable difference in scrolls thought to be copied outside Qumran from those possibly copied at Qumran. Moreover, the variety in the texts of the Scriptures quoted during the late first century by the New Testament authors and by the Jewish historian Josephus reflects the same character as that found in the Scriptures from Qumran."[6]

While the Qumran documents may be regarded as typical of ancient Jewish scribal practices, one characteristic pertaining to some of the Qumran texts has continued bearing on the origin of the SP. The extant Qumran corpus includes eleven or twelve texts written in a paleo-Hebrew script; ten of these are texts from the Pentateuch. Since this script was favored by the Samaritans, and a point of contention already in the Babylonian Talmud, these texts have attracted special attention by scholars investigating the origin of the SP.[7] Do the Qumran manuscripts written in paleo-Hebrew script give additional evidence of Samaritan presence and activity?

Concerning the paleo-Hebrew script at Qumran, Tov cautions:

> The great majority of texts from Qumran and the other sites in the Judean Desert are written in the square script, and they reflect a textual variety. A similar variety, though on a smaller scale, is reflected in the texts written in the paleo-Hebrew script, so that the textual character of these texts cannot serve as a key for unscrambling the riddle of the writing.[8]

Esther and Hanan Eshel conclude their examination of inscriptions in the paleo-Hebrew script by stating, "The inscriptions mentioned above substantiate the widespread use of the paleo-Hebrew script among the Jews

6. Ulrich, "Dead Sea Scrolls and the Hebrew Scriptural Texts," 99. Yet see Emanuel Tov, *Hebrew Bible, Greek Bible, and Qumran*, 146.

7. Jacob Shachter, trans., *The Babylonian Talmud: Seder Nezikin* (ed. I. Epstein; 8 vols.; London: Soncino Press, 1935; repr., 1987), 3:119 (b. Sanh. 21b).

8. Tov, "Hebrew Bible, Greek Bible, and Qumran," 141. Kartveit (*Origin of the Samaritans*, 288) counts fifteen to sixteen biblical manuscripts written in paleo-Hebrew. This is confirmed also by Tov, *The Texts from the Judaean Desert: Indices and an Introduction to the Discoveries in the Judaean Desert Series* (Clarendon Press: Oxford, 2002), 214; see most recently Tov, *Revised Lists of the Texts from the Judaean Desert* (Leiden: Brill, 2010), 113.

during the Second Temple period."[9] Thus, the pre-Samaritan text type is present in Qumran in different scripts, and the paleo-Hebrew script is used for texts of various text types. Consequently, script alone cannot be used to identify the text type tradition assumed by the Samaritans. So the question remains, why and when did the Samaritans settle on the paleo-Hebrew script for sacred texts? Magnar Kartveit offers the following suggestion:

> The Qumran manuscripts in the palaeo-Hebrew script include the following only: pentateuchal manuscripts, one of Joshua, three unidentified, and one manuscript of the book of Job. The theory is that the pentateuchal books and Job were thought to have been written by Moses, and therefore were rendered in the ancient script. This could well be the case of the choice of the palaeo-Hebrew script for the Samaritan manuscripts also, and be another sign of the emphasis upon Moses as the most important person in the Pentateuch. If so, the Samaritans chose the palaeo-Hebrew script to emphasize the Mosaic character of the Pentateuch, and they used it for a specific version of the Pentateuch where the prophetic status of Moses was made explicit. The script seems therefore to be the result of a choice and not due to the manuscript situation of the time. The use of the Samaritan script later spread to other Samaritan texts, which may be another sign of the fundamental Mosaic character of the Samaritan religious literature. Eventually, the original significance of the script was lost.[10]

Select Pre-Samaritan/Harmonistic Qumran Scripture Scrolls

The following description of the Qumran texts most relevant to the development of the SP is intended to serve as a summary, presenting the most significant findings published in the Discoveries in the Judean Desert series and by other scholars conducting exhaustive research on the scrolls. The pre-Samaritan text group from Qumran is most generally identified as 4QExod-Lev^{f} (4Q17), 4QpaleoExod^{m} (4Q22), 4QNum^{b} (4Q27), 4QRP (4Q158 = 4QRP^{a}, 4Q364 = 4QRP^{b}, 4Q365 = 4QRP^{c}, 4Q366 = 4QRP^{d}, 4Q367 = 4QRP^{e}) and perhaps 4QLev^{d}.[11] As will be noted later in this

9. Eshel and Eshel, "Dating the Samaritan Pentateuch's Compilation," 226.

10. Kartveit, *Origin of the Samaritans*, 288–89.

11. Kartveit, "Major Expansions," 117. Michael Segal ("4QReworked Pentateuch or 4QPentateuch?" in Schiffman et al., *Dead Sea Scrolls Fifty Years after Their Discovery*, 393) contends that 4Q364–367 and 4Q158 do not belong to one composition but reflect "three different categories reflecting independent compositions." See Emanuel

chapter, the authoritative status of 4QRP is debated.[12] The pre-Samaritan texts are sometimes characterized as "harmonizing" texts, that is, "texts which seek to bring disparate elements of the text into harmony with each other."[13] Several other texts—4QDeut^{j}, 4QDeut^{k1}, and 4QDeut^{n}—will be included in the survey here, despite the fact that these texts reflect a degree of harmonization greater than that appearing in the SP and may also reflect a layer of editing later than the SP.[14] Our goal is to present the broadest spectrum of scholarship relative to the pre-Samaritan group and harmonistic texts.

4QpaleoExod^{m} (4Q22)

This is perhaps the most informative of the pre-Samaritan scrolls from Qumran.[15] The scroll contains portions of Exod 6:25–37:16 on fragments

---

Tov, "4QReworked Pentateuch: A Synopsis of Its Contents," *RevQ* 16 (1995): 647–53. Tov (*Hebrew Bible, Greek Bible, and Qumran*, 147) considers the following pre-Samaritan Qumran texts: 4QpaleoExod^{m}, 4QExod-Lev^{f}, 4QNum^{b} and secondarily 4QDeut^{n} and possibly 4QLev^{d}. Ferdinand Dexinger ("Samaritan Origins and the Qumran Texts," in *Methods of Investigation of the Dead Sea Scrolls and the Khirbet Qumran Site: Present Realities and Future Prospects* [ed. Michael Wise et al.; ANYAS 722; New York: New York Academy of Sciences, 1994], 233) considers the proto-Samaritan (pre-SP) texts to be: 4Q158, 4Q364, 4QNum^{b}, 4QDeut^{n} and 4Qpaleo-Exod^{m}.

12. But see Segal ("4QReworked Pentateuch or 4QPentateuch," 392), who believes the designation "pre-Samaritan" is misleading, and points out that texts with harmonistic features "appear to have been fairly common in this period [late Second Temple] and played an important role in the textual history of the Hebrew Bible." Similarly, Esther Eshel ("4QDeut^{n}: A Text That Has Undergone Harmonistic Editing," *HUCA* 62 [1991]: 121) advocates the label "harmonistic texts" be used in reference to these Qumran manuscripts rather than either "proto-Samaritan" or "pre-Samaritan." See also Eshel and Eshel, "Dating the Samaritan Pentateuch's Compilation," 220. Tov (*Hebrew Bible, Greek Bible, and Qumran*, 148) considers 4QRP (4Q158, 4Q364–67) one of the non-aligned texts, although he concludes the pre-SP text is "clearly the underlying text of 4Q158 and 4Q364, and possibly so in the case of 4Q365."

13. Sidnie White Crawford, "The 'Rewritten' Bible at Qumran: A Look at Three Texts," in *Eretz-Israel* (ed. Baruch Levine et al.; Archaeological, Historical and Geographical Studies 26; Jerusalem: Israel Exploration Society, 1999), 2. See also Emanuel Tov, "The Nature and Background of Harmonizations in Biblical Manuscripts," *JSOT* 31 (1985): 3–29.

14. Eshel and Eshel, "Dating the Samaritan Pentateuch's Compilation," 237–38.

15. See Patrick Skehan, "Exodus in the Samaritan Recension from Qumran," *JBL* 74 (1955): 182–87.

surviving from forty-three columns. The scroll has been dated variously between 225 and 25 B.C.E., with most scholars favoring a date between 100 and 75 B.C.E. for the scroll itself and ca. 50 B.C.E. for the patch in column VIII.[16] This patch, written in a different hand, indicates that the scroll was well used and considered valuable enough to repair, thus suggesting that it was regarded to have some authority. Presumably, this means that the textual tradition recorded on 4QpaleoExod^{m} was accepted outside the Samaritan community.

4QpaleoExod^{m} demonstrates the same sort of expanded and harmonizing textual tradition that characterizes SP.[17] Skehan, Ulrich, and Sanderson conclude:

> The text of Exod^{m} [4Qpaleo-Exod^{m}] belongs to the text type or tradition which previously was known to us only in its later representative, the Samaritan Exodus. The scroll shares all major typological features with SP, including all the major expansions of that tradition where it is extant (twelve), with the single exception of the new tenth commandment inserted in Exod 20 from Deut 11 and 27 regarding the altar on Mount Gerizim.[18]

Although the place in the scroll where the Samaritan tenth commandment would appear requires reconstruction, it is important to note that this commandment does not seem to have been included in the scroll.[19] This means that a pre-Samaritan expansionist form of Exodus, minus the expressly sectarian Samaritan layer of editing, was in use in the first century B.C.E.

Skehan, Ulrich, and Sanderson further suggest that the expansions found in SP Exod 20, taken from Deut 5:28–31 and 18:18–22 and relating the people's request for Moses as a mediator and YHWH's response, were originally present in the Qumran scroll, while the expansion concerning

---

16. Patrick Skehan et al., eds., *Qumran Cave 4.IV: Palaeo-Hebrew and Greek Biblical Manuscripts* (DJD 9; Oxford: Clarendon, 1992), 62. Tov (*Texts from the Judaean Desert*, 372) dates 4Q22 to the mid to late Hasmonaean period.

17. Skehan et al., *Qumran Cave 4.IV*, 53.

18. Ibid., 66. See also Schiffman, *Reclaiming the Dead Sea Scrolls*, 178.

19. "Briefly stated, fragments from cols. XX and XXII which are securely placed leave too much room between them for the text of Exod 20:1–21:6 as in MT, but too little room for the text as in SP, which includes three major expansions taken from Deuteronomy" (Skehan et al., *Qumran Cave 4.IV*, 66).

the construction of an altar on Mount Gerizim was not present.[20] This proposal is supported by 4Q158, a paraphrase of Exod 20, and 4Q175, which "contain precisely this combination of Deut 5:28–29 and 18:18–19."[21]

The evidence from 4QpaleoExod^{m} thus offers an important clue in understanding the early history of the SP. Comparisons between this text, other Qumran documents, and the SP suggest that the Samaritan Pentateuch, rather than being a creation *de novo* of the community that worshiped at Mount Gerizim, is instead a somewhat later representative of a tradition that was already known elsewhere in Palestine and used in religious communities with no allegiance to Gerizim. The Gerizim expansion, proper to Samaritan theology, was made only in the Samaritan community, and that was the only major expansion this community made to the text of Exodus.[22]

4QExod-Lev^{f} (4Q17)

4QExod-Lev^{f} is one of the oldest manuscripts recovered from Qumran, dating to the mid-third century B.C.E.[23] Cross has determined that 4QExod-Lev^{f} is affiliated with the Samaritan tradition and is an "early, direct, or better collateral, witness to the textual family which has been called Proto-Samaritan [pre-Samaritan]."[24] 4QExod-Lev^{f} demonstrates a tendency toward expansion, especially evident in Exod 39–40. Significantly, 4QExod-Lev^{f} agrees with SP and MT (and thus with modern translations) in placing Exod 39:3–24 just prior to chapter 40; the LXX locates this material at 36:10–32.

4QLev^{d} (4Q26)

4QLev^{d} is a collection of at least four (and perhaps as many as eleven) fragments containing portions of Lev 14, 15, and 17. The fragments have been dated to the early Herodian period (30 B.C.E.–20 C.E.). At Lev 17:4, 4QLev^{d} contains an expansion that is also represented in the SP and LXX but not

20. Ibid., 67–68.
21. Ibid., 68.
22. Ibid.
23. Frank Moore Cross, "4QExod-Lev^{f}," in *Qumran Cave 4.VII: Genesis to Numbers* (ed. Eugene Ulrich; DJD 12; Oxford: Clarendon, 1994), 134.
24. Cross, "4QExod-Lev^{f}," 136.

in the MT; the parallels between 4QLev^{d} and SP are indicated in italics in the quote below:[25]

> Any man from the house of Israel and the stranger who resides in Israel who slaughters an ox, or lamb, or goat, in the camp, or who slaughters it outside the camp, and has not brought it to the door of the tent of meeting *so as to sacrifice it as a burnt offering or an offering of well-being to the Lord to be acceptable as a pleasing odor, and has slaughtered it without and does not bring it to the door of the tent of meeting to offer it* as an offering to the Lord before the tabernacle of the Lord, that man shall be guilty of bloodshed.

It could be argued that the inserted material gives expression to a trajectory leading to the recognition of one divinely approved place of worship and sacrifice by disqualifying sacrifices slaughtered in unapproved locations.

4QNum^{b} (4Q27)

This scroll, which dates to about 25 B.C.E., also exhibits the expansionist tendency found in other pre-Samaritan texts.[26] In fact, some have characterized 4QNum^{b} as "the Qumran manuscript most closely exhibiting pre-Samaritan characteristics."[27] Nathan Jastram says:

> Of the secondary readings in 4QNum^{b}, the most significant are the major interpolations shared with SP. 4QNum^{b} preserves the interpolations in five places (20:13b; 21:12a, 13a, 21a; 27:23b) and requires their reconstruction in four other places (12:16b; 21:22b, 23b; 31:21a). The remaining five major interpolations of SP occur in sections too far removed from the preserved fragments for certain conclusions, but there is no reason to suppose their absence.[28]

The expansions found in the SP provide a significant connection to 4QNum^{b}. In addition to the expansions shared with SP, 4QNum^{b} also con-

25.Tov classifies 4QLev^{d} with texts close to the presumed Hebrew source of LXX (*Textual Criticism of the Hebrew Bible*, 115). See also Emanuel Tov, "4QLev^{d}," in Ulrich et al., *Qumran Cave 4.VII*, 195.

26. Ulrich, "Dead Sea Scrolls and the Hebrew Scriptural Texts," 83.

27. Tov, "4QLev^{d}," 205.

28. Nathan Jastram, "4QNum^{b}," in Ulrich et al., *Qumran Cave 4.VII*, 215.

tains an expansion (36:2–5) not shared by SP or LXX, along with a number of divergent readings and expansions that are shared with LXX. Yet, as Jastram points out, "4QNum^{b} is not merely a conflated text combining the expansions of the other witnesses; it has a significant number of unique readings, and often has shorter readings than LXX."[29] The expansion in Num 36:1–5, not shared by the SP, suggests that the Samaritans may have chosen the pre-Samaritan text tradition of Numbers prior to 4QNum^{b}.[30]

4QpaleoDeut^{r} (4Q45)

This scroll, preserved in sixty-five fragments, dates to 100–25 B.C.E., making it a contemporary of 4QpaleoExod^{m}.[31] The scroll lacks the sectarian features and the expansions found in the SP, agreeing with MT and LXX. There are twenty-three variants preserved in the scroll, only one of which (the exclusion of Deut 28:19) involves more than a single word or part of a word. In minor variants, the scroll often presents unique readings (twelve times), but among these minor variants, the scroll agrees with SP against MT eight times, and with MT against SP three times.[32] Although a reconstruction, fragments 15–16 suggest that 4QpaleoDeut^{r} reads יבחר ("will choose") at Deut 12:5, parallel to MT, against בחר ("has chosen") in SP.[33]

4QDeut^{j} (4Q37)

4QDeut^{j} is a collection of fragments of Deuteronomy and Exodus, written in the same hand and so presumably belonging to one scroll, or at least copied by one scribe.[34] The fragments date to the late Herodian period (ca. 50 C.E.). 4QDeut^{j} contains an expansion not found in any other manuscript: at Deut 11:21, an interpolation reflecting Exod 12:43–51 and 13:1–5

29. Ibid., 215. See also Crawford, *Rewriting Scripture*, 21.

30. Nathan Jastram, "Text of 4QNum^{b}," in Trebolle Barrera and Vegas Montaner, *Madrid Qumran Congress*, 196–98.

31. Tov, *Texts from the Judaean Desert*, 372.

32. Skehan et al., *Qumran Cave 4.IV*, 135. See also Bernard Levinson, "Textual Criticism, Assyriology, and the History of Interpretation: Deuteronomy 13:7a as a Test Case in Method," *JBL* 120 (2001): 211–43.

33. Skehan et al., *Qumran Cave 4.IV*, 134.

34. But see alternative possibilities provided by Julie Ann Duncan, "4QDeut^{j}," in *Qumran Cave 4.IX: Deuteronomy, Joshua, Judges, Kings* (ed. Eugene Ulrich et al.; DJD 14; Oxford: Clarendon, 1995), 75.

adds the promise of a long life to the circumcision requirement for Passover.[35] This interpolation is unusual, inasmuch as pre-Samaritan texts and the SP generally insert interpolations from Deuteronomy into Exodus and Numbers, rather than vice versa as here in 4QDeut^{j}.

4QDeut^{k1} (4Q38)

This manuscript, written in an early Herodian hand (30–1 B.C.E.), consists of five fragments preserving portions of Deut 5, 11, and 32.[36] The orthography of this manuscript is generally fuller than either the MT or SP. It has been suggested that 4QDeut^{k1} is a catena of passages that may have been used for liturgical purposes, a proposal that raises questions as to its value as a witness to the pre-Samaritan scriptural text tradition.[37]

4QDeut^{n} (4Q41)

This scroll, written in six columns, dates to the early Herodian period (30–1 B.C.E.).[38] Esther Eshel has made a compelling argument that 4QDeut^{n} is not a Torah scroll, but rather a collection of prayers used in community liturgies.[39] Consequently, the scroll may not have been intended to present an authoritative text, and thus should perhaps be categorized as an independent composition. Nevertheless, some of the characteristics of the scroll, especially the harmonizations present in the text, give expression to editorial practices seen in the SP, so that the document may be considered a "harmonized text in the pre-Samaritan tradition."[40]

Deuteronomy 27:4

The recent publication of a fragment of Deut 27:4–6 by James Charlesworth seems to confirm the SP version, reading "Gerizim" against the

35. Ibid., 88–89.

36. Ibid., 94.

37. Ibid., 95; Eshel, "4QDeut^{n}," 151.

38. Sidnie White Crawford, "4QDeut^{n}," in Ulrich et al., *Qumran Cave 4.IX*, 117.

39. Eshel, "4QDeut^{n}," 30.

40. Ibid., 120. Charlesworth ("What Is a Variant," 8 n. 8) is of the opinion that 4QDeut^{n} should not be included among the "Proto-Samaritan" texts, owing to the different style of interpolation evident in 4QDeut^{n}.

MT's "Ebal."[41] Although the fragment is small, it is provisionally dated to the middle of the first century B.C.E. The only other Qumran text containing Deut 27:1–10, 4QDeut^{f}, has a gap at verse 4 where the name of the location of the altar would appear.[42] If the tradition represented by the MT is the variant, then it was intended to detract from the Gerizim site, but if the SP is the variant tradition, then this change must have been made by Samaritan scribes in order to emphasize the priority of Gerizim against all competing places of worship. In this instance, the SP seems to preserve the original reading, "Gerizim" having been changed to "Ebal" in reaction to the Samaritan preference for Gerizim.[43] "One may therefore conclude that there once was a Hebrew text with 'Mount Gerizim' in Deut 27:4. This was the earlier reading. The change to 'Ebal' must have been made at the hands of the Jews and could be a polemical alteration: an altar in the north was to be built on the mountain of curse."[44]

4QRP (4Q158, 4Q364, 4Q365, 4Q366, 4Q367)

4QRP is a group of five manuscripts (4Q158, 4Q364–67).[45] The two most extensively preserved members of this group, 4Q364 and 4Q365, were copied sometime between 75–50 B.C.E., and both probably contained all five books of the Pentateuch.[46] Although fragmentary, the manuscripts contain portions of the entire Pentateuch from Genesis through Deu-

41. Ibid., 3.

42. Crawford, "4QDeut^{n}," 52.

43. Kartveit, *Origin of the Samaritans*, 292; Charlesworth, "What Is a Variant?"; Christophe Nihan, "The Torah between Samaria and Judah," in Knoppers and Levinson, *Pentateuch as Torah*, 213.

44. Kartveit, *Origin of the Samaritans*, 303.

45. Segal ("4QReworked Pentateuch or 4QPentateuch," 391–99) is of the opinion that 4Q158 does not belong to the group. Kartveit (*Origin of the Samaritans*, 271) refers to the 4QRP group as fragments of a manuscript.

46. 4Q364: Gen 25:18–21; 26:7–8; 27:39; 28:6; 29:32–33; 30:1–4; 30:26–36; 31:47–53; 32:18–20; 32:26–30; 34:2; 35:28; 37:7–8; 38:14–21; 44: 30–45:1; 45:21–27; 48:14–15; Exod 21:14–22; 24:12–14; 24:18; 25:1–2; 26:1; 26:33–35; Num 14:16–20; 20:17–18; 33:31–49; Deut 1:1–6; 1:17–33; 1:45–46; 2:8–14; 2:30–3:2; 3:18–23; 9:6–7; 9:12–18; 9:22–24; 9:27–29; 10:6–7; 10:10–13; 10:22–11:2; 11:6–9; 11:23–24; 14:24–26.

4Q365: Gen 21:9–10; Exod 8:13–19; 9:9–12; 10:19–20; 14:10; 14:12–21; 15:16–20; 15:22–26; 17:3–5; 36:32–38; 37:29–38:7; 39:1–16; 29:17–19; Lev 11:1–2; 11:17–24; 11:32; 11:40–45; 13:6–8; 13:15–18; 13:51–52; 16:6–7 (11–12?); Lev 18:26–28; 23:42–24:2; 25:7–9; 26:17–32; 27:34; Num 1:1–5; 3:26–30; 3:47–49; 7:1; 7:78–80; 8:11–12;

teronomy (4Q364 lacks Lev). The scrolls in the 4QRP group reflect a common "exegetical tradition" in which "an individual scribe (or group of scribes) had freedom to manipulate a received text within a broader body of tradition."[47] These "manipulations" include insertion of previously unknown material, thematic regrouping of material, short editorial comments that clarify narrative passages, and major harmonizations (some of which are shared by the SP and some that are not shared with the SP). None of the preserved insertions or regrouped materials are identified or marked off in any way. This leads one to believe that the scribe expected his document to be received with the same level of authority as other pentateuchal texts.

The complexities of the biblical textual tradition at Qumran and the authority thought to have been recognized in the different versions are conveniently illustrated by scholarly discussions about 4QRP. Unlike the other pre-Samaritan biblical texts noted above (4QpaleoExod^{m} and 4QNum^{b}), the 4QRP group represents a new literary composition that incorporates material not found elsewhere in the pentateuchal texts.[48] According to Crawford's spectrum as outlined in chapter 2, the presence of this new material identifies 4QRP more as "commentary" than as scriptural composition.[49] Crawford is of the opinion that "4QRP was thus recognized as an expansion of the already stable text of the Torah and relegated to the ranks of commentary," and consequently, the text of 4QRP may be of limited value when describing the pre-Samaritan "biblical" text type.[50] But as we will see, this conclusion is not shared by all.

A similar conclusion was reached by Emanuel Tov (a conclusion he has since reversed), whose approach has added substantial precision to

---

9:15–10:3; 13:12–25; 13:29–30; 15:26–28; 17:20–24; 27:11; 36:1–2; Deut 2:24 (36?); 19:20–20:1.

47. Crawford, *Rewriting Scripture*, 42–54, here 41. See also Sidnie White Crawford, "The Rewritten Bible at Qumran," in Charlesworth, *Scripture and the Scrolls*, 140.

48. Crawford (*Rewriting Scripture*, 39) has most recently revised her earlier descriptions of the 4QRP group. The group should not be considered a single composition by a single author but a group of texts that may have include more than the preserved five manuscripts.

49. Crawford, "Rewritten Bible at Qumran," 3–5. Emanuel Tov shares Crawford's assessment ("Biblical Texts as Reworked in Some Qumran Manuscripts with Special Attention to 4QRP and 4QParaGen-Exod," in Ulrich and VanderKam, *Community of the Renewed Covenant*, 114).

50. Crawford, "Rewritten Bible at Qumran," 3.

the discussion of "rewritten Bible" texts such as 4QRP. Tov identifies three groups of "rewritten" biblical texts among the Qumran scrolls: liturgical texts composed of selections from biblical books, at times in combination with non-biblical selections; abbreviated and excerpted biblical texts prepared for special occasions; and new literary compositions that overlap with biblical texts.[51] The third of these categories is of special interest here and has immediate bearing on the problem of 4QRP. The insertion of new, non-pentateuchal material into 4QRP significantly distinguishes this text from those in the established pre-Samaritan group.[52] Noting this point, in his earlier work Tov affirmed Crawford's assessment of 4QRP, emphasizing that the pre-Samaritan group limited its reworking to "the addition of sentences or pericopes from elsewhere in the Bible" while the rewritten Bible compositions "freely added new details and probably were not considered authoritative."[53] Tov's conclusion here notably moves beyond questions of content to consider the Qumran community's assessment of the text: Was it understood to be an authoritative text or a commentary on an authoritative text? In the late 1990s, Tov concluded that while 4QRP is based on a pre-SP biblical text, the document should not be considered a "biblical" manuscript.[54] Eugene Ulrich, on the other hand, contends that 4Q364–67 should be viewed as a new composition, yet another "variant literary edition of the Pentateuch, parallel to the traditional MT, and parallel to that other Jewish variant edition of the Pentateuch that was at home in Second Temple Judaism and used as the basis for the Samaritan Pentateuch."[55] Crawford, by contrast, concludes that "we have in the Reworked Pentateuch group the end of a very long tradition of innerscriptural scribal exegesis, soon to be replaced by another tradition of separating the authoritative text from its commentary."[56]

Michael Segal, however, proposes a different approach. Segal argues that 4Q364–367 (4QRP^{b-e}) should be considered "biblical" texts despite the fact that they include "new" expanded material that does not appear in

51. Emanuel Tov, "Rewritten Bible Compositions and Biblical Manuscripts, with Special Attention to the Samaritan Pentateuch," *DSD* 5 (1998): 336–37.

52. Ibid., 339.

53. Ibid., 354.

54. Ibid., 341, 354.

55. Ulrich, "The Qumran Scrolls and the Biblical Text," 57.

56. Crawford, *Rewriting Scripture*, 57.

other manuscripts of the authoritative Pentateuch.[57] Likening the expansions of 4Q364–367 to expansions found in the MT text of Jeremiah when compared to the LXX version of Jeremiah, Segal concludes that "these scrolls should be viewed as later editions of the text of the Torah."[58] Following a similar logic, Tov has more recently revised his conclusion on 4QRP, suggesting that the scrolls in this group should be included among the "biblical" texts from Qumran and thus "studied as Hebrew Scripture."[59]

The manner in which 4QRP has undergone transitions in scholarly opinion illustrates our developing awareness of the fluidity of the scriptural tradition in the late Second Temple period. While most scholars agree that 4QRP is an example of a harmonistic text type, and while most would also recognize the "scriptural" status of the 4QRP group, debate continues over the authority attributed to this scroll by the Qumran community and the appropriateness of grouping it with other recognized pre-Samaritan biblical scrolls (4QpaleoExod^{m}, 4QNum^{b}).

Whether it represents a new composition or the extension of a long tradition, 4QRP demonstrates that the tendency toward harmonization and expansion did not stop with the pre-Samaritan group, but was continued even further without affecting the received authority of the text.[60] The multiple versions of scriptural texts, including the pre-Samaritan texts, present at Qumran, remind us that the editing soon to produce the SP was at home within the biblical tradition, not foreign to that tradition.

---

57. Segal, "Between Bible and Rewritten Bible," 15–16. See also Segal, "4QReworked Pentateuch or 4QPentateuch?" 391–99.

58. Segal, "Between Bible and Rewritten Bible," 15–16.

59. Emanuel Tov, "The Many Forms of Hebrew Scripture: Reflections in Light of the LXX and 4QReworked Pentateuch," in Lange et al., *From Qumran to Aleppo*, 28. See also Tov, *Revised Lists of the Texts from the Judaean Desert*, 113.

60. The authoritative status of 4Q364 and 4Q365 is affirmed by Ulrich ("Qumran Scrolls and the Biblical Text," 57). Michael Segal is of the opinion that the group represents three different compositions ("4QReworked Pentateuch or 4QPentateuch," 393). See also Armin Lange, "The Status of the Biblical Texts in the Qumran Corpus and the Canonical Process," in *The Bible as Book: The Hebrew Bible and the Judaean Desert Discoveries* (ed. Edward D. Herbert and Emanuel Tov; London: British Library, 2002), 27; Tov, "Reflections on the Many Forms of Hebrew Scripture," 11–28.

A Fluid Text at Qumran

This brief survey of just a few of the Qumran texts indicates that the pre-Samaritan tradition was fluid during the first century B.C.E., developing side by side with other textual traditions that would not develop into the SP.[61] The Qumran community seems to have accepted "a certain amount of textual flux, even to the point of accepting two [or more] parallel literary editions of the same text as valid Scripture."[62] This is especially true of Exodus, Numbers, and Deuteronomy, but also, to a greater or lesser extent, of other books of the Pentateuch. For example, 4QpaleoGen-Exod^{l} (100–50 B.C.E.), a fragmentary scroll presumed to have contained the whole of Genesis and Exodus, preserves a reading quite different from that in 4QpaleoExod^{m}.[63] 4QpaleoGen-Exod^{l} lacks the harmonizing expansions found in 4QpaleoExod^{m} and the SP, but "in smaller variants sometimes agrees with MT, sometimes with SP, sometimes with Exod^{m} [4QpaleoExod^{m}], and sometimes preserves a unique reading."[64]

The available evidence suggests that the text of both Genesis and Leviticus was fairly stable by the late Second Temple period. Leviticus is present in the Qumran scrolls but with "no major differences among the various witnesses."[65] Although Genesis does exhibit variation, "none of the differences are systematic enough to posit a second (or third) literary edition for the entire book.[66] The same is not true of Exodus, Numbers, and Deuteronomy. As Crawford notes:

> Exodus and Numbers circulated in two literary editions in antiquity, and copies of both editions were recovered at Qumran. The second version was an intentionally expanded version of the first, primarily through the technique of harmonization. The most complete witnesses to the short version of Exodus are the Masoretic Text and the Septuagint, while the most complete witness to the expanded version of Exodus is the Samaritan Pentateuch.[67]

61. Ulrich, "Bible in the Making," 85–86.

62. Crawford, *Rewriting Scripture*, 37. Tov makes the same point in *Hebrew Bible, Greek Bible, and Qumran*, 150.

63. Skehan et al., *Qumran Cave 4.IV*, 23.

64. Ibid., 23.

65. Crawford, *Rewriting Scripture*, 21.

66. Ibid.

67. Ibid.

Crawford concludes that the harmonization technique applied to Exodus was thorough. At least one scribal tradition, evident in the Qumran texts, considered updating, harmonizing, and perfecting the text an important scribal task. Crawford writes, "Any possible hint of inconsistency in the scriptural text, unthinkable in this approach to the text, is thus eliminated and a harmonized narrative is the result."[68]

But is this truly the case? Were all inconsistencies considered "unthinkable" and removed through a harmonizing edit? And what prevented the application of this harmonizing technique to the "stable text of Genesis and Leviticus" even though ample opportunity, or need, exists in these texts? Closer examination of this harmonization technique will lead us further down the stream of textual tradition leading to the SP.

68. Ibid., 29.

4
From Pre-Samaritan to Samaritan Pentateuch

The last chapter concluded with a brief summary of the harmonistic and the pre-Samaritan group of manuscripts recovered at Qumran. These texts existed side by side with other scriptural text traditions, forming a fluid and dynamic textual environment. This observation provides the starting point for our examination of the transition from the pre-Samaritan group of texts to the SP. For Samaritan studies, one of the most significant findings resulting from the examination of the Qumran scrolls is the awareness that "the Second Temple communities behind the Septuagint, the biblical texts discovered at Qumran, and the Samaritan Pentateuch employed the same methods and techniques to interpret and expand the biblical text."[1] Put another way, the examination of the SP must begin with awareness that the Pentateuch as we know it is a product of Judea *and* Samaria.

This observation takes us back to the discussion of Samaritan origins in chapter 1. The Assyrian conquest did not totally depopulate Samaria of YHWH worshipers who shared religious sensibilities and traditions in common with Judeans. These shared beliefs cannot be adequately explained in terms of a group of Jerusalem priests migrating to Gerizim and taking their Pentateuch with them (see Neh 13:28). Neither does the theory of a Persian *Reichsautorisation* seem to adequately explain the common pentateuchal traditions in Judah and Samaria.[2] Without a convincing theory of common origins, we are left with the simple fact that the Pentateuch of the Jews and the Pentateuch used by the Samaritans share much in common,

---

1. Pummer, "Samaritans and Their Pentateuch," 264. See also Levinson, "Textual Criticism, Assyriology, and the History of Interpretation," 211–43.

2. Even in modified form suggested by James Watts (*Reading Law: The Rhetorical Shaping of the Pentateuch* [Biblical Seminar 59; Sheffield: Sheffield Academic Press, 1999], 140–43).

and this commonality is where we must begin our consideration of the development of the SP.[3]

Harmonization in the Biblical Traditions

One of the chief characteristics of the SP is a trend toward internal harmonization. Yet, as Emanuel Tov has noted, this trend is by no means unique: "Almost all Qumran MSS contain sporadic harmonizing readings."[4] The editorial practice of harmonization found in the pre-Samaritan texts is evidenced throughout the Hebrew Bible and in the Synoptic Gospels of the New Testament. Harmonization is not an exclusively Samaritan or pre-Samaritan phenomenon. In broad strokes, scribal harmonizations fall into two patterns. First, details from one parallel passage may be inserted into the other to "fill out" the passage missing those details. Second, details in one parallel passage may be changed in order to bring it into agreement with the other, thus eliminating the impression of contradiction.[5] Both of these procedures are found in the pre-Samaritan text group and the SP. Looking deeper, Tov has offered a useful classification of harmonizations that reflects both the *source* and the *effect* of the harmonizing material. In terms of source, Tov notes that the harmonizing material may be derived from within the same immediate context or the same biblical book or from other biblical books.[6] In the particular case of the pre-Samaritan texts and the SP, this scheme is helpful for distinguishing harmonizing interpolations that originate from within pentateuchal sources from those interpolations that originate outside pentateuchal sources. In terms of effect, Tov notes that efforts at harmonization generally seek to "correct" one of the

---

3. Dexinger ("Samaritan Origins and the Qumran Texts," 231–46) notes that "the religion of the proto-Samaritans was essentially the religion of Jerusalem. It is the common Jewish heritage, then, which forms the similar background of Qumran and the Samaritans as well. And it is the Qumran material that enables us to reach a fresh scholarly view of Samaritan origins" (244). See also Hjelm ("Samaria, Samaritans," 99), who writes, "The non-centralistic aspects as well as ambiguities about halachic rules and the exact meaning about the chosen place or places, mentioned in Deuteronomy 12, challenge traditional assumptions about the Pentateuch's origin in Jerusalem."

4. Tov, "Nature and Background of Harmonizations," 15.

5. Jeffrey Tigay, "Conflation as a Redactional Technique," in *Empirical Models for Biblical Criticism* (ed. Jeffrey Tigay; Philadelphia: University of Pennsylvania Press, 1985), 62.

6. Tov, "Nature and Background of Harmonizations," 5.

following textual problems: syntactical incongruities; minor contextual differences; discrepancies between command and fulfillment; references to earlier statements; or differences in major detail.[7]

Chief among the editorial harmonizations in the pre-Samaritan texts and SP are forty expansions that have resulted from the interpolation of material taken from parallel passages within the Pentateuch in an effort to harmonize command and fulfillment episodes, make reference to earlier statements, and resolve differences in major detail. These expansions are summarized on the table below.[8]

Number	Expanded Passage	Source of Expansion	DSS witness
1	Gen 30:36+	Gen 31:11–13	4QRP^{b} (4Q364)
2	Gen 42:16+	Gen 44:22	
3	Exod 6:9+	Exod 14:12	
4	Exod 7:18+	Exod 7:16–18	4QpaleoExod^{m} (4Q22)
5	Exod 7:29+	Exod 7:26–29	4Q22
6	Exod 8:1+	Exod 8:1	4Q22
7	Exod 8:19+	Exod 8:16b–19	4Q22
8	Exod 9:5+	Exod 9:1–5	4Q22
9	Exod 9:19+	Exod 9:13–19	4Q22
10	Exod 10:2+	Exod 10:3–6	4Q22

7. Ibid., 6–11.

8. Kartveit, *Origin of the Samaritans*, 310–12 and "Major Expansions," 117–24. The + before the biblical reference indicates that the interpolation appears before the reference and the + after the reference indicates the interpolation appears after the reference.

11	Exod 11:3	Exod 11:4b–7	4Q22
12	Exod 11:3+	Exod 4:22–23	4Q22
13	Exod 18:25	Deut 1:9b–18	4Q22
14	Exod 20:17+	Deut 27:2b–7; 11:29–30	
15	Exod 20:19	Deut 5:24–27	4Q22
16	Exod 20:21	Deut 5:28–29; 18:18–22; 5:30–31	4Q22
17	Exod 26:35+	Exod 30:1–10	4Q22
18	Exod 27:19+	Exod 39:1	4Q22
19	Exod 28:29+	Exod 28:30	
20	Exod 29:28+	Exod 29:21	4Q22
21	Exod 32:10+	Deut 9:20	4Q22
22	Exod 39:21+	Exod 28:30	4QExod–Lev^{f} (4Q17)
23	Num 4:14+	Num 4:13–14; Exod 31:9	
24	Num 10:10+	Deut 1:6–8	
25	Num 12:16+	Deut 1:20–22	4QNum^{b} (4Q27)
26	Num 13:33+	Deut 1:27–33	
27	Num 14:40+	Deut 1:42	
28	Num 14:45+	Deut 1:44b–45	

29	Num 20:13+	Deut 3:24–25; 26b–28	4Q27
30	Num 20:13+	Deut 2:2–6	4Q27
31	Num 21:+12	Deut 2:9	4Q27
32	Num 21:+13	Deut 2:17–19	4Q27
33	Num 21:20+	Deut 2:24–25	4Q27
34	Num 21:+21	Deut 2:26–27	
35	Num 21:22	Deut 2:28–29a	4Q27
36	Num 21:23	Deut 2:31	4Q27
37	Num 27:23+	Deut 3:21b–22	4Q27
38	Num 31:20+	Num 31:21–24	4Q27
39	Deut 2:7+	Num 20:14, 17–18	4QRP^{b} (4Q364)
40	Deut 10:6	Deut 10:7; Num 33:31–37	4Q364

Several general observations can be made about the pre-Samaritan expansions:

(1) A significant amount of harmonizing appears in the plague story of Exod 7–11.

(2) The language of Moses' speech in Deut 1–3 is extensively borrowed in the narration of the relevant parallel stories in Exodus and Numbers.[9] In one notable instance, Num 13:33+, the inser-

9. Tov ("Rewritten Bible Compositions," 347) writes, "The reviser of the text in the SP group focused on the first three chapters of Deuteronomy which in his mind should have reflected an exact summary of the events and speeches described in the earlier books."

tion creates a difficulty rather than resolving one, producing a very awkward duplication with the material following in Num 14. A similar problem appears in Num 14:40b, which incorporates material from Deut 1:42. The inserted material duplicates Num 14:42–43, requiring the editor to rephrase the insertion, with the result that Moses repeats the words that God has just spoken.

(3) The most conspicuous SP expansion missing in the 4Q texts is the expansion of the tenth commandment with material inserted after Exod 20:17 as it appears in the MT.

(4) Expansions do not appear in the legal material.

The expansive interpolations found in the pre-Samaritan group and SP all share the same formal characteristic: they are interpolations taken from other places within the Pentateuch. In this one characteristic, the interpolations are similar to other interpolations found in the MT and LXX. For example, Exod 32:9 is copied from Deut 9:13 and is found in the SP, MT, and 4Q22, but not the LXX. Likewise, MT Jeremiah and MT and LXX Joshua, Ezekiel, and Proverbs all evidence this tendency toward expansion. The expansions may also help us date the pre-Samaritan tradition. Expansions are present in four Qumran texts: 4Q17 (mid-third century B.C.E.), 4Q22 (100–225 B.C.E.), 4Q27 (late first century B.C.E.), and 4Q364 (75–50 B.C.E.). Consequently, the expansions must be dated before the third to first century B.C.E.; at the same time, none are found in the LXX, so we may assume the expansions were constructed after the LXX (ca. 275 B.C.E.). The pre-Samaritan textual tradition, at least including the forty expansions identified above, must have been in use between the mid-third and the mid-first century B.C.E.[10]

The Moses Factor

The presence of these forty extensive expansions begs the question, Why are they here? Sidnie White Crawford suggests that the harmonization process evident in the interpolated expansions sought to eliminate differences between parallel passages.[11] Similarly, Magnar Kartviet observes that there has been general agreement that the expansions remove "internal conflict or irregularity."[12] The two expansions found in Genesis illustrate this principle. Both of the Genesis expansions (Gen 30:36+; 42:16+) make later actions more understandable by adjusting the presentation of earlier material. Thus, a divine revelation to Jacob in a dream appears following Gen 30:36. This material is taken from Gen 31:11–13, making the two stories in Gen 30 and 31 agree more explicitly. Similarly, an insertion following Gen 42:16, taken from Gen 44:22, expands the discussion among Jacob's sons in a way that makes Joseph explicitly aware of their reasons for not bringing Benjamin back to Egypt. These two expansive interpolations, although perhaps effecting a harmonizing element, make explicit previously unknown details.

But this rule clearly does not apply to every case. As noted by Kartveit, there are two major problems in attempting to explain the expan-

---

10. See Kartveit, *Origin of the Samaritans*, 276. Eshel and Eshel ("Dating the Samaritan Pentateuch's Compilation," 230, 238–39) make an interesting observation concerning the harmonistic editing in the SP: "Significantly, the SP is the only text-type with comprehensive harmonistic editing in all five books of the Pentateuch." This, they suggest, was not accidental, but a deliberate choice by the Samaritan "sect," providing a biblical version that "corresponded to the Samaritan outlook" and was "prevalent when the authoritative version of their Pentateuch was established." They conclude: "Those scrolls with more comprehensive editing than the SP appear to reflect a version the editing of which was concluded after the Samaritan adoption of the scrolls which formed the basis for the SP.… Consequently, the discovery of texts with more comprehensive editing than the SP, which are written in Hasmonean and Herodian script, as well as the harmonistic section in 4QTest, prove that the primary version of the SP was created in the second century B.C.E."

11. Crawford, *Rewriting Scripture*, 23.

12. Kartveit, *Origin of the Samaritans*, 274–75.

sions solely in terms of a trend toward harmonization.[13] First, the notion of harmonization presupposes an attempt to make the text more "consistent." But consistent in what sense—in its literary style, narrative details, or theological themes? Second, why are there places where no harmonization takes place? The harmonization, even in the highly interpolated sections, is uneven, and some sections of the Pentateuch are devoid of harmonization, most notably the legal material and the creation accounts. For example, within the Exodus plague narrative of the pre-Samaritan and SP tradition, two stories of the death of the animals remain unharmonized; the firstborn cattle die twice (Exod 9:6, 25; 12:29); Moses apparently meets Pharaoh for the last time in 10:29, but then meets him again in 11:8; and the people believe Moses in 4:31, yet he complains of their unbelief in 6:9.[14] If the harmonizing interpolations were intended to remove inconsistencies, the task was only incompletely performed.

The inconsistent nature of the harmonizations in the Qumran pre-Samaritan texts and the SP itself has been a persistent problem for SP studies. As Emanuel Tov notes, the pre-Samaritan texts reflect a great deal of content editing. The editing involved is of a specific nature, meant to impart a more perfect and internally consistent structure to the text, and the editing is idiosyncratic, that is, certain details were changed, while others of a similar nature were left untouched.[15] Overall, a great deal of effort was spent on the content editing with a specific intent, but the final result was inconsistent and idiosyncratic—on the face of it, the editing process appears to have been unsuccessful. Noting these difficulties, Tov admits that "it is hard to know why certain units [of text] were altered … while others were not, and the only explanation for this phenomenon is the personal taste of the editor."[16] The words "the editor" in the preceding quote reflect a significant element of Tov's conclusion. In his view, the apparently haphazard nature of the editing "ought to be conceived of as the work of a single person and not of a school or textual family." The few instances "in which the editor deviated from the sequence of the verses show the personal involvement of a single person, which is reflected in more than one textual source. It seems that a single text must be assumed

13. Ibid., 275–76.

14. Ibid., 275.

15. Tov, "Rewritten Bible Compositions," 341.

16. Ibid., 342.

at the base of the SP texts reflecting the work of a single person."[17] In other words, the expansions are best explained in terms of a single scribe "correcting" a single text.

But are the edits as idiosyncratic as Tov suggests, necessarily confined to the work of a single scribe? A closer look at the distribution of the expansive interpolations may offer clues to their purpose and origin. First, as noted above, expansions do not appear at all in the legal material of Exod 21–23 or Leviticus, and only two expansions appear in Num 1–10. Second, expansions are rare in the Genesis stories—only two appear there. Third, the expansions are concentrated in specific texts, through an uneven distribution: ten expansions appear in Exod 7–11; fifteen are drawn from Deut 1–3 and inserted into Exodus, and fourteen into Numbers; five expansions appear in Exod 25–40, the discussion of the details of the tabernacle's construction. Fourth and finally here, Exod 20 includes two long expansions. Overall, the expansions are concentrated in four contexts: the plague narrative of Exod 7–11; the theophany at Mount Sinai; the details for the construction of the tabernacle; and, the narratives of events mentioned in Moses' summary of Israel's history in Deut 1–3. Common to all four groupings is the prominent presence of *Moses*.

A similar trend is evident in the insertions into the plague narrative, which deal mostly with the communication of a divine message to Pharaoh by Moses. The insertions standardize the introductory formula "Thus says the Lord" and describe a faithful transmission of the divine message delivered by Moses to Pharaoh. Combining this observation with the above notes on the Genesis narratives, one may say that the Genesis and plague expansions tend to appear in passages that involve divine revelations. The phrase "Thus says the Lord," repeated in ten of the twelve expansions, is a notable characteristic of the interpolations. The repeated insertion of this introductory phrase is particularly significant, since many of the small irregularities in the narrative are not smoothed out by the expansions. The harmonization is uneven and incomplete, and there are three instances where harmonization between command and execution of command does not appear (Exod 14:2; 16:11; 17:14).[18] Although a degree of harmonization is accomplished by the interpolations in the plague nar-

17. Ibid., 351. Samaritan tradition also affirms a single author/editor of the revered Abisha Scroll, but for reasons other than that identified by Tov.

18. Kartveit, *Origin of the Samaritans*, 277.

rative, the elevation of Moses as a faithful representative of God may be the more immediate purpose for the edits.

The same emphasis on Moses as God's faithful representative perhaps explains why Deuteronomy serves as the source for fifteen insertions into Exodus and Numbers. In Deut 1–3, Moses recalls incidents and events that occurred during the time of the narratives related in Exodus and Numbers. Some of these events do not appear in the MT and LXX texts of Exodus and Numbers, and the insertions in the SP and pre-Samaritan texts fill this gap. As Kartveit observes, in the SP "Moses in Deut 1–3 is depicted as a truthful history-teller. He does not report an event or a divine revelation in Deuteronomy unless it actually took place according to Exodus and Numbers."[19] This need for the primary narrative to appear in Exodus and Numbers is quite understandable: since Deuteronomy is postured as a recap of the earlier narrative, all of the events described there should also appear in the primary narrative of Exodus-Numbers, but not all of the details in Exodus-Numbers need appear in Deuteronomy, as Moses could have abridged the story.[20] While the vast majority of insertions are taken from Deuteronomy and added to Exodus-Numbers, two additions were made to Deuteronomy: Deut 2:7 incorporates material from Num 20:14, 17, and Deut 10:6 adds material from Num 33:31–34. The former insertion adds an explicit reference to Edom, while the latter corrects an inconsistency regarding the site of Aaron's death. Overall, the pre-Samaritan insertions into Exodus and Numbers do not simply harmonize the details of these books with the words of Moses in Deut 1–3. The insertions reinforce the veracity of Moses and present him as an unequaled source of truth and guidance.

The "Moses layer" of editing in the pre-Samaritan texts provides a key to understanding the editorial practices behind them.[21] Moses becomes the standard by which all subsequent prophets are measured, and prophecy after Moses is defined as simply proclaiming the law of Moses. The central role assigned to Moses in the pre-Samaritan texts may provide some insight into the dialogue concerning the canonization of the second part of the Hebrew Bible. The earliest extant witness to the pre-Samaritan text type (texts with the expansions) is 4Q17, dating to about the middle

---

19. Ibid., 278.

20. Tov, "Nature and Background of Harmonizations," 8.

21. Kartveit (*Origin of the Samaritans*, 287) says, "The pre-Samaritan manuscripts were reworked on one principle, Moses the prophet and his successor."

of the third century B.C.E.; thus the development of the pre-Samaritan Moses Layer predates the mid-third century B.C.E. This timeframe coincides with the rising importance of the prophetic corpus in the Hebrew Bible and suggests a lively debate concerning the value of that body of prophetic texts. In the context of this debate, the pre-Samaritan tradition reaffirms the authority of Moses, an authority to which all other prophets must defer.[22]

From Pre-Samaritan Texts to the Samaritan Pentateuch

The most conspicuous expansive interpolation missing from the pre-Samaritan group of texts is the SP's distinctive version of the tenth commandment of the Decalogue, which specifically names Mount Gerizim as the appropriate place of worship. Tov is of the opinion that the sectarian editing of the pre-Samaritan text was accomplished by the insertion of the Samaritan tenth commandment and the "small change in the centralization formula in the book of Deuteronomy."[23] This thin layer of editing marks the move from the pre-Samaritan texts to the SP. "When this very slight sectarian layer is removed, its underlying base can easily be recognized as an early pre-sectarian text, parallel with any of the Qumran texts."[24] At their core, those sectarian edits involve the composition of a new tenth commandment, composed entirely of material taken from elsewhere in the Torah (Deut 11:29a; Deut 27:4a; Deut 27:5–7; Deut 11:30), and a change in the centralization of the cult effected by the change of the verb יבחר ("will choose" as in present MT) to בחר ("has chosen" in the SP). These trends will be examined in greater detail in the next chapter.

22. Ibid., 299.

23. Tov, "Rewritten Bible Compositions," 340. See also Ulrich, "Pluriformity in the Biblical Text," 27.

24. Tov, "Rewritten Bible Compositions," 340. See also Tigay ("Conflation as a Redactional Technique," 62): "The Samaritan Pentateuch itself is not an exclusively Samaritan text, apart from a few sectarian additions and changes; rather, it is essentially an early Hebrew text type which is sometimes reflected in early manuscripts of the Mishna, a decidedly non-Samaritan composition, as well as in the proto-Samaritan manuscripts from Qumran."

5
Textual Characteristics of the Samaritan Pentateuch[1]

Early in the last century, the influential Samaritan scholar James Montgomery suggested that the SP's "variations will never be of interest to more than the textual scholar."[2] Given the opportunity today, Montgomery would doubtless revise his opinion, for in recent years the SP has been widely recognized as an important participant in the literary milieu of the Second Temple period. In fairness, of course, Montgomery could not have foreseen the discovery of the Qumran scrolls, nor could he have imagined that those materials would shine new light not only upon the SP but also upon the very nature of textual transmission in the late Second Temple period.

In many respects, Montgomery was articulating a widespread view of the SP that had resulted from the work of biblical scholar and text critic H. F. W. Gesenius (1786–1842). In 1815, Gesenius published an extensive examination of the SP in which he attempted to classify the differences between the SP and MT, a classification that was standard until the late twentieth century and that remains influential in some text-critical studies.[3] Using the MT as the standard, Gesenius identified eight classes

1. An earlier version of portions of the material contained in this chapter appeared in Anderson and Giles, *Tradition Kept*, 17–48.

2. Montgomery, *The Samaritans*, 290.

3. H. F. W. Gesenius, *De Pentateuchi Samaritani Origine Indole et Auctorite: Commentatio Philologico-Critica* (Halle: Rengerianae, 1815). See also Bruce Waltke, "Prolegomena to the Samaritan Pentateuch" (Ph.D. diss., Harvard University, 1965) and Waltke, "The Samaritan Pentateuch and the Text of the Old Testament," in *New Perspectives on the Old Testament* (ed. J. Barton Payne; Waco, Tex.: Word, 1970), 213. See also Jean Margain, "Samaritain (Pentateuque)," *Dictionnaire de la Bible* 11:762–69 (Paris: Le Touzey & Ané, 1978); and James VanderKam and Peter Flint, *The Meaning of the Dead Sea Scrolls* (San Francisco: HarperCollins, 2002), 93–94. Recent comparisons

of variant readings in the SP that he considered to be secondary, and used this scheme to categorize more than six thousand variations between the SP and the MT:

(1) scribal error
(2) a linguistic tradition different from that preserved by the Tiberian grammarians, as formulated in the MT
(3) modernization of the text by updating archaic Hebrew forms and constructions
(4) exegetical smoothing of grammatical difficulties by removing rare grammatical forms
(5) interpolations from parallel biblical passages to supplement, clarify, and correct
(6) clarification and interpretation by small textual changes
(7) corrections to remove historical difficulties or objectionable passages
(8) changes to adapt and conform to Samaritan theology

It is telling that Gesenius considered only four distinctive readings from the SP to be preferable to the MT version (Gen 4:6–8; 14:14; 22:13; and 49:14). Although Gesenius's classification scheme has required modification, his generally negative assessment of the SP persisted for the better part of two centuries. In the early 1990s, Bruce Waltke contended that "the Sam. Pent. is of little value for establishing original readings" of the biblical text.[4]

Waltke's conclusion is no longer sufficient today. Although it is still common to describe SP "variants," "differences," "changes," or "alternate readings" using the MT as the standard, with the publication of the Dead Sea Scrolls, it has become obvious that simple comparisons between the MT and SP are inadequate. The SP shares a considerable part of its textual tradition with the pre-Samaritan group from Qumran, and the plurifor-

---

with the materials from Qumran, especially 4QpaleoExod^{m}, are refining Gesenius's categories. See Judith Sanderson, *An Exodus Scroll from Qumran: 4QpaleoExodm and the Samaritan Tradition* (Atlanta: Scholars Press, 1986). Categorizations have also been proposed by Abraham Geiger ("Einleitung in die biblischen Schriften 11: Der samaritanische Pentateuch," in *Abraham Geiger's Nachgelassene Schriften* [5 vols.; ed. Ludwig Giger; Berlin: Gerschel, 1877], 4:54–67); and by Kahle ("Untersuchungun zur Geschichte des Pentateuchtextes," 399–439).

4. Bruce Waltke, "Samaritan Pentateuch," *ABD* 5:938.

mity of the biblical textual tradition serves as warning against assuming any of the various renditions as the standard by which to judge the others.[5] Examination of the Qumran materials since the last decades of the twentieth century has called for a revision (although not an abandonment) of Gesenius's categories. Esther and Hanan Eshel, for example, suggest the classification system shown on page 74.[6]

Classification systems such as that proposed by the Eshels have the advantage of accounting for editorial purpose in the description of SP readings. Thus, the first level of classification differentiates between intentional and unintentional variants, distinguishing between variants with "some significant value and those without."[7] "Significant value" seems an important distinction, but in our view it is not wholly captured by the label "intention"—an attitude of an editor that is very difficult to prove.

More recently, Tal and Florentin have proposed the categories "intentional change" and "unintentional change."[8] The unintentional changes (comprising the vast majority of differences between the SP and MT) are subdivided into orthographic and morphological changes; the intentional changes are subdivided into linguistic changes that correct unusual morphological or syntactic forms and content editing. Content editing includes four identifiable types of editorial activity: logical rearrangement; harmonizing changes; apologetic changes; and ideological or sectarian changes. The taxonomy of Tal and Florentin may be diagramed as shown on page 75.

We recommend the following modification to the classification systems offered by Eshel and Eshel and Tal and Florentin, relating the various variants to a larger chronological development (see p. 76). In the taxon-

---

5. Two recent publications of the SP present it in parallel with the more widely used MT: Mark Shoulson, *The Torah: Jewish and Samaritan Versions Compared* (Westport, Co. Mayo, Ireland: Evertype, 2006–2008); and Benyamin Tsedaka and Sharon Sullivan, *The Israelite Version of the Torah: First English Translation Compared with the Masoretic Version* (Grand Rapids: Eerdmans, 2012).

6. Eshel and Eshel, "Dating the Samaritan Pentateuch's Compilation," 216–18. Note that the chart shown here reflecting Eshel and Eshel's categories is our own.

7. Ibid., 216. This categorization is perhaps borrowed from Ze'ev Ben-Hayyim, *The Literary and Oral Tradition of Hebrew and Aramaic among the Samaritans* (5 vols.; Jerusalem: Hebrew University Magnes Press, 1957–1977), 5:2–3. [Hebrew]

8. Abraham Tal and Moshe Florentin, eds., *The Pentateuch: The Samaritan Version and the Masoretic Version* (Tel Aviv: The Haim Rubin Tel Aviv University Press, 2010), 25–38.

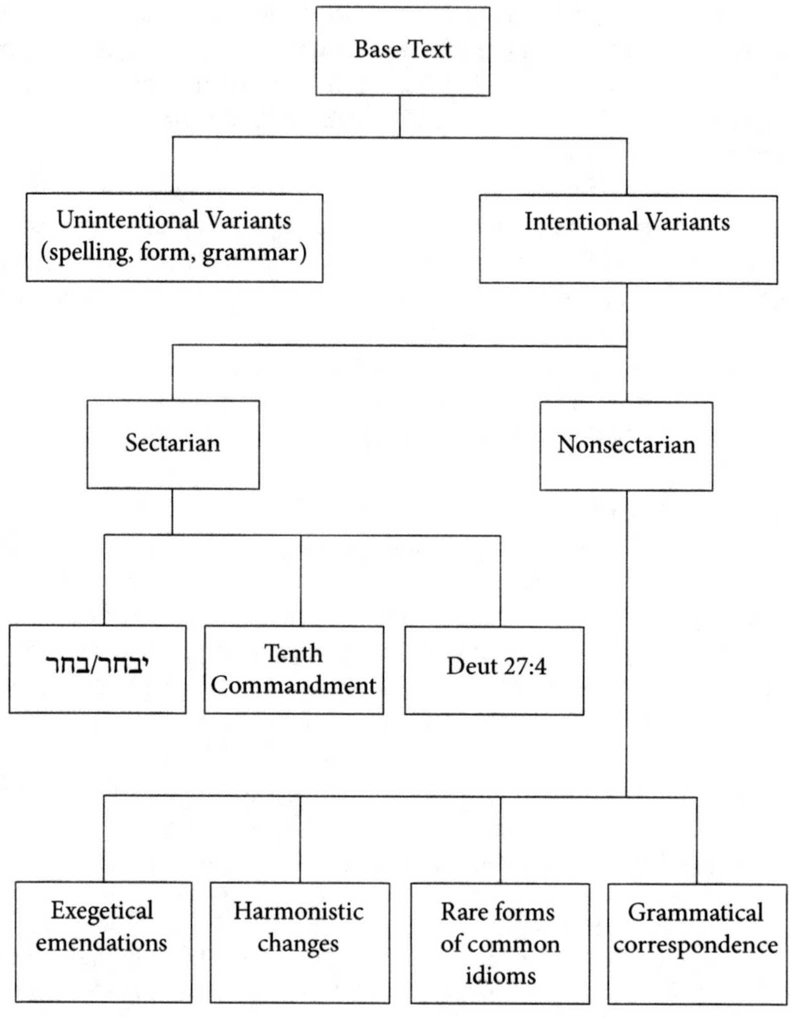

omy, the word "variant" is intended to express simply a textual difference, distinguishing the pre-Samaritan or SP text type from other renditions of the biblical text. The word is not intended to indicate which of those renditions should be given priority, although at times that priority can be surmised. The diagram below provides a visualization of the kinds of variants evident in the Qumran pre-Samaritan group of texts and the sectarian editing of those texts leading to the SP.

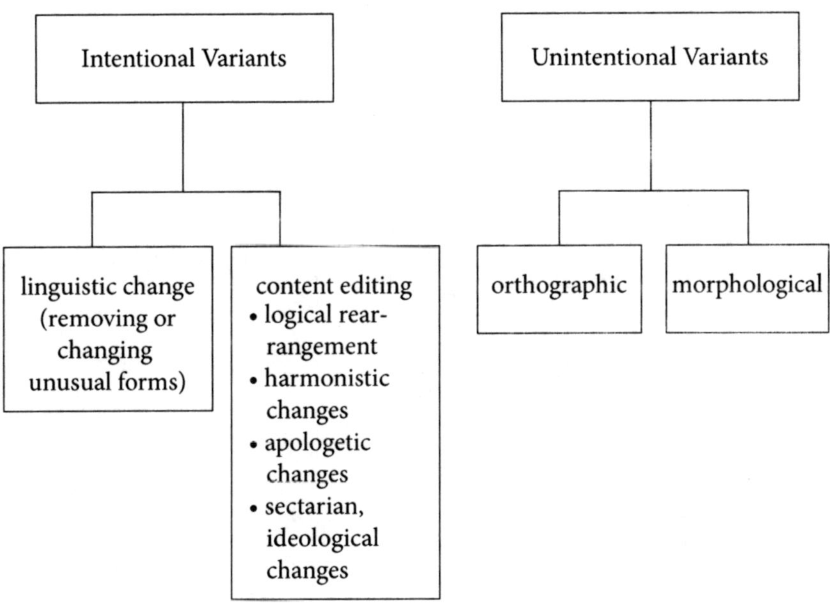

Nonexegetical Variations

For diagramming purposes, we have categorized the first level of variations as either "nonexegetical" or "exegetical" (labels that attempt to emphasize the effect of the variation, viewed from the reader's perspective, rather than its intent).[9] While we believe this to be a helpful distinction, caution is advised. Nonexegetical (orthographic) differences usually do not constitute differences in the meaning of the text, yet an orthographic difference can lead to exegetical differences if it is open to various readings (i.e., susceptible to more than one vowel pointing or pronunciation).[10]

Our heading "Nonexegetical Differences" emphasizes obvious variations in grammar and style. In attempting to explain the grammatical dif-

9. Tov (review of Abraham Tal and Moshe Florentin, *The Pentateuch: The Samaritan Version and the Masoretic Version*. *DSD* 18 [2010]: 389) suggests the initial binary description "important and unimportant."

10. See Ulrich, "Pluriformity in the Biblical Text," 30. See also Benjamin Tsedeka, "Different Pronunciations of the Same Word in the Torah Reading of the Israelite Samaritans in Comparison to Its Significant Attributes," in Zsengellér, *Samaria, Samarians, Samaritans*, 217–22.

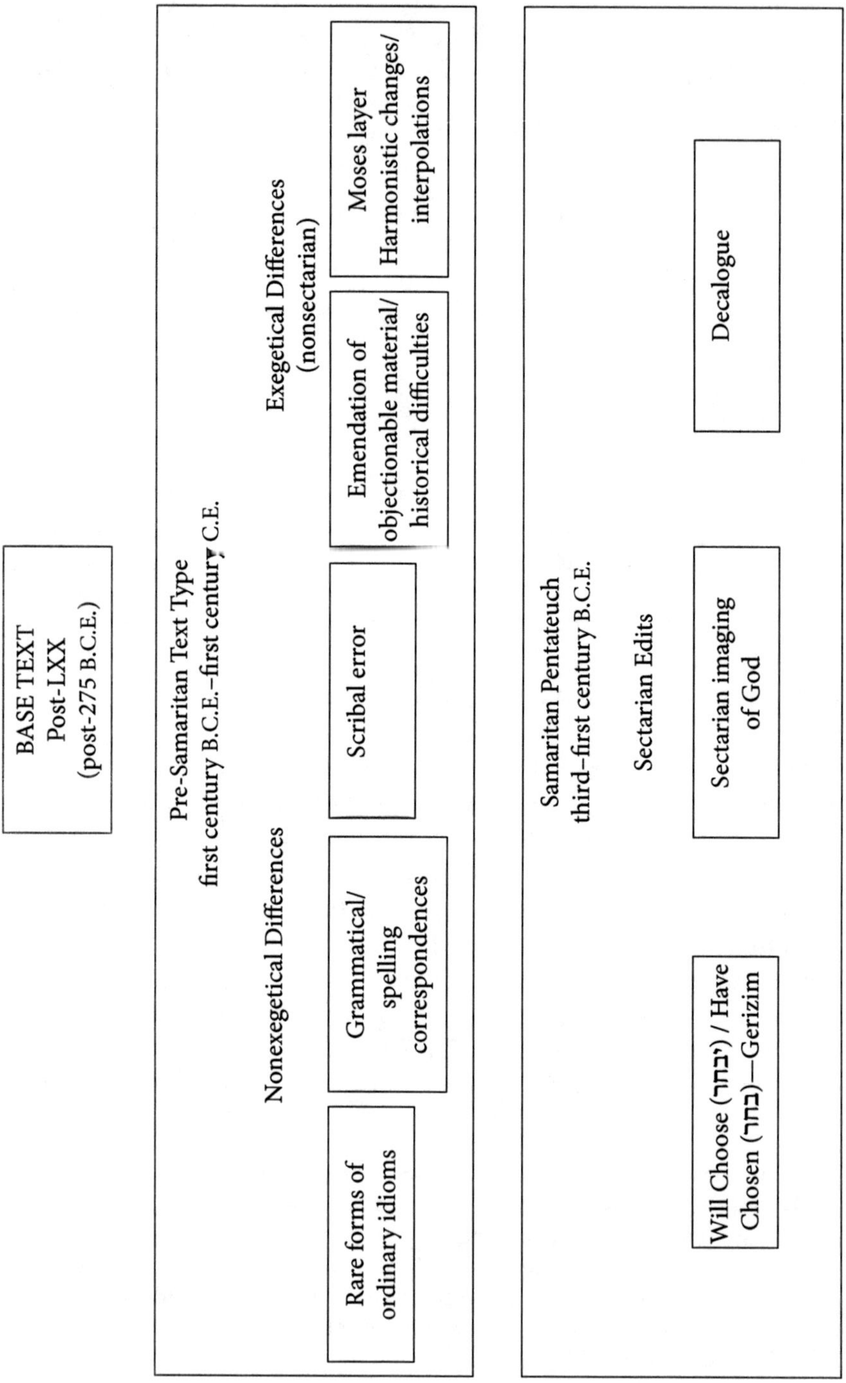

BASE TEXT
Post-LXX
(post-275 B.C.E.)

Pre-Samaritan Text Type
first century B.C.E.–first century C.E.

Nonexegetical Differences

- Rare forms of ordinary idioms
- Grammatical/ spelling correspondences
- Scribal error

Exegetical Differences (nonsectarian)

- Emendation of objectionable material/ historical difficulties
- Moses layer Harmonistic changes/ interpolations

Samaritan Pentateuch
third–first century B.C.E.

Sectarian Edits

- Will Choose (יבחר) / Have Chosen (בחר)—Gerizim
- Sectarian imaging of God
- Decalogue

ferences between the SP and the MT, Gesenius contended that "the Samaritan scribes [acted] according to the norms of an unlearned and inaccurate grammar."[11] Generalizations of this kind are no longer regarded as helpful, and several more recent theories have attempted to explain the grammatical differences between the MT and the SP. Some suggest that SP reflects a northern dialect, while others have considered the differences to be chronological, with the SP readings either preceding or, more recently, following the tradition now resident in the MT.[12] The SP reflects a vocalization later than the MT tradition, but nevertheless incorporates elements (particularly in morphology) of an older stage.[13] Regardless of their origins, the grammatical differences between the SP and the MT are numerous.

- In the SP, all vowels in open syllables are long, while vowels in closed syllables are short (except for those closed at a late stage of linguistic development). Final closed syllables, which may contain long vowels in the MT because of the stress on the final syllable, are short in the SP, which places stress on the penultimate (next to last) syllable.[14] The SP avoids consonant clusters at the beginning and end of a word.[15]

- Many of the variations between the MT and the SP involve morphological differences that are quite consistent and predictable and do not alter the meaning of the text. For example, generally the MT prefers a "long" form of second-person masculine singular and third-person feminine singular pronominal suffix endings, while the SP shows a preference for the "short" forms (forms without a final vowel). Some of the most common morphological differences occur in verbal forms. While generally not affecting the meaning of the text, the morphological forms are important

11. Gesenius, *De pentateuchi samaritani origine*, 26.

12. On the northern dialect theory, see D. W. Thomas, "The Textual Criticism of the Old Testament," in *The Old Testament and Modern Study* (ed. H. H. Rowley; Oxford: Clarendon, 1951), 238–63. On chronological explanations, see Ze'ev Ben-Hayyim, *A Grammar of Samaritan Hebrew* (Jerusalem: Magnes, 2000), 4.

13. Ze'ev Ben-Hayyim, *The Literary and Oral Tradition of Hebrew and Aramaic among the Samaritans* (5 vols.; Jerusalem: Magnes, 1957–1962), 3:7; James Purvis, *Samaritan Pentateuch and the Origin of the Samaritan Sect*, 71.

14. Waltke, "Prolegomena to the Samaritan Pentateuch," 283.

15. Ben-Hayyim, *Grammar of Samaritan Hebrew*, 60–61.

nonetheless, providing significant information relative to the history of the grammar used in both the MT and the SP. Ben-Hayyim provides a comprehensive discussion of the morphology of the SP, noting differences between the MT and SP, and providing chronological notations.[16]

• Certain particles[17] (for example: SP כן for the MT אִם, the SP לו לא for the MT אלולא, prepositions,[18] and nominal forms (typically, the vowels of a word tend to remain constant throughout its declension in SP) also attest to the grammatical variations between the SP and the MT.

• Sentence syntax in the SP is, at times, different from that found in the MT. As noted by Ben-Hayyim, these syntactical differences sometimes seem to result from differences of interpretation, while in other instances the different readings may have given rise to differences in interpretation (e.g., Gen 42:22 *we will be called to account for his blood or a reckoning will come for his blood*; Deut 24:5 *either finding pleasure in or giving pleasure to his new wife*).[19]

Alongside these basic differences in morphology and syntax, some grammatical variations between the SP and the MT emerge from the fact that the SP seems to reflect an "updated" form of the Hebrew linguistic tradition when compared to the MT. Ben-Hayyim concludes that the "SP in its written form displays some features of the language as we know it from Second Temple times—more specifically, from the end of that period."[20] Some of the linguistic characteristics that were previously thought to be peculiar to the SP tradition are now recognized as typical features of the language from the Second Temple period. The grammar of the SP is closer to Mishnaic Hebrew than is the Tiberian (i.e., MT) tradition. A great many of the differences between the SP and the MT are a result of this grammatical updating.

---

16. Ibid., 96–224.
17. Ibid., 314–22.
18. Ibid., 239.
19. Ibid., 328–29.
20. Ibid., 4.

Consistent with this process of "updating," the SP also eliminates some of the grammatical difficulties found in the MT. The SP tends toward producing a more consistent presentation, eliminating the differences between full and defective spellings (see Gen 1:14, 15, 16) and correcting verbal forms to agree with their nouns (see Gen 13:6; 49:20; 49:15), subjects (see Gen 30:42; Exod 4:29; Num 9:6), and other syntactically related verbs (see Exod 39:3; Lev 14:42; Num 13:2; 21:32). The SP regularly replaces passive verbal constructions with active ones (Exod 27:7; Num 3:16; 28:15, 17; Lev 11:13). The SP also tends to even out various forms of spelling. Where the MT may render the same word with two different spellings, the SP opts for a single rendition (Gen 1:14, 15, 16; 7:2; 8:20).

Finally, some of the "nonexegetical differences" between the SP and the MT may be explained in terms of simple scribal error. Many of the consonantal variations between the MT and the SP represent a confusion of letters that sound the same (i.e. between labials, gutturals, dentals, or palatals; for example: ס and שׂ, צ and ז) or a confusion between letters that appear similar (ד and ר, י, and ו). Often, the confusion results in a nonsensical construction that is easily remedied. For example, in Gen 10:27 the SP reads א in אדורם for the ה in the MT rendition, הדורם (both reading the personal name *Hadoram*). Similarly, the SP of Gen 31:40 reads a nonsensical חרף having placed a ף for the ב in חרב (harvest) as found in the MT. A common scribal error is illustrated in Gen 14:2, where ד has become substituted for ר in the SP reading שמאבד for the MT reading שמאבר, the name of a king: *Shemeber* in the MT and *Shemebed* in the SP.[21]

Exegetical Variations

Some differences between the MT and the pre-Samaritan texts may be explained in terms of exegetical activity on the part of the scribes. Many variations in this category are the result of emendations of objectionable material or attempts to correct historical difficulties. The variations resident in this category are interesting, for they seem to be guided by the scribe's sense of propriety. Several examples will illustrate this trend.[22]

21. See also Gen 47:21 and Num 24:17.

22. Several of the following examples involve passages that are not represented in any of the extant pre-Samaritan texts; consequently, variants are referred to simply as "Samaritan."

• In MT Gen 50:23, the births of Joseph's grandchildren are described as occurring "on Joseph's knees" (על־ברכי יוסף). The SP changes "knees" to "in Joseph's days" (בימי יוסף). The reason for the change is unclear. Perhaps, as some have suggested, the connection to childbearing was considered unseemly for the Patriarch. Or the verse may refer to an adoption custom that placed the children of Machir in a special position of privilege with the patriarch, with the scribe wishing to eliminate this privilege.[23]

• A sense of propriety must have guided the scribe writing SP Deut 25:11. Considering it improper to describe a brawl in which a woman grabbed a male opponent's genitals (MT), a simple substitution rendered the verse more appropriate:

> MT: If men get into a fight with one another, and the wife of one intervenes to rescue her husband from the grip of his opponent by reaching out and grabbing his genitals (במבשיו)....

> SP: If men get into a fight with one another, and the wife of one intervenes to rescue her husband from the grip of his opponent by reaching out and grabbing his flesh (בבשרו)....

• The SP reading of Gen 2:2 reflects a desire to clarify the biblical text so as to avoid possible misunderstandings of its meaning:[24]

> MT: And God completed on the seventh day the work that he had done, and he rested on the seventh day from all the work which he had done.

> SP: And God completed on the sixth day the work that he had done, and he rested on the seventh day from all the work which he had done.

The MT reading might give the impression that God concluded his work on the seventh day, finishing up perhaps by mid-morning or a little later, and then took the rest of the day off. The Samaritan scribes apparently wanted no such confusion to take place and so made it clear that the divine labor was concluded on the sixth day.

• The genealogies of Gen 5 and 11:10–26 are well known for the problems they pose. The systems of reckoning that were used to construct the

---

23. A similar episode is recorded in Gen 30:3, where Rachel seeks to establish a special closeness to the anticipated child of Bilhah.

24. 4QGen^k reads with MT.

genealogical tables as presented in the MT, LXX, and SP are not the same and, at least according to Gesenius, seem to operate according to their own patterns of "physiological and chronological knowledge which were sometimes similar and sometimes contradictory to each other."[25] Whatever these patterns of knowledge, it is evident that the end result is different for each textual tradition. The reasons for the differences are yet to be explained.[26]

• Another chronological notation that has caused considerable debate is found in Exod 12:40. The MT and 4QExod[c] of Exod 12:40 read:

> ומושב בני ישראל אשר ישבו במצרים שלשים שנה וארבע מאות שנה
> And the time that the people of Israel dwelt in the land of Egypt was 430 years.

Compare here the SP:

> ומושב בני ישראל ואבותם אשר ישבו בארץ כנען ובארץ מרצים שלשים שנה וארבע מאות שנה
> The time that the children of Israel and their fathers dwelt in the land of Canaan and the land of Egypt was 430 years.

The LXX agrees with the SP but simply reverses the order of the land of Canaan and the land of Egypt. The tradition of the 430-year stay in Egypt appears also in Ezek 4:5, but the Apostle Paul appears to favor the chronology now rendered in the SP and LXX (Gal 3:17).

A number of variants in the SP seem to reflect a desire to avoid discrepancies in parallel passages. At times the variants, when compared to the MT, are quite simple, ranging from the insertion of a preposition (Gen 48:5; Exod 12:43), a noun (Exod 15:22; Lev 5:4; Num 23:26), the sign of a direct object (Gen 44:26; Lev 4:17), or one of a variety of particles (Gen 2:12, 19; Exod 29:33) in order to render a sentence clearer. On other occasions, the variations result in the harmonization of parallel passages without altering the meaning of either. For example, the SP of Gen 18:29

25. Gesenius, *De pentateuchi samaritani origine,* 48.

26. Waltke ("Prolegomena to the Samaritan Pentateuch," 314–15) provides helpful charts showing the differences in the three traditions. Tov (*Hebrew Bible, Greek Bible, and Qumran,* 61) describes the pre-Samaritan rendition of the genealogy as "streamlined by the addition of summaries of the number of years that each person lived."

reads לא אשחית (*I will not destroy…*) for the MT לא אעשה (*I will not do …*), importing information from verses 28, 31, and 32 to harmonize the entire passage. Similarly, the MT gives several different names for Moses' father-in-law, whereas the SP consistently refers to him as Jethro (יתרו). A number of similar examples may be cited.

• In Exod 21:20–21, an ambiguity is clarified by an apparent change in the text when compared to the MT.[27] The paragraph concerns capital offenses and considers the appropriate punishment for injury to a slave or a pregnant woman. The MT of verse 20 reads נקם ינקם ("shall be punished") and uses the verb יקם ("punish") in verse 21 while the SP reads מות ימות ("shall be put to death") and יומת ("put to death") in these verses. While the SP may represent a simple removal of ambiguity, clarifying the intent of the MT, this seeming clarification may go beyond what the MT writers meant to imply, thus beginning an interpretive trajectory carried further by the LXX.

• An example of a harmonistic interpolation, apparently not shared by 4QGen[j], is found in Gen 42:16. Here the SP adds material from Gen 44:22, harmonizing the two passages by making explicit what otherwise is only imperfectly implicit in 42:16:

> "Let one of you go and bring your brother, while the rest of you remain in prison, in order that your words may be tested, whether there is truth in you; or else, as Pharaoh lives, surely you are spies." And they said to him, "The boy cannot leave his father, for if he leaves his father, his father will die."

On several occasions, clarification is rendered through the insertion of an introductory sentence or phrase. In the SP and 4QpaleoExod[m] versions of Exod 24:1 and 24:9, Aaron's sons Eleazar and Ithamar are introduced as accompanying the procession summoned to meet the Lord. The inclusion of these two sons of Aaron is not found in the MT or LXX. This expansion seems calculated to insure that the younger sons of Aaron, who would eventually replace their older brothers, Nadab and Abihu, in their religious offices (Lev 10:1–7), were present at the great theophany at Sinai.[28]

---

27. 4QpaleoExod[m] is unclear here.

28. Sanderson (*An Exodus Scroll from Qumran*, 213) uses these two insertions in Exod 24 to make a convincing argument for the literary affiliation between the SP and the 4QpaleoExod[m] text.

A similar expansion is found in Exod 27:19. In the SP, the verse ends with the phrase: ועשית בגדי תכלת וארגמן ותולעת שני לשרת בהם בקדש ("And you will make garments blue and purple of fine linen for their holy service"). The reading seems oddly out of place: it follows a lengthy discussion about the tabernacle, its measurements, and its utensils (27:9–19), and introduces a paragraph describing the oil used to keep the lamp in the tabernacle continually burning. The paragraph discussing the priestly vestments begins at 28:2; consequently, the expansion of 27:19 seems to appear two verses too soon. Although fragmentary, 4QpaleoExod^{m} seems to share the SP reading. This shared reading stands in contrast to that reading preserved in MT and LXX.[29]

As noted in the diagram above, a number of the exegetical variants in the SP reflect a general tendency to elevate Moses (see discussion in ch. 4). In fact, one of the distinctive characteristics of the SP, shared with the pre-Samaritan Qumran manuscripts,[30] is an editorial layer giving prominence to Moses through a series of insertions and expansions.[31] The material in all these insertions is taken from other passages within the Pentateuch; no new, nonpentateuchal material is added. Once labeled "harmonistic insertions," Kartveit had more recently identified these as forming a "Moses layer" of editing. "Most of the insertions have the effect that Moses is portrayed as a reliable mediator of divine messages to Pharaoh and to the people, and that relates history of the people in a correct and truthful manner."[32] Each expansion or insertion emphasizes Moses' role, not only by its simple content but also by the already recognized authority of the material inserted into the expansion.[33]

Yet it would be wrong to conclude that all of the material in this "Moses layer" is expressly concerned with Moses. At times, the editorial activity was intent on simply emphasizing the role of the prophetic mediator—a role that came to be synonymous with Moses. For example, SP Gen 30:36

29. Ibid., 209–10.

30. Most noticeably, 4QpaleoExod^{m} and 4QNum^{b}; see also 4Q175 and 4Q364 (4QRP^{b}).

31. Kartveit, "Major Expansions," 117.

32. Kartveit (*Origin of the Samaritans*, 280) notes that the major insertions "share the same characteristics as far as content is concerned. The impression is that they form one distinct layer in the pre-Samaritan texts and in the SP. This layer had Moses as its primary figure, and we may term it the 'Moses layer.'"

33. Ibid., 281.

includes material from 31:11–13; the inserted material concerns a divine message given to Jacob and provides the "revelatory background for a later report to his wives."[34]

> SP: And he set a distance of three days' journey between himself and Jacob, while Jacob was pasturing the rest of Laban's flock. *And the Angel of God said to Jacob in a dream, "Jacob," and Jacob replied, "Here I am." He said, "Lift up your eyes and look, all the goats that leap on the flock are striped, speckled or spotted for I have seen all that Laben is doing to you. I am the God of Beth-El where you anointed a pillar and made a vow to me. And now rise up and leave this land, return to the land of your father, to the land of your birth."*

It is striking that several insertions in the "Moses layer" are prefaced by כה אמר יהוה ("thus says the Lord") or ויבדר/ויאמר יהוה אל ("the Lord spoke/said to…").[35] Both phrases are frequently found in the source text of the insertion, but are not always needed in the target passage for the insertion, and may give a clue regarding the editor's intent. By the time the insertions were formed, both phrases had long since become associated with prophetic activity, and found an easy connection with Moses.

A further clue concerning the purpose of the Moses layer may be found in the insertion of material from Deut 18:18 into Exod 20:22. The addition explicitly identifies Moses as a prophet and, as a prophet, Moses faithfully transmits everything that God had commanded:

> SP: *"I will raise up for them a prophet like you from among their brethren; and I will put my words in his mouth, and he shall speak to them all that I command him. And whoever will not give heed to his words while he shall speak in my name, I myself will require it of him. But the prophet who presumes to speak in my name that which I have not commanded him to speak, or who speaks in the name of other gods, that same prophet shall die. And if you say in your heart, 'How may we know the word which the Lord has not spoken?,' when a prophet speaks in the name of the Lord, if the word does not come to pass or come true, that is a word which the Lord has not spoken; the prophet has spoken presumptuously, you need not be afraid of him."*

---

34. Ibid., 279.

35. Gen 7:18, 29; 8:19; 9:5, 19; 10:2; 11:3; Exod 18:24; 20:21; 26:35; 27:19;28:29; 29:28: Num 4:1; 10:10; 14:40; 20:13; 21:11, 12; 20; 21:23; 31:20.

The impact of this insertion extends far beyond the personal status of Moses. The insertion also makes mention of a Moses-like successor who will carry on the prophetic task and, most significantly, identifies that anticipated figure with the preaching of the law. Those who fail to listen to this successor will be held accountable, and any would-be prophet advocating anything at variance with the law, now codified in Exod 20, has proven himself or herself unreliable and should be put to death. Prophets to come will follow the pattern of Moses and will be first and foremost preachers of the law.[36]

This characterization of "prophets yet to come" has immediate significance, helping to determine the status given to the later prophets in the pre-Masoretic tradition. Unlike so many of the Hebrew Bible prophets, who rarely refer to established Mosaic law, and unlike 1 Macc 4:44–46; 14:41, which anticipates a prophet giving new prophecies, the SP remarkably limits the function of the expected prophet to interpretation of the Mosaic law. In so doing, not only is Moses emphasized, but the nature of prophecy is defined and modeled by the faithful transmission of the law communicated through Moses. The Writing Prophets—indeed, the whole second section of the Hebrew Bible, must go unrecognized, for the prophets in the pre-Masoretic tradition do not conform to the pattern now established in SP Exod 20. Consequently, the version of Exod 20:22 found in 4QpaleoExod^{m} (4Q22) and the SP contribute to a lively deliberation, fixing the nature and extent of the sacred canon and confirming the Samaritan insistence that only Torah is sacred text.

The following offers a sampling of some of the passages where "Moses layer" interpolations are found. In a number of instances, text from Deuteronomy is inserted into Exodus or Numbers. The insertion has the effect of expanding or amplifying the corresponding story in Exodus or Numbers, usually bringing it into agreement with Deuteronomy.[37]

• In the SP, Num 10:11 is proceeded by Deut 1:6–8:

> *And the Lord God spoke to Moses saying, "You have stayed long enough at this mountain. Resume your journey, and go into the hill country of the Amorites as well as into the neighboring regions; the Arabah, the hill country, the Shephelah, the Negeb, and the seacoast—the land of the Canaanites*

36. Kartveit, *Origin of the Samaritans*, 284.

37. In addition to the examples cited above, see also Num1:12 followed by Deut 2:17–19; Num 21:20 followed by Deut 2:24–29, 31; Num 27:23 followed by Deut 3:21–22; Num 20:13 followed by Deut 3:17–18.

> *and the Lebanon, as far as the great river, the river Euphrates. See I have set the land before you; go in and take possession of the land that I swore to your fathers, to Abraham, to Isaac, and to Jacob, to give to them and to their children after them.*" In the second year, in the second month, on the twentieth day of the month, the cloud lifted from over the tabernacle of the covenant.

It is interesting to note that this interpolation also contains several other editorial marks. In both the MT and SP version of Deut 1:6, God speaks to the people, not to Moses, and identifies Horeb as the location of the camp. In the interpolated version that finds its way into SP Numbers, God speaks to Moses and there is no mention of Horeb.

• In the SP, Num 13:33 is followed by Deut 1:27–33:

> "There we saw the Nephilim (the Anakites descend from the Nephilim)." *And the children of Israel grumbled before God and they said, "It is because the Lord hates us that he brought us from the land of Egypt to give us into the hands of the Amorites to destroy us. And now, where are we going? Our brothers have made out hearts melt by saying, 'The people are greater and more numerous than we are. The cities are greater and fortified up to the heavens. And also, the sons of the Anakim we saw there.'" And Moses said to the sons of Israel, "Do not have dread or be afraid on account of them. The Lord your God who goes before you will fight for you just as he did in Egypt before your eyes and in the wilderness where you saw the Lord your God carried you just as a man carries his son all the way that you traveled until you reached this place. But still you do not trust the Lord your God, who goes before you in the way to seek a place for you to camp in fire by night and in a cloud by day to show you the route to take.*"

• In the SP, Num 14:41 is preceded by Deut 1:42:

> *The Lord said to Moses, "Say to them, Do not go up and do not fight, For I am not in the midst of you; otherwise you will be defeated by your enemies.*" And Moses said, "Why do you continue to transgress the command of the Lord? That will not succeed."

It should be noted that the process of interpolation does not always involve the insertion of material from Deuteronomy into Numbers. Much less frequently, Deuteronomy borrows from Numbers.

• In both the SP and 4Q364, Deut 2:8 is preceded by material taken from Num 20:14–18:

> *"And I sent messengers to the king of Edom saying, 'Permit us to pass through your land. We will not trample your field or vineyard or drink from your well. We will go along the King's Highway, not turning aside to the right hand or to the left until we have passed through your borders.' And he said, 'You may not pass through or we will come against you with the sword.'* We passed by our relatives, the sons of Esau who live in Seir, leaving the way of the Arabah that comes from Elath and Ezion Geber. And we headed out along the route of the wilderness of Moab."

• In both the SP and 4Q363, Deut 10:6–8 incorporates material from Num 33:31–38a:

> *The Israelites journeyed from Moserah and came to Bene-Jaakan. From there they journeyed and came to Gudgodah. From there they journeyed to Jotbathah, a land with flowing streams of water. From there they traveled and came to Abronah. From there they traveled and came to Ezion Geber. From there they traveled and came to the wilderness of Zin, that is Kadesh. From there they traveled and came to Mount Hor.* There Aaron died. There he was buried. And Eleazar was made priest after him.

A "large harvest" of interpolations is found in SP Exodus, where the redactor has added passages taken from elsewhere in Exodus or other books in the Pentateuch (often Deut 1–3).[38] The insertion of passages from one part of the Pentateuch into another generally effects a change in emphasis of the modified text.

• In SP and 4Q22, Exod 6:9 adds Exod 14:12.

> Moses told this to the sons of Israel but they would not listen to Moses because of their broken spirit and their cruel slavery. *And they said to Moses, "Let us alone and let us serve the Egyptians. It would have been better for use to serve the Egyptians than to die in the wilderness."*

As was suggested in chapter 3, this insertion does nothing to harmonize this text with Exod 4:31, in which the people are described as "believing" and apparently willing to follow Moses' direction. The insertion in 6:9 does, however, serve to emphasize the role of Moses as mediator and prophet.

• SP Exod 18:25 incorporates Deut 1:9–18, with appropriate changes in verbal forms and other small variations allowing a smooth narrative.

---

38. Gesenius, *De pentateuchi samaritani origine*, 45.

> *Moses said to the people, "I am unable by myself to bear you. The Lord has multiplied you so that today you are as numerous as the stars of the heavens. May the Lord God of your fathers increase you a thousand times more and bless you as he has said. How can I by myself bear the burden of your disputes?* Choose for each of your tribes men who are wise discerning and knowledgeable to be your leaders." *They replied and said, "What you have said is good."* He took the leaders of the tribes, men who were wise and knowledgeable and gave them as leaders over them, officers of thousands, officers of hundreds, officers of fifties, officers of tens and officers throughout the tribes. *He made them judges and said to them, "Listen fairly between your brothers and judge righteously between a man and his brother and between the sojourner. Do not be partial in judgment between the small and the great. Do not fear any man because judgment is God's. If a matter is too great for you, bring it to me and I will hear it."* He *commanded them at that time all that they should do.*

• In SP and 4Q22, Exod 32:10 includes a portion lifted from Deut 9:20:

> "Now therefore let me alone, that my anger may burn against them and I will consume them. But of you [Moses] I will make a great nation." *The Lord was very angry against Aaron and was ready to destroy him, but Moses prayed for Aaron.*

It has been observed that many of the alterations, insertions, and expansions noted above enhance the narrative in some way.[39] Some have suggested that these alterations make more explicit some valued idea or belief, and thus produce a text more suitable for sectarian purposes.[40] While the "sectarian" purpose is less sure, certainly there is an ideological interest at work in the Exod 32:10 passage. Aaron is cast in a role dependent upon Moses; by extension, the expected prophet, the *Taheb*, because of his connection to Moses, is to be preferred over a priesthood that relies upon its Aaronic descent.

One common type of interpolation takes the form of a repeating phrase that does not appear in the corresponding MT texts. A fascinating example of this type of repetition is found in the plague narratives of Exodus (see 7:18, 29; 8:19; 9:5, 19; 10:2). Although constructed with variations, all of

39. Sanderson, *An Exodus Scroll from Qumran*, 313.

40. Jeff Tigay ("An Empirical Basis for the Documentary Hypothesis," *JBL* [1975]: 334–35) notes that the interpolations of Deut 1:9–18 into Exod 18:21–27 allows the redactor to "preserve the version of Deuteronomy and drop that of Exodus."

these repetitions include a description of Moses and Aaron (although the verbal forms are at times awkward) approaching Pharaoh and pronouncing a message from the Lord (כה אמר יהוה, "thus says the Lord"). The pronouncement is a repetition of the command given by God earlier to Moses. The expansion commands the release of the Hebrews, the people of God, so that they may go and serve the Lord (sometimes in the desert and sometimes under threat of retribution from the hand of the Lord). The elements of the repeated insertion seem to rehearse the formula found in Exod 7:16: "The Lord, the God of the Hebrews, sent me to you saying, 'Let my people go that they may serve me in the wilderness: and behold you have not yet obeyed me.'" Sanderson observes that these expansions emphasize the conflict between the Lord and Pharaoh.[41] As in other Exodus readings, the expansion found in the SP shares characteristics with readings preserved in 4QpaleoExod[m] (4Q22). Sanderson argues that this common reading was produced by a single author prior to the separation of these two text traditions, and suggests that they may have been intended to assist in a dramatic recitation of the text or its liturgical use.[42]

Samaritan Sectarian Editing: From Pre-Samaritan Texts to the Samaritan Pentateuch

The specifically sectarian readings now present in the SP are best understood as steps along a path, a path that began even earlier than the Moses layer editing shared by the SP and the pre-Samaritan Qumran manuscripts. One step on that path emphasizing Moses and the Mosaic law, and seen quite clearly in the reading of Exod 20:22 shared by SP and 4QpaleoExod[m], may be seen in the insertion of "today" in three places: Deut 4:2; 12:28; and 13:1 (NRSV 12:32).[43] These three insertions emphasize the law of Moses while deemphasizing any rendition of the law that might follow. The LXX shares this reading, suggesting that the insertions may have been made prior to the Moses layer.[44] This trajectory is continued further in Deut 34:10. The SP, by a subtle change in word order (compared to the MT) enhances the status of Moses by asserting his lasting uniqueness.

---

41. Sanderson, *An Exodus Scroll from Qumran*, 204.
42. Ibid., 203–4.
43. Absent also in 1QDeut[a].
44. Kartveit, *Origin of the Samaritans*, 285.

The SP further insures that Moses will remain uniquely positioned, never eclipsed by any prophet yet to come.[45]

MT: Never since has there arisen a prophet like Moses....
ולא־קם נביא עוד בישראל כמשה

SP: Never again will there arise a prophet like Moses....
ולא־קם עוד נביא בישראל כמשה

Not only does this rendition of Deut 34:10 enhance the stature of Moses, it charts a trajectory for the future. The *Taheb*, the one who will restore the Divine Favor to the Samaritans, will come in the tradition of Moses, but will not replace Moses. All others—prophets, priests, and kings alike, regardless of their stature and influence—must assume secondary positions in light of the divinely sanctioned role played by Moses and the One to Come. It is easy to imagine that texts of this kind were part of a lively conversation concerning the status of the prophets within the Hebrew Bible and the Samaritan insistence that only Torah be granted sacred authority.

Most of the remaining sectarian edits in the SP can be categorized into three broad groups: identification of Gerizim as the proper place of worship; sectarian references to God; and, a sectarian rendition of the Decalogue of Exod 20.

Gerizim as the "Chosen" Place of Worship

Many of the sectarian changes in the SP concern themselves with the identification of Mount Gerizim (one word: הרגריזים) as the appropriate place for worship. Perhaps the best-known group of variants in this category read the past tense of the verb "choose" to elevate Gerizim as God's chosen site. Thus, MT Deut 12:5 reads, "But you shall seek the place that the Lord your God *will choose* (יבחר) out of all your tribes as his habitation to put his name there." The SP version of the same verse reads, "But you shall seek the place that the Lord your God *has chosen* (בחר) out of all your tribes

45. In a fashion, this continues a trajectory already seen in earlier editing of Deuteronomy. See Konrad Schmid, "The Late Persian Formation of the Torah: Observations on Deuteronomy 34," in Lipschits et al., *Judah and the Judeans in the Fourth Century B.C.E.*, 237–51.

as his habitation to put his name there." The SP affirms God's past choice, Gerizim (identified in 11:29–30), and replaces the future "will choose" with the reading "has chosen." The SP reading implies that Jerusalem is not a legitimate location for the proper worship of God, since that city was not "chosen" prior to the crossing of the Jordan by the wandering Israelite nation. None of the pre-Samaritan texts can be confirmed to agree with the SP in any of the twenty-one possible instances of this shift (Deut 12:5, 11, 14, 18, 21, 26; 14:23, 24, 25; 15:20; 16:2, 6, 7, 11, 15, 16; 17:8, 10; 18:6, 26:2; 31:11).[46] The unnamed place of God's choosing in the MT will eventually be identified as Jerusalem and cannot possibly be known to Moses. In the SP, the place already chosen by God is Mount Gerizim, which was chosen by God prior to the entrance of the Israelites into the Promised Land.

The majority view, at present, is that the SP represents the variant reading. Yet there is a minority opinion that deems the MT's "will choose" as the later variant.[47] Observing that the SP reading ("has chosen") is also found in some LXX manuscripts, the Coptic, and in the Latin translation of the Old Greek, Stefan Schorch contends that "בחר [has chosen] is therefore certainly the original reading, while the Masoretic reading יבחר [will choose] is secondary, being an ideological and maybe an anti-Samaritan correction."[48] Schorch, noting that the SP reading is perhaps supported by 4QMMT while the MT reading is reinforced by the Temple Scroll, concludes that the MT reading may have been produced "in the period between 4QMMT and the Temple Scroll, i.e., around the middle of the 2nd century B.C.E."[49]

Several other sectarian edits further support Gerizim as the appropriate place of worship. In Gen 22:2, the place of Abraham's sacrifice of Isaac is rendered in the MT as המריה ("Moriah"), while in the SP the place is המורה ("Morah"). The effect of this small variant is to change the association of the place of sacrifice from the temple mount of Jerusalem (by way of 2 Chr 3:1) to the preferred Samaritan site, Shechem (a city often associated with Morah). Exod 20:21 presents a reading that has much the same effect. The MT of this verse reads, "You need make for me only an altar of

46. Contra Hjelm, *Samaritans and Early Judaism*, 92; *Jerusalem's Rise to Sovereignty*, 295.

47. Stefan Schorch, "The Samaritan Version of Deuteronomy and the Origin of Deuteronomy," in Zsengellér, *Samaria, Samarians, Samaritans*, 23–37.

48. Ibid., 32.

49. Ibid., 34.

earth and sacrifice on it your burnt offerings and your fellowship offerings, your sheep and your oxen; in every place where I will cause my name to be remembered I will come to you and bless you." The SP, by contrast, reads, "You shall make for me an altar of earth and sacrifice on it your burnt offerings and your fellowship offerings, your sheep and your oxen; *in the place where I have caused my name to be remembered* I will come to you and bless you." The variants here are relatively simple—במקום ("in *the* place") for the MT בכל־המקום ("in every place") and אזכרתי ("I *have chosen*") for the MT אזכיר ("I will choose")—but make quite plain that there is one proper place of worship, and it is there that God's blessing can be expected.

Complementary to the emphasis on Gerizim as the divinely chosen site, the SP stresses that there is only one appropriate place for worship. Slight variations ensure this singularity. For example, the MT and 4QLev-Num[a] of Lev 26:31 reads, "I will lay your cities waste, will make your sanctuaries desolate, and I will not smell your pleasing odors." The SP version reads, "I will lay your cities waste, will make your *sanctuary* desolate, and I will not smell your pleasing odors." Here the point of a single, divinely approved place of worship is made by a simple change of the plural form "sanctuaries" to the singular form "sanctuary." Even in the midst of threatened divine punishment, the text asserts only one place of legitimate and actual worship—Gerizim. Similarly, MT Deut 11:30[50] reads, "As you know, they are beyond the Jordan, some distance to the west, in the land of the Canaanites who live in the Arabah, opposite Gilgal, beside the oak of Moriah." In the SP version, Moses says, "As you know, they are beyond the Jordan, some distance to the west, in the land of the Canaanites who live in the Arabah, opposite Gilgal, beside the oak of Morah *opposite Shechem*." The MT verse is identical in the SP except for the all important ending (מורא מול שכם): after "Morah," and to make sure that the location is clear to all, the phrase "opposite Shechem" is added. The association of Morah and Jerusalem is given no opportunity to flourish here.

Sectarian References to God

Occasionally, plural verbal forms are used with the noun "Elohim" (God) in the MT. The SP tends to avoid these plural verbal forms, using singular

50. 4QpaleoDeut[r] is fragmentary.

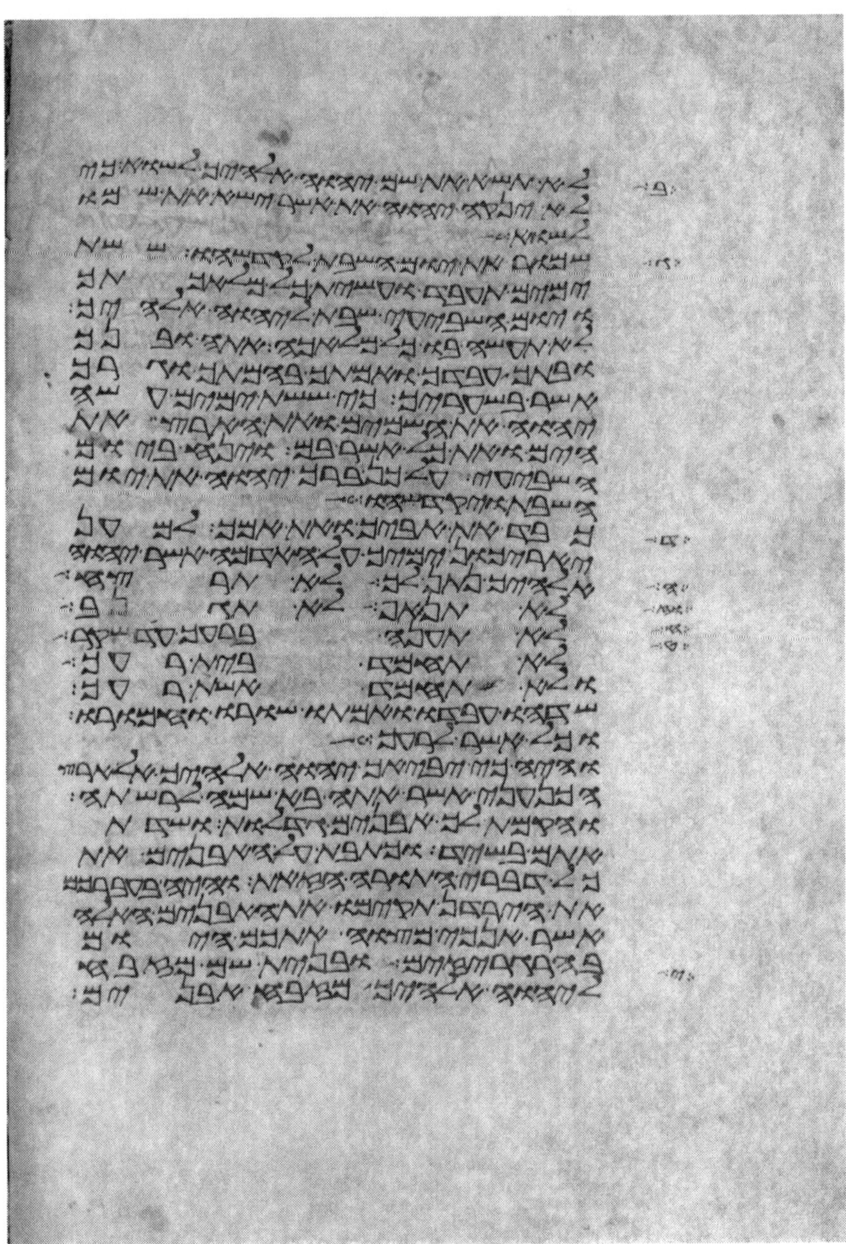

The Decalogue in CW 2484 in Exodus. Letters in the margin enumerate the commandments. The last one (*yod*) is the distinctive Samaritan commandment that an altar be built on Mount Gerizim. Courtesy of Special Collections, Michigan State Universities Libraries.

forms and so asserting the singularity of God. For example, MT Gen 20:13 reads התעו (third person plural; "they caused to go"). The SP eliminates the plural, using instead the 3rd person singular form התעה ("he caused to go"). Similar variations in verbal form are found in Gen 31:53; 35:7, and a nominative singular noun with the same effect is found in Exod 22:8.

Just as the SP occasionally shows care to preserve the singularity of references to God, the text also eliminates certain anthropomorphic representations of God. Exod 15:3, a text favored by the Samaritans and used in liturgies and appearing on stone inscriptions, illustrates this trend. MT Exod 15:3 reads, "The Lord is a man of war (יהוה איש מלחמה). The Lord is his name (יהוה משו)." The SP renders the same verse, "The Lord is mighty in warfare (יהוה גיבור במלחמה). The Lord is his name (יהוה משו)". Similar examples appear in SP Exod 15:8, where the SP renders the MT's "breath from your nostrils" with "breath from you," and in SP Deut 32:6, where the SP renders the MT's "your father" with "your creator." Similarly, in certain episodes, the Angel or Messenger of the Lord appears as the actor in the SP where, in the MT, the Lord acts or speaks directly without the benefit of mediation (Num 22:20; 23:4, 5, 16).[51] This presentation of God's transcendence is quite in line with the theology of the Samaritans.

The Samaritan Decalogue

The SP version of the Decalogue of Exod 20 is a composite literary piece, inserting into the Exodus text selections from Deut 5, 11, and 27. The resulting rendition of the Ten Commandments accomplishes three important tasks. First, with clarity and geographical precision, Mount Gerizim is identified as the only legitimate and divinely ordained place of sacrifice. Worship on Gerizim becomes the concern of the tenth and final command, and in this manner the importance of Gerizim, the distinctive place for Samaritan worship, is secured. Second, Moses is elevated to an even higher status than that presented in the MT. Only Moses can speak with God, and the community grants only to Moses the status of intermediary to the Divine. The third accomplishment of this text is to invest the promised prophet to come with all the authority of the ten sacred words. The promise of the prophet, in Samaritan theology, becomes a significant social construct by which the Samaritans critique the Davidic dynasty and

51. 4QNum[b] is uneven, supplying mediation only in Num 23:4.

all social power structures that detract from the centrality of the one who will restore the Divine Favor, the *Taheb*.

The SP version of Exod 20 presented below is that produced by Benyamin Tsedaka and Sharon Sullivan.[52] Variations from the MT marked by *italics* signify material present in the SP but not in the MT, while ellipses (…) indicate the location of material that appears in the MT but not in the SP. Verses that contain significant expansions (interpolations) when compared to the MT are signified by the inclusion of letters following the verse number (14, 14a, 14b, etc.). The word "God" (אלהים) is spelled "Eloowwem," reflecting a Samaritan pronunciation that is also indicated in proper nouns throughout the translation (see "Missrem" for מצרים/Egypt in verse 2; "Moosha" for the more recognizable Moses). "YHWH" (יהוה) is shown deferential respect in the translation "Shehmaa," in a fashion similar to the vowel pointing of the MT and in the translation "Lord" as in many English translations. The reader will also notice that Mount Gerizim (Har Gerizim: הר גריזים) is rendered in one word, "AARGAAREEZEM" (a typical Samaritan rendering). Traditionally, the SP is divided into sections, qissem (קצים), signified here by double stars (**).

1 And Eloowwem spoke all these words saying,
2 I am Shehmaa your Eloowwem, who brought you out of the land of Missrem (Egypt), out of the house of slavery.
3 You shall have no other gods besides Me.
4 You shall not make for yourself an idol, or any image, of what is in heavens above, or on the earth beneath, or in the water under the earth.
5 You shall not worship them or serve them. For I Shehmaa your Eloowwem am a devoted Eloowwem, counting the iniquity of the fathers on the children, on the third and the fourth generations of those who hate Me.
6 And showing loving kindness to thousands, to those who love Me and keep My commandments.
7 You shall not take the name of Shehmaa your Eloowwem in vain. For Shehmaa will not leave him unpunished who takes His name in vain.**

52. Benyamin Tsedaka and Sharon Sullivan, *The Israelite Version of the Torah: First English Translation Compared with the Masoretic Version* (Grand Rapids: Eerdmans, forthcoming).

8 *Keep* the Sabbath day, to keep it holy.
9 Six days you shall labor and do all your work.
10 And the seventh day is a Sabbath of Shehmaa your Eloowwem. *In it* you shall not do any work, you, or your son, or your
daughter, your male or your female slave, or … *your cattle*, or
your proselyte who stays in your gates.
11 For in six days Shehmaa made the heavens and the earth, the
sea, and all that is in them, and rested on the seventh day.
Therefore Shehmaa blessed the Sabbath day and made it holy.
**
12 Honor your father and your mother, that your days may be
prolonged in the land which Shehmaa your Eloowwem gives
you.
13 You shall not murder.
You shall not commit adultery.
You shall not steal.
You shall not bear false witness against your neighbor.
14 You shall not covet your neighbor's house, *and* you shall *not*
covet of your neighbor *his field* and wife or … *his male slave*
or his female slave … *his bull* and his donkey or anything that
belongs to your neighbor.**
14a *And when Shehmaa your Eloowwem will bring you to the land
of the Kaanannee which you are going to inherit it* 14b *you shall
set yourself up great stones and lime them with lime. And you
shall write on them all the words of this law.* 14c *And when you
have passed over the Yaardaan (Jordan) you shall set up these
stones, which I command you today, in Aargaareezem (Mt Gerizim).* 14d *And there you shall build an altar to Shehmaa your
Eloowwem, an altar of stones. You shall lift no iron on them.*
14e *And you shall build the altar of Shehmaa your Eloowwem
of complete (uncut) stones.* 14f *And you shall offer burnt offerings thereupon to Shehmaa your Eloowwem* 14g *and you shall
sacrifice offerings and shall eat there. And you shall rejoice
before Shehmaa your Eloowwem.*
14h *That mountain, in the other side of the Yaardaan, beyond the
way toward the sunset, in the land of the Kaanannee who dwell
in the prairie, before the Gaalgaal, beside the Aalone Moora,
before Ashkem.***
15 And all the people *heard the voices, and the ram's horn voice,*

and saw the lightning flashes, and the Mountain smoking. *And* when *all* the people *saw,* they trembled and stood at a distance.

16 And they said to Mooshe, *Surely Shehmaa our Eloowwem has shown us his glory and his greatness.* 16a *And we heard his voice from the midst of the fire.* 16b *We have seen this day that Eloowwem speaks with man, yet he still lives.* 16c *And now, why should we die, for this great fire will consume us.* 16d *If we hear the voice of Shehmaa our Eloowwem any more, then we shall die.* 16e *For who is there of all flesh who has heard the voice of the living Eloowwem speaking from the midst of the fire, as we have, and lived?* 16f *You go near and hear all that Shehmaa our Eloowwem may say. And tell us all that Shehmaa our Eloowwem says to you, and we will hear and do it.* 16g And let not *the Eloowwem* speak with us, or we will die.

17 And Mooshe said to the people, Do not be afraid, for Eloowwem has come in order to test you, and in order that the fear of Him may be before you, that you sin not.

18 And the people stood at a distance, while Mooshe approached the fog where Eloowwem was.**

18a *And Shehmaa spoke to Mooshe saying,* 18b *I have heard the voice of the words of this people which they have spoken to you.* 18c *They are right in all that they have spoken. Who will wish that they had such a heart in them that they would fear me, and all the days keep my commandments* 18d *that it will be well unto them and unto their children forever?* 18e *I will raise up for them a prophet like you from among their brethren and will put my words in his mouth. And he shall speak to them all that I will command him.* 18f *And it shall be that the man who will not hear his words which he will* 18g *speak in my name, I will require it from him. But the prophet who will dare with malignity to speak a word on my behalf which I have not commanded him to speak, and he speaks on behalf of other gods, that prophet shall die.*

18h *And if you say in your heart, How will it be known the word which Shehmaa has not spoken?* 18i *That the prophet speaking on behalf of Shehmaa, the thing will not happen and will not come, this is the thing which Shehmaa has not spoken.* 18j *The prophet has spoken in malignity.* 18k *You shall not be afraid of him. Go say to them, Return to your tents.* 18l *And you stand here by me, and I will speak to you all the commandments and statutes, and the judgments which you shall teach them.* 18m *And they will do so in the land which I am giving them to inherit.* **

19 And Shehmaa *spoke* to Mooshe *saying, Speak* to the Sons of Yishraael. You have seen that I have spoken with you from the heavens.

20 You shall not make with Me gods, of silver and gods of gold you shall not make for yourselves.

21 You shall make an altar of earth for Me, and you shall sacrifice on it your burnt offerings, and your peace offerings, *some of your* sheep, *and some of your* bulls. 21a *In … the place* where *I have mentioned* My name, *there* I will come to you and bless you.

22 And if you make an altar of stone for Me, you shall not build it of cut stones, for if you wield your sword *on it, you have profaned it.*

23 … You shall *not* go up by stairs to My altar, that your nakedness will not be exposed *to it.***

Several interesting observations are evident when a comparison is made between the SP Decalogue in Exod 20 and Deut 5 and the corresponding passages in the MT. First, the commands that prohibit other gods, prohibit the vain use of God's name, prohibit killing, prohibit committing adultery, prohibit stealing, and prohibit bearing false witness are the same in the MT and the SP renditions. Beyond these instances of verbatim agreement, there are occasions where it seems that the SP has chosen a "middle road," negotiating between the differences resident in the MT. John Bowman characterizes the Samaritan treatment of the Ten Commandments as "no more than the result of the application of a general principle which … affects the whole Pentateuch … that principle is harmonization."[53] While there is certainly harmonization at work, the exact nature and purpose of the harmonization is not as simple as one

53. John Bowman, *Samaritan Documents Relating to Their History, Religion, and Life* (POTTS 2; Pittsburgh: Pickwick, 1977), 16.

might suppose. The harmonization is uneven and, if designed to eliminate differences, only partially successful—at times the SP eliminates tensions in the MT presentation, and at other times preserves them. Several examples will illustrate this trend.

- SP Deut 5:7 differs from the MT Deut 5 by inserting ו before כל, in agreement with SP Exodus and MT Exodus.

- SP Deut 5:9 agrees with MT Exod 20:5 (על שלישים ועל וביעים) while MT Deut 5:9 differs from SP Exod 20:5.

- SP Deut 5:12 reads לקדשהו in agreement with SP Exod 20:8, rather than לקדשו as in MT Deut 5:12. The SP verb שמר will be considered below.

- SP Deut 5:13 and SP Exod 20:9 insert בו in distinction from the MT readings.

- SP Deut 5:13 lacks ו before "servant" and "donkey," agreeing with both SP and MT Exod 20:10.

The point of these simple comparisons is to demonstrate that if harmonization was the goal of the SP editing, it was done very inconsistently. Some of the differences in readings are due to grammatical characteristics of Samaritan Hebrew, while others appear to reflect scribal preferences. The SP makes great use of MT Deuteronomy, but the preference is not consistent.

A comparison of two of the commandments proves especially interesting. SP Exodus is closer to MT Exodus for the Sabbath commandment, but SP Exodus parallels MT Deuteronomy in the prohibition against coveting. On the former, SP Deut 5:12–15 reads:[54]

12 Keep the sabbath day to keep it holy, as Shehmaa your Eloowwem commanded you.
13 Six days you shall labor and do all your work.

54. Tsedaka and Sullivan, forthcoming.

14 And on the seventh day is a sabbath of Shehmaa your Eloowwem. *Don't make in it* any labor, you and your son and your daughter, … *your male slave* and your female slave, … *your bull* and your donkey, and any of your cattle, and your proselyte who stays with you, that your male slave and your female slave may rest as well as you.

15 And you shall remember that you were a slave in the land of Missrem, and Shehmaa your Eloowwem brought you out of there by a mighty hand and by an outstretched arm. Therefore, Shehmaa your Eloowwem commanded you to do the sabbath day.

This command offers an interesting example of Samaritan scribal editing. Like the MT, SP Deut 5:11 (NRSV 5:12) inserts כאשר צוך יהוה אלהיך ("as the Lord your God commanded you"), a phrase not found in the SP or MT versions of Exod 20:8. Yet in the same verse, SP Exodus prefers MT Deuteronomy over MT Exodus. SP Exodus begins with שמור ("guard" or "keep"), as do SP and MT Deuteronomy, MT Exodus begins with זכור ("remember"). The preference for שמור ("keep") over זכור ("remember") is quite understandable, for שומרים ("Keepers") is the self-designation of the Samaritans.

The second command that shows interesting comparisons is the prohibition of coveting. As the following comparison reveals, the relationship between the Deuteronomy and Exodus renditions of the covet command is multifaceted.[55]

SP Deut 5:17:

לא תחמד בית רעך ולא תחמד אשת רעך שדהו עבדו

Do not covet your neighbor's house, do not covet your neighbor's wife, his field, or his servant.…

SP Exod 20:13:

לא תחמד בית רעך ולא תחמד אשת רעך שדהו עבדו

Do not covet your neighbor's house, do not covet your neighbor's wife, his field or his servant.…

55. Bowman (*Samaritan Documents*, 19) is aware of the above differences but does not consider the range of implications that arise from these textual observations.

MT Exod 20:13:

לא תחמד בית רעך לא תחמד אשת רעך ועבדו

Do not covet your neighbor's house, do not covet your neighbor's wife or his servant....

MT Deut 5:17

ולא תחמד אשת רעך ולא תתאוה בית רעך שדהו ועבדו

Do not covet your neighbor's wife, do not covet your neighbor's house, his field or his servant....

SP Exodus and SP Deuteronomy present the same reading. Both are at variance with MT Deuteronomy (changing the order of "house" and "wife" and inserting תתאוה to name the offense against the neighbor's house and property to follow) in the first part of the commandment, agreeing instead with the MT Exodus reading. The MT Deuteronomy version itemizes the neighbor's field as one of the things that should not be coveted. Both Samaritan renditions mention the neighbor's field as well. Apparently, the Samaritan scribe felt free to follow the reading presented in either MT Deuteronomy or MT Exodus as the need demanded. The inclusion of "field" is also found in 4QDeut^{n} (which does not insert תתאוה as in MT), a scroll dated to the early Herodian period (30–1 B.C.E.), perhaps suggesting a first century B.C.E. or first century C.E. date for the Samaritan recension of the Decalogue.[56]

By contrast, it should be noted that Fragments 7–8 of 4Q158 (40–1 B.C.E.) do not include the insertion of "field" while agreeing with the SP reading in other respects.[57] The lengthy text is presented here to provide a comparison to the SP rendition.[58] These texts provide valuable information in attempts to understand the development of the SP in its own literary context.

(Honor) your [father] and your mother, [so that your days may be long in the land that the Lord your God is about to give to you. You shall not murder. You shall not commit adultery. You shall not steal. You shall not bear] false witness [against] your [neighbor]. You shall not covet [your] nei[ghbor's] wife, [male or female slave, ox, donkey, or anything that

---

56. Ulrich et al., *Deuteronomy, Joshua, Judges, Kings*, 117.

57. Tov, *Texts from the Judaean Desert*, 410.

58. Michael Wise et al., *Dead Sea Scrolls* (San Francisco: Harper Collins, 1996), 202.

> belongs to your neighbor]. And the Lord said to Moses, "Go say to them, 'Return to [your tents.' But you, stand here by Me, and I will tell you all the commandments, the statutes] and the ordinances that you shall teach them, so that they may do them in the land that [I am about to give them as a possession." …]
>
> So the people returned to their individual tents, but Moses remained before [the Lord, who said to him, "Thus shall you say to the Israelites,] 'You have seen for yourselves that I spoke with you from heaven. You are not to mak[e gods of silver alongside Me, nor make for yourselves gods of gold. You need make for Me only an altar of earth, and sacrifice] on it your burnt offerings and offerings of well-being, your sheep [and oxen; in every place where I cause My name to be remembered I will come to you and bless you. But if] you make for Me [an altar of stone], do not build it of hewn stones; for by [using] a chisel [upon it you profane it. You are not to go up by steps to My altar lest your nakedness be exposed] on it.' "

As shown in Fragments 7–8, 4Q158 (4QRPa) does not include "field" in its rendition of the Exodus passage but reads much more like the MT rendition. Later in Exod 20, however, 4Q158 does share substantial agreement with the SP. Does the agreement with MT in the covet command mean that, unlike the Samaritan editors, the 4Q158 editors felt no such threat to their cherished land holdings? Does deliberate inclusion of "field" in SP Exodus indicate that the SP Exodus recension can be dated to a time when the Samaritans were threatened with losing their property to the hands of pious neighbors, with the specification that a "field" may not be coveted serving as a protest against this threatened loss? If so, can this be taken as evidence that the recension of the covet prohibition, like that of the Sabbath command, took place after a sense of self-awareness had developed for the Samaritan sect, and not prior to that self-awareness?

Finally, particular attention should be given to the SP's distinctive tenth commandment. The Samaritan Tenth Commandment is a conflation of texts, including material from Exod 13:11a; Deut 11:29b; 27:2b–3a, 4a, 5–7; 11:30.[59] It was added to both versions of the Decalogue, in SP Exod 20 and Deut 5. The number of ten commandments is maintained by making the MT's first commandment an introduction to the law code.

When was the tenth commandment insertion completed? Suggestions among Samaritan scholars vary. James Purvis dates the insertion

59. See Tigay, "Conflation as a Redactional Technique, 78–83.

to the time of the Maccabees (second century B.C.E.) and Alan Crown to the time of the great Samaritan theologian Baba Rabba (222–254 C.E.).[60] Ben-Hayyim thinks the commandment is a response to a Christian notion that the ten commandments should be viewed as a collection of moral statements devoid of concrete practical observance.[61] Kartveit observes that the repair patch on 4Q22 (a scroll without the Samaritan tenth commandment), dated to the mid-first century B.C.E., extended the continued use of the scroll in the first century B.C.E.; this being the case, the addition of the tenth commandment may have occurred after the turn of the eras.[62] Kartviet further suggests that Josephus (*A.J.* 5.68–70) uses language now in the core of the tenth commandment (from the Deut 27 insertion) to counter Samaritan claims about Mount Gerizim by rendering MT Deut 27 with the mountain of cursing—Ebal.[63] If so, the Samaritan tenth commandment should be dated after the repair of 4Q22 and before the composition of *Antiquities*—that is, sometime in the first century C.E.

---

60. Purvis, *Samaritan Pentateuch and the Origin of the Samaritan Sect*, 85; Alan Crown, *Samaritan Scribes and Manuscripts* (TSAJ 80; Tübingen: Mohr Siebeck, 2001), 11.

61. Ze'ev Ben-Hayyim, "The Tenth Commandment in the Samaritan Pentateuch," in *New Samaritan Studies of the Sociétè d'Études Samaritaines III and IV: Essays in Honour of G. D. Sixdenier* (ed. Alan Crown and Lucy Davey; Studies in Judaica 5; Sydney: Mandelbaum, 1995), 487–91.

62. Kartveit, *Origin of the Samaritans*, 295.

63. Ibid., 308. See also Charlesworth, "What Is a Variant?"

6
The Samaritan Pentateuch and Emerging First-Century Sectarianism

The fluid nature of the pluriform scriptural tradition in the first century C.E. means that identifying the presence of the SP in the New Testament and other early Christian literature is at times tenuous and provisional. In this chapter we will survey the cultural complexities that have a bearing on the use or nonuse of the SP and pre-Samaritan literary tradition by New Testament authors. Ideological points of contact between the Samaritan sect and the emerging Christian sect will provide a context within which to consider the function of the SP in the New Testament. The possible existence of a Greek SP will also be considered in our attempt to identify quotes and allusions from the SP and pre-Samaritan tradition within the New Testament literature.

The Samaritan Pentateuch in Its Geographical and Cultural Setting

The various textual developments described in the previous chapters occurred in the midst of geographical and cultural conditions as fluid and dynamic as the texts themselves. Particularly significant were the well-established tensions between north and south in Palestine, the dominance of Hellenism, and the struggling sectarianism among Samaritan, Jewish, and Christian groups. Long-term geographical, political, and cultural tensions between northern and southern Palestine play a significant role in the complex relationship between the emerging movements as reflected in the development of the New Testament, the Samaritan Pentateuch, and the Hebrew Bible.

Palestine, a common designation of the territory between the Mediterranean Sea on the west and the Jordan valley on the east and from current Lebanon in the north extending into the Sinai Peninsula in the south, is the central stage for early Jewish, Christian, and Samaritan history. The northern part of Palestine, centered on the valley of Jezreel, cutting generally from east to west through the Palestinian hill country, is much better suited to profitable agriculture than the more arid and hilly southern part of Palestine. This basic fact of geography helped form deep cultural differences between the northern and southern reaches of this relatively small land.

The North

Because of its rich agricultural resources, the north was economically and politically stronger than the south. The biblical memory recalls that the territories were united early in Israel's history under Saul, David, and Solomon, but a civil war followed Solomon's death and the north effectively seceded from the union. In the biblical story, it retained the name Israel with its capital city of Samaria, while the weaker southern territory became Judah, retaining the capital city of Jerusalem. The northern kingdom with its resources and access to the sea dominated Judah while attracting the coveting interest of stronger powers to the East, notably Assyria. The northern kingdom fell to the Assyrians late in the eighth century and lost its sovereignty. The Samaritans claim to be remnants of that occupied territory.

The region has a long history of hosting eclectic, multicultural, dynamic peoples. The early biblical case study is the Israelite King Ahab, who married the Phoenician Jezebel, reflecting intercultural relations that included extensive penetration by the Baal fertility cult, which was related to agriculture. After Israel fell, according to the biblical story, the Assyrians deported masses of Israelites and replaced them with peoples from other territories they had conquered. The Samaritan side of that story is told in their chronicles and is recited in chapter 1. Hebrew prophets from the south continually condemned the heterodoxy of the north, which included the Hellenism brought in by Alexander the Great and his successors.

According to the biblical narrative, the surviving northern population became visible as a distinct group when the Jews returned from the Babylonian Exile and, with Persian support, set about rebuilding the city of Jerusalem under the leadership of Nehemiah. A coalition of Israelites who had not been part of the exile tried to deter Nehemiah, and were successfully thwarted by Nehemiah. One of the coalition members, a northerner opposed to Nehemiah named Sanballat, was governor of Samaria under the Persians and may have been concerned that a rejuvenated Judean autonomy would threaten his own power.

Josephus claims that Sanballat switched his allegiance to Alexander, who was making his appearance into the region, and was rewarded by Alexander with approval to build a Samaritan sanctuary on Mount Gerizim.[1] As we have seen, a central distinction of the SP is the insistence that the central sanctuary for the Israelites should be on Mount Gerizim.

Once it was clear that the Greeks were taking over, both Samaritans and Jews sought Greek favor, which was ultimately not forthcoming to either. Sanballat's family was deposed from leadership in Samaria. This led to a Samaritan revolt that compromised their standing with the Greeks. Some think the Jews may have aided the Greeks in putting down the revolt. In any case it became clear that the much more tolerable reign of the Persians had yielded to the oppressive reign of the Greeks, and in their polemics both Samaritans and Jews sought to portray the other as allied with the despised Greeks.

The Hellenists, both Jewish and Samaritan, welcomed the Hellenistic culture brought in by Alexander and his successors. The Hellenists of both Jewish and Samaritan communities were disposed to read the Hebrew Scriptures in Greek translation rather than in Hebrew, the Septuagint for Jews and, as we will see, a likely Greek Samaritan Pentateuch. The Hellenists spoke Greek rather than Aramaic. This Hellenistic bent may have spawned a synagogue-based religion among both Samaritans and Jews, as is implied in Acts 6:9. A minority within New Testament scholarship, represented by Henry Cadbury, think the Hellenists were indeed Gentiles. E. C. Blackman believes the Hellenists were proselytes.[2] Acts 6:5 does identify Nicolaus as a proselyte, but he is the only one so designated.

Hellenistic culture was strong in cities, not villages, and Galilee had few cities—though Lower Galilee was more cosmopolitan and open to Hellenism.[3] Appropriately, for example, the early Christian missionary,

---

1. Josephus, *Ant.* 11.321–24.

2. Thomas W. Martin, "Hellenists," *ABD* 3:136.

3. Eric Meyers, "Galilean Regionalism as a Factor in Historical Reconstruction," *BASOR* 221 (1976): 93–101.

Philip, went directly to an unnamed Samaritan city (Acts 8:5).[4] There were degrees of acceptance of Hellenism among Samaritans, Jews, and Christians, resulting in both strong "Hebrew" and strong "Hellenistic" parties within each group.

The more heterodox culture of the north adapted to the Greeks more easily than the more monolithic and conservative south. So various Hellenistic influences increased tension between north and south, further inflaming schisms among the Israelite Samaritans. There were many variables in the developing Palestinian heterodoxies: holy place at Jerusalem or Gerizim, emphasis on Temple or synagogue, authority with priests or laity, limits of Scripture (fewer books or more, including the apocrypha), emphasis on Moses and/or David, and definitions of cleanliness, for example.

The fact that the Samaritan Scripture contained only the Pentateuch was itself a radical departure from the direction taken by rabbinic Judaism. Most of the latter effectively included the Prophets and the Writings in their canon, as did the Christian groups, while the Samaritans did not expand on the Pentateuch, the law of Moses.

The Samaritans were more focused on the rituals of the Pentateuch, and schism arose among them over issues of cleanliness and purity. Some Samaritan groups were more lenient, for example, interpreting Lev 16:19 so that women were regarded as unclean for a shorter period during menstruation, and some were more strict, saying that Lev 11:36 should be interpreted to read that water was rendered unclean if it was touched by anything unclean. Some sects deemphasized the sacrifices on Mount Gerizim when it was inaccessible during political turmoil, and centered more on the synagogues and laity.

Since the Scripture of each group was still quite fluid, some Samaritan sects believed they had the truest version of the Pentateuch and, of course, rejected the additions (the Prophets and the Writings) that most Jewish groups added. The Hebrew Bible was modified at least in partial response to the claims of the Samaritans: Gerizim/Ebal (Deut 27: 4), the Prophets and Writings were added along with likely anti-Samaritan polemics like "the crime of Gibeah" of Judg 19 and anonymous taunts in several books, such as that found in chapter 65 of Isaiah.

---

4. Mark A. Chancey, *Greco-Roman Culture and the Galilee of Jesus* (SNTSMS 134; Cambridge: Cambridge University Press, 2009), 33.

The largest splinter group, the Dositheans, which itself continued to splinter even more, added many texts that took on canonical status in some circles. Described in some of those texts was the Ascension of Moses after death, a doctrine that eventually gained currency among most Samaritans and added emphasis to the "Moses layer" described in chapter 3. From this story about Moses, some sectarian Samaritan groups extrapolated and affirmed a general resurrection of the dead.

The date of the origin of these sects cannot be determined, but it is argued that the major impetus came with the destruction of the holy place on Mount Gerizim by John Hyrcanus in the late second century B.C.E. These early splits are attributed to "Dustan," but little more can be said of them. Sometime in the first century, major splits were initiated by "Dositheus," as just described. The leader of at least one Dosithean sect is known to us from both Samaritan and Christian sources: Simon Magus. Simon's story is intertwined sometimes positively, sometimes negatively with the Dosithean Samaritan sect, early Christianity, and the origins of Gnosticism, an early heresy within both Samaritanism and Christianity.

Simon Magus

When Philip, a first century member of a Christian sect, began his missionary work in a certain Samarian city, he found himself in competition with Simon, who already had developed a large sectarian following (Acts 8:8–11). Simon's leadership capabilities are confirmed by the second century bishop of Lyon, Irenaeus, who is the earliest to identify Simon as one of the founders of Gnosticism.[5] Most traditions identify him as a Samaritan from the village of Gitta, not far from Flavia Neapolis.[6]

Simon was certainly in the right location to be a Samaritan, and his thought intertwines with that of some Samaritan sectarians. That Simon was a Samaritan is implied by the Samaritan Chronicler, Abu'l Fath,[7] and by the early church fathers[8] who, with Irenaeus, identified him as a gnostic, though both labels are still debated (as is the identification of the Simon present in the book of Acts with the Simon condemned by the church

5. Irenaeus, *Haer.* 1.13.

6. Justin, *Apol.* 1.26; *Dial.* 120.

7. Paul Stenhouse, *The Kitāb al-Tarīkh of Abū'l Fath, Translated with Notes* (Sidney: Mandelbaum Trust, 1985), 221.

8. I.e., Justin, *Apol.* 1.26; Irenaeus, *Haer.* 1.23.4.

fathers).[9] The confusion may arise from the different polemical descriptions made of the same Simon.

The role of Simon Magus in the New Testament, the testimony of the church fathers that Simon is the father of Gnosticism, the extensive work done on Samaritan sects, and the likelihood of an early gnostic Christianity hinted at by the Johannine literature, all converge to imply a tendency toward Gnosticism in some Samaritan sects, and supply good reason why the literature of the New Testament, particularly in the Pauline and Johannine schools, has an anti-gnostic posture. Gnosticism would have allowed some Samaritan Christians to "de-Judaize" Jesus by denying him a biological entity, and it is possible that the Gnosticism that Paul seems so often to attack is a form of Samaritanism.[10]

Jarl Fossum[11] suggests various Samaritan influences on Simon: particularly, use of God's hypostasized thought (*Ennoia*) and the use of the divine epithet "the Great Power,"[12] and Simon's title of "The Standing One."[13] Simon could also have been influenced by Philo.[14] Further, some church fathers directly associate him with Dositheus,[15] and Fossum believes that Simon was himself influenced by their beliefs.[16] The early church did associate Simon with the Samaritans, so it seems likely that Simon is associated with the Samaritans by the earlier New Testament writers and, as with the church fathers, made the gnostic-associated Samaritans seem a threat to orthodox Christianity. Significantly, Simon is also identified as a

---

9. See for example Edwin M. Yamauchi, *Pre-Christian Gnosticism: A Survey of Proposed Evidences* (Grand Rapids: Eerdmans, 1973).

10. William Albright–Abram Spiro Correspondence (SAC). Special Collections, Michigan State University Libraries, East Lansing, Michigan.

11. Jarl Fossum, "Sects and Movements," in Crown, *The Samaritans*, 239–389.

12. Both Robert Grant (*Gnosticism and Early Christianity* [New York: Columbia University Press, 1959], 27–38) and Klaus Haacker ("Samaritan, Samaria," *NIDNTT* 3:457) say the term was more widespread.

13. Alan Crown ("Qumran or the Samaritans: Which Has the Closer Relationship to Early Christianity?" in *Proceedings of the Tenth World Congress of Jewish Studies* [Jerusalem; World Union of Jewish Studies, 1990], A:221–28) believes this term could be derived from Christian tradition.

14. Pieter R. Goedendorp, "If You Are the Standing One, I Also Will Worship You," in *Proceedings of the First International Congress of the Sociétè d'Études Samaritaines* (ed. Abraham Tal and Moshe Florentin; Tel Aviv: Chaim Rosenberg School for Jewish Studies, 1991), 61–78.

15. E.g., Eusebius, *Hist. Eccl.* 4.22.4ff.

16. Fossum, "Sects and Movements," 363–89.

Samaritan in the Samaritan Chronicles.[17] Simon's appellation as a "magus" (magician) invites associations with the portrayal of Jesus as a "magus," strongly implied both in John (by Jesus' power to bestow eternal life),[18] and in Mark.[19] The linkages among Mark, John, Simon, the magus title, and the Samaritans seem more than coincidental.

Melchizedek joins Simon Magus as a focus of the Jewish/Christian sectarian foment in first century Samaria. Melchizedek is an elusive character who appears twice in the Hebrew Scripture, once in a section included in the SP, the other in a section not recognized by the Samaritans. He intrudes into a scene with Abraham in Gen 14 where he is identified as king of Salem, and gives Abraham bread, wine, and a blessing. Psalm 110, speaking of the Messiah, says, "You are a priest for ever according to the order of Melchizedek." This is an appropriate rendering of the LXX version of Ps 110. The MT is more ambiguous and may not even contain the proper name "Melchizedek."

Amid this set of cultural dynamics and widespread sectarianism, the SP, the MT, the LXX and the New Testament were taking shape. In spite of their deep mutual dislike, the geographical proximity of Jews and Samaritans, and the awkward separation of the Jewish populations of Judea and Galilee by Samaria, would necessitate at least a minimal level of interaction, some mutual influence, and at least pockets of cooperation. Two major manifestations of cooperation among all the sectarians, either witting or unwitting, would be the direct or indirect northern influence on the sources of Samaritan, Jewish, and New Testament texts, and an obvious, easily available, and tempting mission field for all the sectarians within the Samarian/Samaritan communities. There is much debate over the cultural identification of the populations throughout Galilee. Without doubt, there was extensive Hellenistic influence in Galilee, and the Samaritans and Jews may have been highly Hellenized,[20] though Mark Chancey believes

17. Stenhouse, *Kitâb*, 219–22.

18. James Purvis, "The Fourth Gospel and the Samaritans." *NovT* 17 (1975): 197.

19. That Jesus was a "magus" is a major theme in Morton Smith, *The Secret Gospel: The Discovery and Interpretation of the Secret Gospel according to Mark* (London: Victor Gollancz, 1974). This work is, however, challenged by many, including Stephen C. Carlson, in *Gospel Hoax: Morton Smith's Invention of Secret Mark* (Waco, Tex.: Baylor University Press, 2005).

20. Purvis, "Fourth Gospel," 174

the Hellenists were primarily Jewish.[21] Galileans and Samaritans accepted Jesus more decidedly than Jews of other regions. John equated Galileans and Samaritans in their sympathies and antipathies.[22]

Sources

According to substantial literary criticism, the large Samaria/Galilean region to the north was particularly fertile in the creation of traditions that would affect each of the evolving Scriptures, including the New Testament. It evidenced great heterogeneity within its Jewish, Samaritan, and Christian communities. Five traditional sources are potentially relevant: (1) E, the northern Mosaic tradition that held tenets meaningful to both Samaritans and early Christians; (2) Q, the hypothetical source shared by Matthew and Luke; (3) S, a hypothetical distinctive Samaritan source proposed by Scobie,[23] (4) the Gospel of Mark, and (5) the Gospel of John. Both gospels strongly suggest a northern influence if not provenance. In addition to these five literary traditions, geographic mobility and a continuous emergence of new sects, with their unique interpretations of those traditions, enhanced the cross-fertilization of cultural influences.

E Document

It is likely that Samaritans, as heirs of the northern kingdom and its traditions, would emphasize the E (northern telling of the Mosaic story) traditions over J (southern telling of the Mosaic story) and P (a much later editing of the traditions). This preference seems to be supported in Samaritan literature. The SP and the Jewish MT are alike in including the J, E, and P traditions, but Samaritan liturgical and theological works show preference for the E tradition. MacDonald has noted this both as a generalization and in several notations in the major Samaritan theological work, *Memar Marqah*, written by the third- or fourth-century C.E. theologian Marqah.[24]

21. Mark A. Chancey, *The Myth of Gentile Galilee* (Cambridge: Cambridge University Press, 2002), 61.

22. Purvis, "Fourth Gospel," 171–72.

23. Charles H. H. Scobie, "The Origins and Development of Samaritan Christianity," *NTS* 19 (1973): 397.

24. John MacDonald, ed. and trans., *Memar Marqah: The Teaching of Marqah* (Berlin: Töpelmann, 1963), 1:xliii. For example, *Memar Marqah* 2:16 passes over J in

The latter notations are observations on the explicit Samaritan predisposition for the E or northern traditions in the Pentateuch over the J or southern traditions. E is consistently pro-priestly and antimonarchical, and is initially unknowing of and later unsympathetic to Jerusalem and the temple. The New Testament books most sympathetic to the Samaritans (Luke, John, and Hebrews) share and emphasize antitemple sentiments with later Hebrew traditions in books not recognized by the Samaritans (the Prophets and the Writings), the Deuteronomic equivocation on the choice of Jerusalem (particularly in Deut 12:5, בחר/יבחר discussed in ch. 5), select conciliatory psalms that are not focused on Jerusalem, temple, or kingship (topics that would offend Samaritans), and the more spiritually, rather than ritually, focused Isa 40–66 (e.g., Isa 57:15; 58:1–14; 66:3).

Q

The Q source, a likely product of a distinctively Hebrew-speaking, northern community would have been understandably amenable with Samaritan involvement. First, Q's apocalyptic expectation of an era of peace is not unlike Samaritan expectations of a new era of divine favor. Second, there are indications that the community of Q was the object of Jewish persecution that was comparable to the animosity we experience between Samaritans and Jews in other documents. The Q source is generally thought to represent three layers of community editing: Palestinian, Jewish Hellenistic, and Hellenistic. As many have noted, Q shows some links with the later gnostic work the Gospel of Thomas. [25] As we have seen, both Gnosticism and Hellenism are common links between the Samaritans and early Christians.

Samaritan Source: S

Both Abram Spiro, the one-time professor of Near Eastern studies at Wayne State University in Detroit, and Charles Scobie, professor of religious studies at Mount Allison University, Sackville, New Brunswick pose

Exod 5:3; *Memar Marqah* 2:18 most of P (Exod 6:2–7:13) in narration of Moses and Pharaoh, *Memar Marqah* 2:26. Exod 8:20–35 (J) is passed over in *Memar Marqah* 2:27; Exod 9:1–21 (J and P) abbreviated or passed over; and many other J or P passages throughout the work.

25. Norman Perrin, *The New Testament: An Introduction* (New York: Harcourt Brace Jovanovich, 1974), 46.

a hypothetical source, "S" or Samaritan source. Scobie believes such a source was available to Luke. [26] Spiro assumed such a source was used by Mark, for example, in the temple logion, and to some extent by the other gospels (notably John 8:44).[27] Scobie thought such a source may be a collection of Stephen's views, not necessarily assuming that Stephen was a Samaritan, but that he was in contact with Samaritans. Or, S could have been the work of one of Stephen's followers, perhaps someone active in the mission work under Philip.[28] S may have been a sister tradition to Q, the other repository of early northern Palestinian tradition.

"Galilean Gospels" and Sectarian Compromise

Just as Hosea, a northern Hebrew prophet, reflects an ability to compromise or adapt Mosaic tradition to the Canaanite culture of the north, and just as Samaritans adapted to Gnosticism, there are suggestions that Christian sectarian works most in touch with the northern culture were the most adaptive.

Both the Gospels of John and Mark, the latter particularly on the basis of an examination of the motif of returning to Galilee (14:28) and Mark's editorial activity, have been associated with Galilee.[29] The Johannine school was a prophetic school of a type that may have been the object of criticism in the apocryphal apocalypse, the Ascension of Isaiah,[30] a work produced by another and perhaps rival prophetic school of Jewish-Christian and possibly anti-Samaritan origin.[31] Spiro noted parallels to the charges brought against Jesus and Stephen and assumed that the Gospel of John really says that the Samaritans were responsible for the crucifixion of Jesus. According to Scobie, John's Gospel "shows remarkable knowledge of Samaritan customs, beliefs and topography."[32] John's work may have evolved in a Samaritan Galilean area alienated both from Jerusalem

26. Scobie, "Origins," 397.

27. SAC, March 12, 1965.

28. Charles H. H. Scobie, "The Use of Source Material in the Speeches of Acts III and VII," *NTS* 25 (1979): 399–421, 415.

29. Scobie, "Origins" 398–400, 408, and "Use of Source Material," 399–421, 414–15; Willi Marxsen, *Mark the Evangelist* (Nashville: Abingdon, 1969), 54–95.

30. Robert G. Hall, "The *Ascension of Isaiah*: Community, Situation, Date, and Place in Early Christianity," *JBL* 109 (1990): 289–303.

31. SAC, March 28, 1987.

32. Scobie, "Origins," 403.

and Gerizim, anxious to affirm that Jesus was greater than Moses.[33] The unique vision of Jesus as Son of Man *standing at God's right hand* could be an intentional echo of Moses as the one "who stands before God and intercedes for his people."[34] Certainly John draws on the popular Moses piety of the north.[35]

Christianity was another Palestinian minority sect. Like most Jews, Christians accepted a Scripture of more than the Pentateuch, but, like the Samaritans, they were generally unsympathetic to the Jerusalem temple. Unlike the Jews, Christians were mixed in their attitude to Samaritans. The Gospels of John and, to a slightly lesser degree, Luke defy the general anti-Samaritan Jewish tenor, perhaps because of their own, more pressing troubles with "the Jews." Social memory theory[36] could say that John had good memories of the Samaritan community while other Jewish communities had memories that accumulated into communal prejudice. Maybe John's preoccupation with the Samaritans is an attempt to co-opt and capitalize further on the success of the missions to Samaria. John may also be identifying with the Samaritans against the Jews.

The South

The Jews, primarily inhabitants of the southern territory of Judah, maintained relative cultural and political autonomy and isolation into New Testament times, though the autonomy was seriously compromised by the successive dominant powers: Assyria, Babylon, Persia, Greece and, in New Testament times, Rome. The basically pastoral culture of the south, less touched by the military and commercial activities that were attracted to the north, was culturally and religiously more isolated and stable, tending toward a more conservative way of life.

Both the New Testament and the early Jewish historian Josephus witness to a pervasive hostility toward the Samaritans on the part of Jews. John's comment that Jews do not share things in common with Samaritans

---

33. Purvis, "Fourth Gospel," 191.

34. Scobie, "Origins," 397.

35. Purvis, "Fourth Gospel," 191.

36. Alan Kirk and Tom Thatcher, *Memory, Tradition, and Text: Uses of the Past in Early Christianity* (Atlanta: Society of Biblical Literature, 2005). See also Tom Thatcher, *Why John Wrote a Gospel: Jesus—Memory—History* (Louisville: Westminster John Knox, 2006).

(John 4:9) is echoed by the hostility implied in Jesus' instruction to apostles to enter no town of the Samaritans (Matt 10:5) and the ameliorative stories told by Luke of the Good Samaritan (Luke 10:33) and the healing of the Samaritan (Luke 17:16). The same implication is found in New Testament scholar John Dominic Crossan's understanding of the parable of the Good Samaritan: it forced Jews to conceive unwittingly the oxymoron, "Good Samaritan."[37]

As a Jew, Josephus reflects a general Jewish hostility in his critique of Samaritans. Though some argue that Josephus was impartial in his treatment or, at worst, that his enmity did not distinguish between Samaritans and Samarians,[38] the strong Jewish bias against the Samaritans is noted by many.[39] Among the statements that show this bias are comments that describe the beginning of the Samaritan priesthood, populated by priests from Jerusalem who fled because of moral character,[40] a questionable description of the building of the temple at Gerizim, allusion to Samaritan weakness in defending Mount Gerizim,[41] and a purported Samaritan request to have their temple dedicated to Jupiter.[42] Shaye Cohen speaks for a substantial group of scholars in describing the *Jewish Antiquities* as decidedly "anti-Samaritan."[43]

---

37. John Dominic Crossan, "Parable and Example in the Teaching of Jesus," *NTS* 18 (1971–1972): 294.

38. The best example is Rita Egger, "Josephus Flavius and the Samaritans," in *Proceedings of the First International Congress of the Sociétè d'Études Samaritaines, Tel Aviv, April 11–13, 1988* (ed. Abraham Tal and Moshe Florentin; Chaim Rosenberg School for Jewish Studies, 1991).

39. See R. J. Coggins, "The Samaritans in Josephus," in *Josephus, the Bible, and History* (ed. Louis H. Feldman and Gohei Hata; Detroit: Wayne State University Press, 1989), 257–73; Stanley J. Isser, *The Dositheans: A Samaritan Sect in Late Antiquity* (SJLA 17, Leiden: Brill, 1976), 5–11; Morton Smith, *Palestinian Parties and Politics That Shaped the Old Testament* (New York: Columbia University Press, 1971), 420; Menachem Mor, "Samaritan History: 1. The Persian, Hellenistic, and Hamonean Period," in Crown, *The Samaritans*, 1–18.

40. Coggins, "The Samaritans in Josephus," 259–60.

41. Josephus, *J.W.* 3.307–315.

42. Josephus, *Ant.* 12.257–264.

43. Ibid. See also Shaye J. D. Cohen, *Josephus in Galilee and Rome: His Vita and Development as a Historian* (Leiden: Brill, 1979), 149.

THE EMERGING CHRISTIAN SECT

The emergence of the Christian sect sharing antipathies and kinship with both Samaritans and Jews added a new dimension to the flow of both scriptural and sectarian development of all the parties. The relative abundance of Christian literature in the New Testament provides a unique window into those dynamics.

In the mid-1960s, Abram Spiro confided somewhat ruefully to the renowned archaeologist William F. Albright that he feared his own research on the Samaritans and the New Testament would revolutionize New Testament studies and convert to failure the life work of many New Testament scholars.[44] As it turned out, Spiro's rather modest intrusion into the arena of New Testament studies via his commentary on Acts elicited more discussion among Samaritan scholars than among New Testament scholars, and did little to threaten, challenge, or even affect New Testament scholarship.[45] Ironically, Spiro himself later disowned the condensed and paraphrased version of his work.[46] With similar enthusiasm and considerably more tact, Charles Scobie observed, "Fascinating and valuable though the Qumran and Nag Hammadi finds are, time may yet reveal that in terms of their direct bearing on the study of Christian origins the Samaritan writings are of even greater interest and importance."[47]

Now, more than a half century later, a rather extended survey of current commentaries, New Testament introductions, New Testament dictionaries, and encyclopedias reveals essentially no references to the role of the Samaritans in the early New Testament community or to contemporary Samaritan scholars. The occasional articles by New Testament scholars in journals during the 1960s and 1970s mentioning the SP or the Samaritans have diminished even further. In recent years even Samaritan scholars have focused little of their research on the New Testament. While such studies need not be as dramatic as in Scobie's speculation, or as hostile as Spiro's, they ought to be more visible than the testimony of the last decades. The literature of the 1960s and 1970s regarding the Samaritans

44. SAC, June 30, 1965.

45. William F. Albright and C. S. Mann, "Stephen's Samaritan Background," in Johannes Munck, *The Acts of the Apostles* (AB 31; Garden City, N.Y.: Doubleday, 1967), 285–300.

46. SAC, Nov 14 and 29, 1966.

47. Scobie, "Origins, 390–414.

and the New Testament is far too rich to ignore. The Gospel of John has been the focus of major works by John Bowman, George W. Buchanan, Edwin D. Freed, John MacDonald, Wayne A. Meeks, Hugo Odeburg, and James Purvis.[48] Attention has been given to Stephen's speech by Richard J. Coggins, Simeon Lowy, W. H. Mare, James Purvis, Earl Richard, Abram Spiro, and Denis D. Sylva.[49] The book of Hebrews has been the subject of studies by Robert S. Eccles, Menahem Haran, E. A. Knox, Charles H. H. Scobie, and Robert Trotter.[50] Occasional comments have been made regarding Luke-Acts (beyond Stephen's speech) and Matthew, and perhaps more should be said about Mark and even Paul.

The latter part of the first millennium B.C.E. was the basic incubating time for the SP, the MT, and the LXX in a milieu of great cross-fertilization and fluidity of traditions, as the texts at Qumran demonstrate. The basic text of the SP is so close to the MT that it must be assumed the base text was developed before the schism between Jews and Samaritans.[51] Since a distinctive Samaritan text cannot be firmly established before the first century C.E., the presence of Samaritan influence is deduced from Samaritan tradition, the literary presence of features distinctive to the Samaritan Pentateuch, and explicit references to the Samaritans. Often, it is difficult to determine who affected whom. For example, when similar concepts are used for Moses and Jesus, were Christians applying to Jesus a readily acces-

---

48. John Bowman "Samaritan Studies I: The Fourth Gospel and the Samaritans," *BJRL* 40 (1958): 298–308; George W. Buchanan, "The Samaritan Origin of the Gospel of John," in *Religions in Antiquity: Essays in Memory of Erwin Ramsdell Goodenough* (ed. Jacob Neusner; Leiden: Brill, 1968), 149–75; Edwin D. Freed, "Samaritan Influence in the Gospel of John," *CBQ* 30 (1968): 580–87.

49. Coggins, *Samaritans and Jews*; Simeon Lowy, *The Principles of Samaritan Bible Exegesis* (StPB 28; Leiden: Brill, 1977); W. H. Mare, "Acts 7: Jewish or Samaritan in Character?" *WTJ* 34 (1971): 1–21; Purvis, "Fourth Gospel"; Earl Richard, "Acts 7: An Investigation of the Samaritan Evidence" *CBQ* 39 (1977): 190–208; Albright and Mann, "Stephen's Samaritan Background," 285–300; Denis D. Sylvia, "The Meaning and Function of Acts 7: 46–50," *JBL* 106 (1987): 261–75.

50. Robert S. Eccles, "Hellenistic Patterns in the Epistle to the Hebrews," in Neusner, *Religions in Antiquity*, 207–26; Menachem Haran, "The Song of the Precepts of Aaron ben Manir" [Hebrew], *Proceedings of the Israel Academy of Sciences and Humanities* 5.7 (1974): 1–36; Robert J. F. Trotter, *Did the Samaritans of the Fourth Century Know the Epistle to the Hebrews?* (LUOSMS 1; Leeds: Leeds University Oriental Society, 1961). See also Scobie, "Origins."

51. Zsengellér, "Origin or Originality," 189–202. The base text may be no more "Jewish" than "Samaritan."

sible Samaritan way of talking about Moses, or did later Samaritans co-opt a Christian way of talking about Jesus, modifying speech for Samaritan usage? Such adopted usages by Samaritans could have been picked up by Christians looking for clues about what in Christianity would appeal to Samaritans in the mission field. Identifying lines of influence becomes complex! The complexity of the lines of influence can be illustrated by examining some of the work of the John MacDonald. MacDonald claimed that an early Samaritan theological work, *Memar Marqah*, presents "that most remarkable phenomenon of Samaritanism, the assimilation of Christology and the application of it to Moses."[52] Marqah is the greatly revered Samaritan theologian of the third or fourth century C.E. who wrote poetry and theology during a period of Samaritan renaissance.

On further reflection, it is not at all clear whether it was assimilated directly by the Samaritans or by the spin of Christian missionaries. MacDonald is inclined to think that most Samaritan assimilation of Jesus narratives, such as the birth narrative, comes after Marqah. Marqah himself was not as influenced by Christian stories as were later Samaritans. The dynamic fluidity of sectarian influence continued.

Additionally, when searching for Samaritan presence or influence in the New Testament, care must be taken to distinguish between the term *Samarians*, a reference to any of the inhabitants of the province of Samaria regardless of religious or ethnic status, and *Samaritans*, the Hebrew religious group that focused on Mount Gerizim rather than Jerusalem as the central holy place. This distinction has been made repeatedly in the present book. Samaritans are prominent in the New Testament story, but as we survey New Testament documents and other early Jewish sources, we must be mindful that it is not always easy to determine whether the subject of the writing is *Samarians* in general or the distinctive *Samaritan* religious sect.

Interactions between Christian and Samaritan Groups

Samaritans and Christians interacted frequently and intensely. The story of Pentecost in Acts 2 reflects the likelihood that Christianity initially became a viable movement in Jerusalem and from there spread very rapidly. The proximity of the Samaritans to Jerusalem made them an obvious

52. John MacDonald, *Memar Marqah*, 2:xvii.

object of proselytizing, incidentally if not intentionally, and as outcasts like many of the Christians, they may have found the Christian message appealing. The Samaritan missionary field permeates the gospels and the rest of Acts and is likely evident throughout the New Testament. The initiative for the Samaritan mission is disputed, but there could be more than one Christian group attracted to Samaria. The explicit statement that "Hellenists" and "Hebrews" among the Christians had issues with each other (Acts 6:1) supports the impression that each of those "sects" had their own version of where the initiative for missions began and whom that initiative should include.

George W. Buchanan, among others, says the mission to the Samaritans was led by the apostle John and is initially reflected in John 4:4–42, the account of Jesus' encounter with the Samaritan woman at the well in Samaria.[53] As Buchanan considers it, this was not an intentional moment of mission. To avoid trouble with the Pharisees, Jesus retreats to Galilee via the shortest route, a road that passes through Samaria. He stops to rest in the village of Sychar and is by himself when the disciples arrive on the scene. Where they have been is not described and we cannot deduce missionary activity from that silence—or much at all about their attitude when they arrive. Jesus has been deeply involved in serious talk with the woman at the well. The woman is so impressed by Jesus that she has gone into the city to gather people to come out and see this remarkable man. In this fashion, Jesus unwittingly sets a missionary program in motion.

While the woman is gone off to gather her neighbors and friends, the disciples arrive and Jesus apprises them that they have just come upon a missionary field: "I tell you, lift up your eyes, and see how the fields are already white for harvest. He who reaps receives wages, and gathers fruit for eternal life, so the sower and the reaper rejoice together" (John 4:35–36). When the local Samaritans arrive in response to the woman's solicitation, they find Jesus convincingly charismatic and invite him to stay with them. He stays for two days and wins over many of the Samaritans. As indicated above, John may have intentionally composed or, more likely, "remembered" this rendering of the story in the light of his motivation or agenda at the time of his writing.

By contrast, Charles Scobie and others say the first Christian missions were led by the Galilean and Samaritan Christian community, brought

53. Buchanan, "Samaritan Origin," 149–75.

into focus by the Stephen-Philip group.[54] Following the stoning of Stephen, "a great persecution arose against the church in Jerusalem and they were scattered throughout the region of Judea and Samaria, except the apostles" (Acts 8:1). As Scobie understands it, the phrase "except the apostles" implies that it was the Hellenistic Christians who were the object of this persecution, maybe even at the hands of those who martyred Stephen and maybe with the support of the apostles.

Since Christianity was headed toward a Hellenistic future, this schism between apostolic and Hellenistic Christian sects was important. Hellenistic Christians moved easily into Samaritan territory and the greater Hellenistic world beyond.

Philip

Philip is first brought to our attention as a result of one of the flaps between the Hellenist and Hebrew groups within the early Christian movement. When the Hellenists complain that their widows were neglected in the daily food distribution, the twelve authorize the Hellenists to appoint a group of seven to assure the proper distribution of food (Acts 6:3–6). One of them is Stephen, who is soon martyred. Another is Philip.

Traditions about Philip are preserved by Luke, even though he tends to ignore or forget them in his further discourse about Paul's missionary work. Perhaps he tells Philip's story to indicate the precedent or preparation for what he considers the real beginning of mission work under Paul. Christopher R. Matthews assumes Luke is preserving a familiar Philip tradition originating earlier in the first century, from which we can deduce certain information about Philip's work and its relation to Paul.[55]

Luke's separation of the actions depicted in Acts 8:4–25 and 11:19–24, which logically occur simultaneously, provides an interlude within which Luke can portray several momentous events, notably the conversions of Paul and Cornelius, which in Luke's view must precede the Hellenist breakthrough to the Gentiles signaled in 11:20. [56] When the Philip narrative picks up in Acts 8:4, three important events take place. First, Philip flees to the city of Samaria and many Samaritans are won over by his preaching.

---

54. Scobie, "Origins" 398, 408.

55. Christopher R. Matthews, *Philip: Apostle and Evangelist—Configurations of a Tradition* (Leiden: Brill, 2002), 38–41.

56. Ibid., 37.

Second, Philip usurps the stage from Simon Magus—indeed, Simon himself became a believer in Philip's message. Third, word of Philip's success motivates Peter and John to enter that mission field. Either Peter and John had not supported the preaching of the Hellenist Stephen or, seeing the accomplishments of the Samarian mission, they decide to join and perhaps compete with it, offering their "orthodox" or "Hebrew" Christianity.

Many years later, if the stoning of Stephen took place when Paul was a young man, prior to his conversion and missionary work, which likely ended in his early sixties, Paul, returning from his third missionary journey, stops over in Caesarea and stays in Philip's home (Acts 21:8–9). We do not know why Philip is living in Caesarea or what has happened during the intervening years. More intriguing is the link between Philip, the early Hellenist missionary to the Gentiles, and Paul, the much later Hellenist whose work was with a wider, but similar, population. Had Philip and Paul been in competition? Had Philip laid some ground work for Paul? Was the Caesarean visit a reunion of Hellenistic missionaries? Philip is never mentioned in a Pauline letter. This implies the relationship was not close and may even have been competitive.

Whether these were alternative versions of the gospel or parallel missions, Samaritans may have felt an identity with at least some Christian groups for a number of reasons. There are several intimations that Jesus sought an ultimate unity of all twelve tribes of Israel (e.g., Matt 19:28; Luke 22: 30; John 5:22), the political image at the heart of the Pentateuch, the only Scripture recognized by the Samaritans. Both Samaritans and Christians were negatively disposed toward the Jerusalem temple, and both experienced persecution at the hand of the Jews. Without question, Samaritans would have appreciated a Christian devaluation of the Jerusalem temple in a manner that fit with the Samaritan description of the proper holy place in their Pentateuch.

A second major stage in the development of Hellenistic Christianity is characterized by the Christology of the "Christ Hymns" that share the common feature of a redeemer who descends to earth, redeems humanity, and ascends to heaven (Phil 2:6–11; Col 1:15–20; 1 Pet 3:18–19, 22; 1 Tim 3:16; Eph 2:14–16; Heb 1:3).[57] This is consistent with Samaritan theological expectation of a redeemer (the Taheb) deduced from their Pentateuch whether modeled on Moses or Joshua.

57. Perrin, *New Testament*, 52–53.

Stephen was a member and likely the leader of "the (Hellenistic) Seven," in contrast to "the (apostolic and Hebrew) Twelve." The Twelve had been established by Jesus, probably influenced by Ezekiel and again reflecting Jesus' intention to unite the northern and southern tribes. By contrast, Stephen founded the Seven, whom Spiro saw as representing the seven dispossessed nations of the Hebrew Scriptures. The Seven represented Gentile Christianity in contrast to Jewish Christianity and had Gnosticism as a common denominator.[58] The Seven may have been the vehicle for the movement from Hellenistic Samaritan Christianity to dialogue with, and development of some mutual acceptance of, Hellenistic Jewish missionary Christianity as described in the book of Acts. Scroggs says Stephen was leader of the Hellenistic church and his speech was "a fragment of a Christian proclamation to the Samaritans."[59] Luke, as always, is irenic in spirit (and a Hellenist himself), and tries to include Hellenistic Samaritans,[60] but he diminishes them to the role of "deacons."

Philip's missionary success inspires Peter to come to Samaria, where it is reported that he quarrels with both Philip and Simon. This is a sectarian controversy that includes both Christian and Samaritan sects. Some argue that Peter's disagreement with Simon is a retrojected later argument that really involves Peter's argument with Paul. All of this takes place in Samaritan territory. Simon and the Samaritans in general are won over by Philip against Peter. Against Peter's argument that he himself was a companion of Jesus and is in a better position to interpret Christianity than any competitors (Simon, Philip, or Paul), Simon argues that, like Paul, he had a vision of Jesus and visions are superior to Peter's experiences as a traveling companion to Jesus.

Hellenism, the SP, and the New Testament

The Greek army of Alexander the Great was stronger than any resistance it encountered throughout the Middle East, but in the long run the Judeo-Christian culture swept through the Greek-speaking world. Robin

58. SAC, Aug 10, 1965; Matthews, *Philip*, 18–19.

59. Robin Scroggs, "The Earliest Hellenistic Christianity," in Neusner, *Religions in Antiquity*, 177.

60. Robert T. Anderson, "Hebrew Sources of Stephen's Speech" in *Uncovering Ancient Stones: Essays in Memory of H. Neil Richardson* (ed. Lewis M. Hopfe; Winona Lake, Ind.: Eisenbrauns, 1994), 205–15.

Scroggs calls the Hellenists "the Mother of Western Christianity."[61] It may have been a mixed victory and a troubled pregnancy. To the extent that Christian theology was heavily influenced by Greek thought, possibly including Samaritan concepts from a proto-Gnosticism, Hellenism co-opted apostolic Christianity. Both the language and the theology of early Christianity involved the Samaritans. It seems clear that the Samaritans had an early Greek translation of their Scripture, adapting to Greek as the lingua franca of the culture just as they had adapted to Aramaic as the previous lingua franca. It is possible that the Samaritans made use of a modified LXX.

When searching for the relationship of the SP and the New Testament, we emphasize the difficulty in distinguishing between the Jewish and Samaritan Greek translations in any particular passage. Since the early Christian community was disproportionately Hellenistic, quotations from the Pentateuch (or the rest of the Jewish Scriptures) are essentially all in Greek. It is easy to say that they are all quotes from the LXX, but there are times when it seems clear that some version of the Samaritan Scripture is in use. This will be quite apparent in Stephen's speech in the book of Acts, which will be discussed below.

Explicit Samaritan Presence in the New Testament Writings

The mission to the Samaritans evident in the book of Acts and the Gospel of John is not the only Samaritan issue considered in those books. Samaritan presence is strongly implicit in the book of Hebrews and elsewhere in the New Testament. The following survey highlights the more emphatic evidence of awareness of Samaritan presence in the New Testament.

Luke

Luke's openness to the Samaritans is consistent with his openness to foreigners in general. Unlike John, who considers Samaritans part of the true Israel, Luke considers the Samaritans to be foreigners. And unlike John, who was motivated by an emphasis on a twelve-tribe Israel shared with the SP, Luke is acting out of his general irenic spirit. It is not surprising that subsequent Samaritan writings often cite John and ignore Luke. Neverthe-

61. Scroggs , "Earliest Hellenistic Christianity," 200.

less, Luke is empathetic concerning Samaritans: for example, he explicitly refers to the Samaritan leper, who thanks Jesus for a healing, as a foreigner (Luke 17:18). John Bowman muses that other references to Gentiles in Luke could be references to the Samaritans, since Luke and the early church imply that the Samaritans were Gentiles rather than schismatic Jews.[62] The story of the thankful Samaritan is itself another Lukan narrative of a "good" Samaritan. Bowman believes that the role of the priests in this story, taken with Luke's emphasis on the priestly parenthood of John the Baptist and the priesthood in general, was an intentional Lukan device meant to appeal to the Samaritans.[63] Luke's work is shaped by awareness that the definition of the priesthood is a focal point of the SP, which so explicitly focuses on rituals and laws.

Earlier, in Luke 9:52, Luke indicates Jesus' patience with Samaritans even when Samaritans are hostile to the disciples who in turn are ready to ask God to annihilate the Samaritan communities with a pyrotechnic display from heaven. The story is similar to one told by Josephus, in which a Galilean Jew was murdered by Samaritans on his way to a festival in Jerusalem. The Jews sought retribution from the procurator Cumanus, but he was tolerant of the Samaritans and stayed the Jewish violence.[64] This same tolerant acceptance is where Luke wants to lead the Jewish community in its attitudes toward Samaritans. That story is followed by the parable of the Good Samaritan (Luke 10:25–37), in which Luke, through Jesus, forces the Jews to think the unthinkable: a grudging recognition of a good Samaritan. Both of these narratives may have been told by Luke to encourage the mission work in Samaria.

Stephen's Speech

The most prominent scholarly focus on the Samaritan issues in Luke/Acts is related to Stephen's speech in Acts 7 and Stephen's subsequent martyrdom. Shelly Matthews underscores the value of martyr stories in building and shaping movements, and thinks that with the Stephen story Luke was

62. John Bowman, *The Samaritan Problem: Studies in the Relationship of Samaritanism, Judaism, and Early Christianity* (trans. A. Johnson Jr.; Pittsburgh: Pickwick, 1975).

63. Ibid., 70–71.

64. Josephus, *J.W.* 12.3.

shaping the distinction between Jew and Christian.[65] Accordingly, Matthews wants to date Luke/Acts in the early second century, when martyrdom was more prevalent, and a significant issue for Christians.[66] As important as the distinction was between Jew and Christian, it was at least as important to Luke to shape the difference between Hellenistic and apostolic Christianity as it was to present a narrative preparing for the possibility of a martyr's death. Stephen's Hellenism may have been as important to Luke as his actual martyrdom.

The speech quickly raises the question of Stephen's likely use of the SP (or the pre-Samaritan tradition) in his biblical references and, in turn, the question of why he would use the SP. Stephen's speech reflects a deep awareness, if not use, of the SP and characteristic Samaritan terms and usages that in the twentieth century have been a lightning rod for scholars with a Samaritan interest. Was Stephen a Samaritan? Was he trying to win over or at least not offend Samaritans? Was Luke anticipating a Samaritan audience?

Abram Spiro picked up the Samaritan clues and their significance and, in so doing, initiated the debate of the 1960s and 1970s when his ideas were summarized in Munck's commentary on Acts.[67] For example, Stephen says Abraham left Harran after his father's death (Acts7:4), implying the earlier death of Terah at 145 years of age, in keeping with the SP (Gen 11:24–32). In 7:32, Stephen uses the plural of father, as in the SP, rather than the singular of the MT. Harran itself is much more important to the Samaritans than to the Hebrews, as is Shechem, the Samaritan counterpart to Jerusalem. Both Harran and Shechem are emphasized by Stephen. In addition, a grammatical characteristic common in the SP, the distinctive demonstrative pronoun "this" before a proper name, occurs six times in Stephen's speech (e.g., "this" Moses), and once in the testimony of the witness against Stephen: "this" Jesus (Acts 6:14). Also, *topes* (place), an important concept to the Samaritans, is used both in John (4:20) and in Stephen's speech (Acts 7:7, 33), in a manner not required by the surrounding context.

There are themes within Stephen's speech that also seem to be compatible with Samaritan sensitivities, if not to originate within Samaritan ideology. Stephen's speech, with its criticism of Solomon and his house

---

65. This is the thesis of Shelly Matthews, *Perfect Martyr: The Stoning of Stephen and the Construction of Christian Identity* (Oxford: Oxford University Press, 2010).

66. Mathews, *Perfect Martyr*, 6.

67. Albright and Mann, "Stephen's Samaritan Background," 285–300.

"made with hands" (most commentators agree that the term is pejorative) and acceptance of David's plan for a "tabernacle,"[68] rather than a temple, is amenable to Samaritan sentiments. Like Stephen's speech, the Samaritan portrayal of David is ambiguous, as illustrated by this description taken from a Samaritan chronicle: "Our congregation, too, the community of Samaritan Israelites on Mount Gerizim Bethel, liked David very much … and said, 'A good upright man is David the son of Jesse.'"[69] For Stephen it seemed to be important to note that it was Solomon who built the temple. Further, Jesus, Peter, Paul, and James all got into trouble in the temple, but Stephen did not go to the temple, but rather was arrested in the synagogue.

Scobie and Scroggs argue that Stephen was using the SP.[70] On the other hand, Lowy, Mare, and Richard argue that some of the non-MT used in Stephen's speech can also be found in other recensions, including the LXX.[71] "These variant recensions also find parallels in Jewish and Christian literature originating during the time in question, such as the book of Jubilees (either early or late postexilic) and, most importantly, the New Testament (50–90 C.E.). For example, Stephen's sermon (Acts 7) and Hebrews (ch. 9) are based on the pre-Samaritan recension."[72] With the accumulation of important explicit and circumstantial evidence suggesting the presence of Samaritans in the early Christian story, it may be more relevant to point out that in this period of a fluid and pluriform text, what have been considered Jewish or Christian versions may in fact have been Samaritan.

Stephen's speech helps Luke marshal several contemporary sectarian groups—Hellenists, Samaritans, Essenes, and Christians—against temple-centered Judaism. Thus he prepares the reader for the spread of Christianity among those groups already alienated from orthodox Judaism. That is not to say that Luke is determined to lead the Christians out of Judaism. Rather, it is to emphasize the irenic spirit at work in Luke to link Christianity to Judaism while justifying its expansion beyond sectarian borders.

---

68. Ernst Haenchen, *The Acts of the Apostles: A Commentary* (Philadelphia: Westminster, 1971), 285.

69. John MacDonald, *The Samaritan Chronicle No. II (or: Sepher Ha-Yamim): From Joshua to Nebuchadnezzar* (BZAW 7; Berlin: de Gruyter, 1969), 132.

70. Scobie, "Origins," 411.

71. Lowy, *Principles of Samaritan Bible Exegesis*, 56; Mare, "Acts 7," 1–21; Richard, "Acts 7," 190–208.

72. Waltke, "How We Got the Hebrew Bible," 38–39.

Luke was trying to appeal to Jews while being open to Gentiles. With Paul (notably in Rom 11), he foresees that in the long run Christians, including Gentile Christians, will be reconciled with their roots in Judaism.

John and Hebrews in Direct Dialog with the SP and the Implications

The author of the Fourth Gospel is the New Testament author most explicitly involved with the Samaritans, *sometimes even to their depreciation.* In telling the Samaritan woman at the well that she worships what she "does not know" (John 4:22), John, through Jesus, is not being sympathetic with the Samaritans. He reflects the Jewish bias that Samaritans are stupid or foolish—unknowing—"the foolish people of Shechem" (as described in the apocryphal Sirach 50:26). The expression "do not know" is also used by John against the Jews—and John was certainly critical of the Jews!

But despite his occasional criticism, John knows the Samaritan culture and is generally very sympathetic with it. John is aware of the general Jewish contempt for Samaritans, but his own responses are plentiful and sympathetic. His Gospel mentions Samaritans more than any other book in the New Testament, including Luke. Many of his comments are centered on the episode at the well in Samaria (John 4). And for their part, later Samaritans are aware of John's Gospel. The third or fourth century Samaritan theologian Marqah reflects John's words and ideas, and he and other Samaritan writers even use verbatim quotes.[73] Samaritans acknowledge the empathy that John has for them.

A few have gone so far as to argue that John was in charge of the mission to the Samaritans, if not a Samaritan Christian himself.[74] The peculiar exchange and accusation leveled at Jesus in John 8:48, "You are a Samaritan and have a demon" has been used as evidence suggesting Samaritan identity. Jesus denies that he has a demon, but says nothing about the charge of being a Samaritan. Heinrich Hammer assumes that Jesus says nothing because Jesus is in fact a Samaritan.[75] Hammer's conclusion has yet to be shared by others. It may simply be Jesus did not respond to that charge because he thought it absurd and beneath him. Generally, it is thought

---

73. MacDonald, *Memar Maqah*, 1:xx.

74. Buchanan, "Samaritan Origin," 149–75. Buchanan goes on to say that the Gospel is a product of Samaritan Christians.

75. Hammer, *Traktat vom Samaritanermessianias*, 28–32 and 100–101.

that the charge in John 8:48 is a redundant accusation. Samaritans were believed to be demon possessed, so calling Jesus a Samaritan and demon-possessed was saying the same thing in two different ways.

Unlike so many others, John does not see Samaritans as foreigners; they are part of the original Israel. Bowman believes John designs his Gospel to facilitate the conversion of Samaritans, and that he uses Ezekiel and the vision of a united Israel as bridge between Samaritans and Jews. Bowman is of the opinion that the extensive use of Ezekiel in the Gospel of John could be a reiteration of Ezekiel's vision of a restored whole Israel after the Babylonian captivity, which in terms of the first century could mean a restoration of relationships between Samaritans and Jews. When the Samaritan woman at the well asserts that her people are descendents of Jacob and thus have a legitimate claim to call themselves Israelites (John 4:12), it is the only such claim in the New Testament that goes unchallenged. The incident affirms both the Samaritan theory of their own origin and a tacit acceptance of that theory among at least some Jews.

Countering Bowman, James Purvis is disinclined to think of the Gospel of John as a tract to facilitate mission work with the Samaritans because the Christians are, by allegiance to Jesus, subordinating the great Samaritan hero, Moses, in a fashion never to be accepted by Samaritans.[76] Actually, there are two competing major heroes in the New Testament, as there are in the Hebrew Scriptures. One strain holds David as the great hero, and is seen in the Christian determination to demonstrate the Davidic background of King Jesus. The other strain is focused on Moses, seen in the emphasis on Jesus' having been miraculously saved from a king's massacre to become a law giver and prophet. The Gospel of Matthew sharpens this focus. The gospels, like Paul and the book of Hebrews, argue for the superiority of Jesus as the distinctive thrust of their movement. This superiority was a hard sell to the Samaritans, as it was to the Jews, but it was nevertheless the argument of the new Christ-centered sect. John argues that Jesus himself was well received in Samaria and Galilee, and generally rejected in Jerusalem (e.g., John 5:18, 42, 52; 7:1, 11, 13; 8:42, 57; 9:18; 18:12, 38; 19:7, 12, and 20).

John is one of four New Testament books that are notably silent about any Davidic Christology.[77] Mark, like John, offers no genealogy of Jesus.

76. Purvis, "Fourth Gospel," 191.

77. Ibid., 176.

Stephen's speech in Acts, and the book of Hebrews[78] are likewise silent.[79] This unevenly reported linkage to David may reflect tensions within Judaism and sensitivity to the Samaritans who would not in any fashion link their "Messiah" to David.

The priestly model (Moses-Joshua link for priests or Moses-Joseph link for laity) is significant in John as well, as Purvis has shown.[80] Although the Samaritan religion is heavily focused on the priesthood, the development of synagogues by the various Dosithean factions, after John Hyrcanus destroyed the sanctuary on Mount Gerizim in the late second century B.C.E., raised the leadership status of teachers, elders, and judges. Populating offices in a decentralized fashion by lay people led to various interpretations judged by some to be less than orthodox. There is no obvious single person who led the schism(s), and the range of nominees has even included John the Baptist.[81]

There are several other items in John reflecting possible Samaritan influence or sensitivity. The common Samaritan usage "our Father" appears in several places in the Gospel of John, and Bowman suggests that the *shekinah* appearing to the shepherds in Luke 2:14 would hold special meaning to Samaritans.[82] We saw earlier the distinctive Samaritan term *topes* (place) used in Stephen's speech (Acts 7:7, 33), and note once again its appearance in John (4:20), this time comfortably presented by the Samaritan woman. While the terminology of the SP is usually not distinct from that of the MT, terms and word usage often does distinguish Samaritan influence.

Perhaps John uses the term "Israelite" polemically at times, perhaps akin to the Samaritan usage at places like Delos, as a marker for Christians as opposed to other Jewish groups.[83] Purvis has suggested that the Johannine Christians may have used Samaritans as well as Israelites, not as equivalent, but as parallel markers in a polemic against the Jews in the

---

78. Scobie, "Origins," 411.

79. Bowman, *Samaritan Studies*, 313; Purvis, "Fourth Gospel," 177; and Scobie, "Origins," 404–5.

80. Purvis, "Fourth Gospel," 180.

81. Ibid., 169, 193.

82. Bowman, *Samaritan Problem*, 79–80.

83. Kyung-Rae Kim, "Studies in the Relationship between the Samaritan Pentateuch and the Septuagint" (Ph.D. diss., Hebrew University, 1994), 246.

controversy over who is the true Israel.[84] The attitude of early Christians toward Samaritans, while generally empathetic, is mixed.

The Book of Hebrews

The book of Hebrews is replete with signals that call attention to the Samaritans. The title of the book, whoever assigned it or when, raises questions in itself. "Hebrews" would be an appropriate address for Samaritans as well as Jews, and may be even more appropriate for Samaritans. Jews are consistently called "Jews" in the New Testament, so it is curious why they would here be addressed as Hebrews. Spiro cites Theodor Zahn's (1838–1933) commentary on Acts, which asserts that the Jews even had an aversion to being called Hebrews.[85] This aversion may be illustrated in the LXX reading in Gen 14 referring to Abraham as a "migrant" rather than a "Hebrew," which may be a Jewish polemic against the Samaritans.

Scobie speaks for many who note that the Samaritans referred to themselves, perhaps even preferably, as "Hebrews" [86] (although Lowy insisted that the Samaritans preferred to call themselves "Israelites"[87]). Early Christianity did conserve a tradition of "Jews" as a pejorative term, "Hebrew" as a neutral term, and "Israelite" as a term of honor.[88] By contrast, "Israelite" could refer to a Galilean (e.g., Nathaniel in John 1:47) and, to complicate terminology, Galileans and Samaritans are paralleled in John.[89] Buchanan and others concur that both Samaritans and non-Samaritans acknowledged "Israelite" as an acceptable designation for the Samaritans. [90]

E. A. Knox proposes Philip, the early missionary to the Samaritans, as the author of Hebrews.[91] Scobie states, "Hebrews represents in a highly developed form the theology of one branch of the Stephen-

84. Purvis, "The Fourth Gospel," 161–98, 191.

85. SAC, Nov 1, 1965.

86. Scobie, "Origins," 414; Spiro, SAC, June 6, 1965.

87. Lowy, *Principles*, 56–57.

88. Bernard Blumenkranz, *Die Judenpredigt Augustins: Ein Beitrag zur Geschichte der Jüdisch-Christlichen Beziehungen in den ersten Jahrhunderten* (Basel: Brepols, 1946), 181–86.

89. Purvis, "Fourth Gospel" 171–72.

90. Buchanan, "Samaritan Origins," 149–75.

91. E. A. Knox, "The Samaritans and the Epistle to the Hebrews," *The Churchman* NS 41 (1927): 184–93, here 189, 191, 192.

Philip movement."[92] Derenbourg believes the synagogue at Rome was Samaritan[93] and that this synagogue could be implied by the last verse of Hebrews: "Those who come from Italy send you greetings." There is evidence of a Samaritan synagogue in Rome, as we will see.

More convincing markers of Samaritan influence of presence are necessary to make the case that the book of Hebrews has a significant relationship to the Samaritans, and several have been offered. Heinrich Hammer notes that Heb 10: 8 follows the SP and Samaritan Targum rather than the MT.[94] Most convincingly, it has been noted that Stephen's sermon in Acts 7 and Heb 9:3–4, which reflects Exod 26:31–33 and Exod 30:1–5, are based on a "pre-Samaritan recension "[95] of the Pentateuch and at least show use of a text tradition that would come to be associated with the Samaritans. The ambiguity of the location of the altar of incense in the Hebrews passage, as opposed to the specific location in the temple as defined in the MT, would certainly cause less offense to the Samaritans. Scobie thinks that the Samaritan reading of Exod 30: 1–10 clarifies the confusion implied by a comparison between the book of Hebrews and the Masoretic reading of Exodus.[96] In the MT, the golden altar of incense does not stand within the Holy of Holies as stated in the book of Hebrews and the SP.

The book of Hebrews also thickens the plot of a Christian-Samaritan-gnostic-Hebrews puzzle introduced in Acts. Hebrews 7 introduces the unique appearance of Melchizedek material, including the distinctive Samaritan demonstrative pronoun "this" before Melchizedek in 7:1. The literal meaning of the name Melchizedek, "king of righteousness," and the general ambiguity of each of the texts about Melchizedek, including the Heb 7:3 statement claiming he was without father or mother or ancestors, allows wide-ranging speculation concerning priesthood, kingship, and messiahship that unfortunately cannot be settled by the texts themselves.

The gnostic library found at Nag Hammadi contains a tractate entitled "Melchizedek." It proposes that Melchizedek is Jesus Christ.[97] Jean Doresse seeks to establish a connection between the Samaritan Christians and

92. Scobie, "Origins," 414.

93. SAC, May 6, 1964.

94. Hammer, *Traktat vom Samaritanermessias*, 43.

95. Waltke, "How We Got the Hebrew Bible," 38–39.

96. Scobie, "Origins," 413.

97. James M. Robinson, *The Nag Hamadi Library* (San Francisco: HarperCollins, 1990), 438–44.

the gnostics,[98] suggesting that Melchizedek became a gnostic personality through the work of Samaritan Christians.[99] Robert Eccles describes Moritz Friedlander's position that "Melchizedekianism was the form of early Christian Gnosticism by which Alexandrian philosophical mysticism passed rapidly into Christianity." [100] Scobie includes Psuedo-Eupolemus in the Melchizedek context.

There are several other possible accommodations to the Samaritans in the book of Hebrews. Hebrews calls the temple a tabernacle (*skene*) throughout chapter 9, and echoes the sentiment of the perfect tabernacle "not made with hands" (9:11). Neither Stephen, in his speech in Acts 7, nor Hebrews, in this chapter, speak of the rebuilding of the temple, because of the implication that it would be built on Mount Zion, something that would have been anathema to a Samaritan audience.

Hebrews 11 catalogs the great people of faith in the Hebrew story. Notably this list emphasizes the same heroes emphasized in Samaritan tradition: Abraham, Moses, and Joshua. Curiously, Joshua is noted by deed, but not name (11:30–31), though he is mentioned by name in 4:8. In fact, except for an extended and concluding list of names, the Heb 11 list ends with Joshua—the same spot where the Pentateuch and thus the SP ends.

Richard argues that New Testament theology, including certain articulations of that theology in Hebrews, regarding law and Moses (particularly Jesus' title, "a prophet like Moses") reflects a Samaritan point of view.[101] The book of Hebrews gives special focus, perhaps informed by Samaritan beliefs, to the two distinctive Samaritan heroes, Moses and Joshua. The first six verses of Heb 3 make much of Moses' faithfulness, which is quite relevant to association with the Samaritans. A very common phrase in Samaritan liturgy, and in references to Moses in general, is "Moses, the faithful," a concept also emphasized by the "Moses layer" discussed above in chapter 4. The emphasis on Moses in Hebrews may have been intended to elicit echoes of Moses *redivivus* in the person of Jesus.[102] In Heb 3:1–6, Christ is characterized as "faithful over God's house as a son."

98. Jean Doresse, *The Secret Books of the Egyptian Gnostics: An Introduction to the Gnostic Coptic Manuscripts at Chenoboskian* (London: Hollis & Carter, 1960), 329–332.

99. SAC, Jan 25, 1965.

100. Eccles, "Hellenistic Patterns," 213.

101. Richard, "Acts 7," 194–95.

102. Scobie, "Origins," 410.

Scobie meaningfully compares this characterization with the portrayal in the Samaritan works of *Amram Darah* and *Memar Marqah* of Moses as the son of God's house.[103] It is also noted that the term "apostle" is ascribed both to Moses by Samaritans and to Jesus in Hebrews.[104]

Samaritan interest in the priesthood and the high priestly role assigned to Moses has been heavily explored.[105] Most notable is the major and frequent role assigned to the high priest in the book of Hebrews.[106] Scobie notes a striking parallel to characterizations of Jesus in Hebrews to similar characterizations of Moses in *Memar Marqah* 4:6: "Where is there the like of Moses and who can compare with Moses the servant of God, the faithful one of his House, who dwelt among the angels in the Sanctuary of the Unseen? … He was holy priest in two sanctuaries."[107]

William Manson adds several issues.[108] Hebrews 4:8 and Acts 7:45 represent the only mention of Joshua in the New Testament and may thus provide circumstantial evidence of Samaritan influence.[109] Joshua was particularly important to the Samaritans, who created their own *Book of Joshua* unrelated to the text in the Hebrew Bible. The MT Joshua is echoed in Heb 4:8. Both works make a general note that it was Joshua who finally brought rest to the Hebrews in Palestine by ending the wars. By contrast, Spiro thinks Heb 4:8 combats Samaritan belief that Joshua brought fulfillment and rest and that the future redeemer, the Taheb, was modeled on Joshua.[110]

In an interesting modern parallel, an Arab Anglican priest in Libya said he preached from the book of Hebrews during the protracted uprisings against Muammar Qaddafi in 2011. He found it meaningful to the protes-

103. Ibid., 411.

104. Ibid.

105. Eccles, "Hellenistic Patterns," 210–11.

106. Scobie, "Origins," 411.

107. Ibid.

108. William Manson (*The Epistle to the Hebrews* [London: Hodder & Stoughton, 1951], 56), focuses on eight issues that Hebrews seems to share with Stephen's speech. This list is challenged by Martin Henry Scharlemann in *Stephen: A Singular Saint* (AnBib 34; Rome: Pontifical Biblical Institute, 1968), 166–75.

109. Manson, *Epistle to the Hebrews*, 56.

110. A. Spiro, Commentary on Stephen's Speech (Acts 7:2–50) (unpublished manuscript), 50.

tors who lived and suffered in what to them was a strange land.[111] Earlier Samaritans may have found a similar solace in the message of Hebrews.

Faint Possibilities

Beside the occurrences we surveyed in Luke and John, the remaining gospels make little mention of the Samaritans, and seem neither to influence nor to be influenced by them or the SP. Matthew makes explicit reference to the Samaritans only in 10:5 when Jesus, sending out the twelve, admonishes them to enter no town of the Samaritans but rather to go the lost sheep of the house of Israel. It is not clear why the Samaritans wouldn't fit that category, but certainly the general explanation of the origin of the Samaritans in 2 Kings and Josephus was probably widespread among many Jews, including Matthew, who would not consider the Samaritans as Israelites.

There is no mention of Samaritans at all in Mark, though there are possible clues of sensitivity toward the Samaritans that could be reinforced by Mark's northern geographical location. In addition to the lack of a genealogy that would link Jesus to David and the south, the appellation "son of David" is not used by Mark and there is no mention of Jesus as "son of David" even during the entry into Jerusalem during the final week of his life. The only exception, where the phrase "son of David" appears, is in usage that may have been sympathetic to the Samaritans: Mark has Jesus explicitly deny that the Messiah is a son of David (12:34), citing David himself.

The Samaritans play no part in the writings of Paul. Paul must have encountered Samaritans on his travels. There is ample evidence of Samaritan synagogues in Rome and Thessalonica and he presumably heard Stephen's speech, but Paul does not mention Samaritans.

Conclusion

The relevance of Samaritan studies for New Testament studies is an area of inquiry that has fallen into neglect. Samaritan scholars are almost exclusively from a background in Hebrew Scripture. New Testament scholars

111. Amy Frykholm, "Caught in a Revolution: Tripoli Priest Hamdy Sedky Daoud," *Christian Century* 128:22 (November 1, 2011): 10–11.

tend to focus on the Greek tangents when they move out from the New Testament text. Charles Scobie's attempts to bridge scholarship across Hebrew Scripture and the New Testament provide a particularly admirable model. It is a difficult area of investigation, because the biblical texts are still fluid in the first century, to say nothing of the unsettled history of the period in general.

Just as the tradition preserved in the SP and pre-Samaritan group of Qumran texts has been recognized as a vital participant in the religious and literary world of Hasmonean and Herodian Palestine, so too there is ample evidence to conclude that Samaritan ideology and literature cannot be ignored when exploring the literary and ideological seedbed of the New Testament. The work on John, Stephen, and Hebrews is well advanced and deserves recognition. Mark and even Paul call for further investigation. Samaritans could have influenced almost every sect and geographical location of Christianity, and awareness of their tradition could potentially illuminate the complex sectarian picture of the first century in northern Palestine. In addition, the fluidity of texts and the thin and permeable line between composition and exegesis evident in the Qumran texts aids our understanding of scribal practices used by New Testament authors even where the presence of the SP itself cannot be proven.

7
The Samaritan Pentateuch in the First Millennium

No complete copies of the Samaritan Pentateuch produced in the first millennium C.E. survive. Nevertheless, portions of the text are preserved in Origen's third-century C.E. *Hexapla*, which refers to a *Samareitikon* (a Greek translation of the SP discussed in ch. 8 below), in marble and stone inscriptions dating mainly from the third to the sixth centuries C.E., and in metal and cloth inscriptions dating from the fifteenth century to the present. These witnesses provide valuable clues to the history and use of the SP during the first millennium.

First-Millennium Witnesses to the Samaritan Pentateuch

Apart from the *Samareitikon*, which may have originally contained all of the Pentateuch, the available inscriptions from the first millennium quote parts of the Pentateuch that were most meaningful to the Samaritans: the Ten Words of Creation (an abridgement of Gen 1);[1] the Ten Commandments (usually a conflation of the lists in Exodus and Deuteronomy); the core of the Passover Story (Exod 12:13, 23; 15:3, 11);[2] the priestly benediction (Num 6:22–27); and the scattering of Israel's enemies (Num 10:35).

---

1. In the beginning God created. And God said, / "Let there be light." And God said, / "Let there be firmament." And God said, "Let there be a collection / Of waters." And God said, "Let the earth sprout forth." And God said, "Let there be / Lights." And God said, "Let the waters swarm...." / And God said, "Let earth be brought forth." / And God said, "Let us make / a man." And God said, "Behold I have given / to you." And God saw all that / he made and behold it was very good and he said, "I / am the God of your fathers, the God of Abraham, / the God of Isaac and the God of Jacob" (translated from "Shechem Inscription 2," in Montgomery, *The Samaritans*, pl. 2).

2. "In the name of YHWH, the Deliverer, [His word] spoken by the hand of

Inscriptions can preserve witnesses to SP readings that are not preserved in any existing manuscripts. For example, the special collections archive in the library of Michigan State University includes a fractured marble stone, presumably used as a lintel, bearing an inscription written in paleo-Hebrew.[3] The inscribed fragment reads:

יהוה גיבור ב[ה]
מי כמוך באי
נדרי בקדש נור

YHWH is a hero in [the]. . . .
Who is like you among the [gods]
Majestic in holiness, terrifying. . . .

The text inscribed on the stone is taken from Exod 15:3, 11. The reconstructed definite article in line 1 of the marble inscription, CW 2472, does not appear in other manuscripts and could suggest an application of

A Samaritan Inscription on marble. The text is Exod 15:3 and 11 (CW 2472). Courtesy of Special Collections, Michigan State Universities Libraries.

Moses: / 'I will pass over you and not be smitten.' / YHWH will pass over the door and will not let the Destroyer enter you house to smite you" (translated from John Strugnell, "Quelque inscriptions samaritaines," *RB* 74 [1967]: 573; the passage appears in many other inscriptions as well).

3. Removed from its setting, the inscribed stone is difficult to date, but it may originate from the third to the sixth century C.E. (Terry Giles, "The Chamberlain-Warren Samaritan Inscription CW 2472," *JBL* 114 [1995]: 113).

the verse to a current or anticipated struggle facing the community and their confidence that God will be with them.[4] As such, the inscription is a reminder of the fluidity of texts and the nuance between translation and interpretation that was explored in chapter 2 and will be discussed again in chapter 9.

Amulets, a personalized form of inscription designed to be worn on the body or attached to some part of a home, are also important witnesses to the text of the SP during the first millennium. Like other inscriptions, they focused on and recited the major events in Israel's history and creed. Amulets were usually more or less oval in shape and could be made of stone, metal, parchment, wood, or paper. They had the practical function of protecting the wearer from illness and enemies. Sometimes amulets consisted of a square pattern of numbers, either with supposed magical properties or letter equivalencies to scriptural passages. Edward Robertson describes a five-number by five-number square amulet inscription that incorporates the Hebrew letters of "I am who I am" (Exod 4:14).[5]

During the Renaissance period, scroll cases began to appear decorated with inlaid inscriptions. Although arguably not intended to reproduce the SP text verbatim, functioning more like liturgical or prayer texts, these decorative inscriptions reflect distinctive Samaritan scribal traditions that are well established in extant copies of the SP. An example of these dedicatory inscriptions can be found on the Chamberlain-Warren Scroll Case (CW2465) housed at Michigan State University. According to the dedicatory inscription, the case was crafted in 1524. The case, like the Benguiat Scroll Case in the Jewish Museum of New York, constructed in 1565, is decorated with a number of inlaid inscriptions identifying the craftsman and location of manufacture.[6] On both cases an inscription, circling the case, pronounces the priestly blessing יברכך יהוה וישמרך ("YHWH bless you and keep you") from Num 6:24. Also inscribed on both cases is a selection taken from Num 10:35:

ויהי בנסע
הארון ויאמר

4. Giles, "Chamberlain-Warren Samaritan Inscription," 115–16.

5. Edward Robertson, *Catalogue of the Samaritan Manuscripts in the John Rylands Library* (2 vols. Manchester: Manchester University Press, 1938–1962), 2:22.

6. Robert T. Anderson and Terry Giles, *The Keepers: An Introduction to the History and Culture of the Samaritans* (Peabody, Mass.: Hendrickson, 2002), 83–84.

משה קומה
יהוה ויפוצו
איביך וינוסו
משנאיך מפניך

As the ark departed, Moses said, "Arise, YHWH, and scatter your enemies. The ones who hate you will flee from you."

The Scrolls Entering the Second Millennium

During the long yet mostly hidden period of copying manuscripts in the first millennium, a number of scribal practices and traditions developed that manifest themselves when the first extant manuscripts emerge in the early second millennium. The oldest existing SPs were written on animal skin, while most of the manuscripts in recent centuries are written on paper. The ink is usually carbon black in a gum or oil base. Margins and lines were usually ruled before writing. The text was written from right to left across the page, so the justification of the right margin was easy to control. Justification of the left margin was attained by thoughtful spacing of words and letters and arbitrarily saving the last letter of the line for the extreme left margin. Sometime in the early renaissance period it became customary to save two letters to mark the left margin. This was presumably an aesthetic consideration.

There are many levels of punctuation evident in the early copies of the SP. A dot followed every word, with ends of sentences marked by a more elaborate sign, such as a colon. Paragraph endings were even more elaborate, perhaps a colon, a "c" shape and a dash. Other subdivisions or distinctive phrases might have other markings. The end of a biblical book would be marked by a thick pattern, usually involving sharp wavy lines with dots within the waves. Since manuscripts contain no page, verse, or paragraph numbers, scribal traditions evolved by which to mark important passages. The Ten Commandments are often marked by simply putting the number of each commandment in the margin, but more extensive and subtle markings also developed.

The most frequent marker, which can also serve as a decorative feature, is the use of intentional vertical columns of letters, words, or phrases. When the decorative column consists of words or parts of sentences, there is an internal composition (a reading or design within a reading), for example, lists of tribes or families or descendants placed in columns where each of those generic words leads the phrase. Columns of letters, where the scribe leaves spaces in order to align the same letter in subsequent lines, have no inherent sense, but the creation of a column of letters will catch the eye, and if placed strategically may help a reader find a particular passage. Passages involving covenants, genealogies, and incidents in the life of a patriarch tended to encourage columnization. The columns function like subheadings, underscoring the highlights of the story. Like decorative patterns at the ends of biblical books, the practice of creating columns, often in the same places in different manuscripts, is a phenomenon shared between Samaritan Pentateuchs and the Codex Alexandrinus, a fifth-century Greek Bible, one of the earliest and most complete biblical manuscripts. The relationship between these manuscripts leaves open the question of the nature of the Hebrew Scripture quotations in the New Testament. To say that these quotations are taken from the Septuagint is not to answer the question of whether they are from a Jewish or Samaritan source. Evidence is mounting to suggest that Samaritan sources influenced a substantial number of the scriptural quotations in the New Testament.

The major acrostic or *tasqil* of the great Abisha scroll was mentioned in the preface. The Abisha *tasqil* represents a form that is characteristic of the *tasquilim* of many SPs. The location of the *tasqil* is usually in Deuteronomy, if the scribe is not a priest, or in Leviticus, if the scribe is a priest. A vertical channel that will accommodate a column of letters is ruled down the center of the page. As the biblical text is being copied horizontally across the page, a letter from each appropriate line is dropped into the empty space within the column to create a vertical message. Sometimes the scribe must go several lines without inserting a letter because the desired letter does not appear in the line he is copying. The *tasqil* contains the name of the scribe, several generations of his paternal genealogy, and the date on which the manuscript was completed, using Islamic dating. Often, the scribe will include the location of production, usually Damascus or Egypt. Sometimes he tells who commissioned the scroll, and occasionally the price.

Other acrostics occur in some later manuscripts, particularly a note marking the halfway point in the Torah (in Lev 7) and an occasional "Mount Gerizim." Ab Chisda, son of Jacob, son of Ahron, described as a crippled tailor, included nine acrostics in a manuscript he copied in 1912.[7]

7. CW2482 in the Chamberlain-Warren collection at Michigan State University.

The acrostics record words of praise to God and assurance to the reader of God's mercy.

The rate of production for Samaritan manuscripts depended on the vicissitudes in the life of the scribe, but four hundred lines a day was not unusual, nor was the production of two Pentateuchs per year. Afif, a scribe who produced two of the Pentateuchs in the Chamberlain-Warren collection at Michigan State University, is known to have produced the following extant manuscripts over the time periods indicated below.[8]

Date Copied (C.E.)	Catalogue	Number in Total Number Produced
1468	Sassoon MS. 403	10th
1468	Sassoon MS. 404	12th
1469	Trinity College, Cambridge. MS. R.15.55	15th
1474	Michigan State CW 2484	18th
1476	(15 T2) f=von Gall I	19th
1481	Ben Zvi MS 21	28th
1482	Trinity College, Cambridge, MS. R.15.54 =von Gall Gothic R	29th
1484	Michigan State CW 2478a	31st
1485	Berlin Or. MS. 4 534 = von Gall Gothic P	33rd

8. This information is based on Robert T. Anderson, *Studies in Samaritan Manuscripts and Artifacts: The Chamberlain-Warren Collection* (Cambridge: American Schools of Oriental Research, 1978), 26; and Alan Crown, "Studies in Samaritan Scribal Practices and Manuscript History: The Rate of Writing Samaritan Manuscripts and Scribal Output," *BJRL* 66 (1983–1984): 97–123, 119.

Bills of sale are often appended to empty spaces at the end of biblical books. They identify the seller and buyer of the manuscript and the date, the name of the person recording the sale, and the names of witnesses to the sale. In addition, the note will often include the location of the buyer and/or seller and the price. As an example of prices and price fluctuations, CW2478a, housed at Michigan State University, has four bills of sale. In 1487 the manuscript was sold for 24 gold dinars. It was sold again in 1500 for 22 gold dinars and in 1522 for 14 gold dinars. The last bill of sale records a transaction in 1524 for 300 silver edomi.

Honorific titles are a common feature of both *tasqils* and bills of sale. The honorific titles easily divide into four categories. The first is essentially census data, notably "son" or "daughter," and status as an elder—for example, "upright," "praying," "venerable," "elder," and "elder of Israel." Second are titles of flattery: "generous," "good," "honorable," "exalted," "saintly," and "leader." Third are titles indicating vocation: "good priest," "cantor," "reader of the law," and "keeper of the scroll case." Last are titles of deprecation, used almost always by the scribe himself: "humble," "fallen into sin and transgression," "poor, humble, needy servant." The number of titles ascribed to an individual varies from none to twenty. The status of the addressee is relevant, but the initial addressee (the actual participant in the transaction) usually receives the largest number of honorific titles, with diminishing numbers to his father and grandfather.

There was apparently a set process to check manuscripts for errors. The scribe himself would often realize an error, such as an omission of a word, and squeeze it into the margin or between the lines. Often a later hand is recognized correcting the text in the same manner.

Evidence from the Abisha Scroll

Parts of some manuscripts from the first millennium are possibly preserved in the revered Abisha Scroll, attributed by the Samaritans to Abisha, a great grandson of Aaron, the brother of Moses.[9] No Samaritan history traces the scroll from its creation (supposedly in the latter half of the second millennium B.C.E.) to the fourteenth century C.E., when it was discovered. According to the Samaritan *Book of Joshua*, many of the Samaritan scrolls were either burnt or stolen during the period of Hadrian (early second

9. Kahle, *Cairo Geniza*, 188.

century C.E.), leaving few literary sources for the community, the most precious of which was a copy of the SP.[10] Presumably, this single surviving scroll was the Abisha Scroll, although no further mention of it is made until the fourteenth century.

Over the centuries, the Abisha Scroll could have been lost among the many items in the synagogue library at Nablus. There is ample precedent for misplacing valuable biblical scrolls, perhaps most notably Josiah's discovery in the temple (2 Kgs 22), and the Codex Sinaiticus, a copy of the LXX that disappeared amid the old manuscripts at Saint Catherine's Monastery at the foot of Mount Sinai until it was rediscovered by German archaeologist Constanin von Tischendorf in 1844. John Strugnell believes that the Abisha Scroll was kept in Egypt with an exilic community during the hidden years, but John Bowman and others think that this unlikely, since there would be such strong community resistance to the removal of the Abisha Scroll from the Holy Land.[11] Most scholars today believe that the scroll has little or no history prior to its "discovery" in the fourteenth century. The consensus view understands the Abisha Scroll as a composite constructed in the fourteenth century C.E. from pieces of several different manuscripts representing different scribes and centuries. The oldest texts within the manuscript may date to the twelfth century C.E. According to this scholarly narrative, the Abisha Scroll was intentionally designated as the central rallying artifact for a Samaritan renaissance that sought to invigorate and reconcile the various Samaritan factions. This renaissance was begun in 1352 under the impetus of the high priest Pinhas, who commissioned several works, including two chronicles by Abul-Fath. During a search for Samaritan scrolls that could be helpful in these projects, the soon-to-be famous Abisha Scroll made its appearance (or reappearance) at Nablus. It was Pinhas who claimed that the Scroll was written by Abisha, a great-grandson of Aaron, the brother of Moses.

A sometimes illegible (and therefore, ambiguous) acrostic beginning in Deut 5:6 of the scroll is puzzling. It reads: "I am Abisha, the son of Pinhas, the son of Eleazer, son of Aaron, the priest, to whom be the favor of the Lord and his glory. I have written this Holy Scroll at the gate of the Tent of the Assembly on Mount Garizim, Beth El, in the thirteenth year

---

10. Oliver Trumbull Crane, trans., *The Samaritan Chronicle or Book of Joshua, the Son of Nun, Translated from the Arabic with Notes* (New York: Alden, 1890), 126.

11. Strugnell, "Quelque inscriptions samaritaines," 557–80; Bowman, *Samaritan Problem*, 9.

of the settlement of the children of Israel in the land of Canaan. I thank the Lord." The Abisha Scroll is written in a form of paleo-Hebrew on sewn lambskin or goatskin from a peace offering. All paleographic evidence suggests a much later date than that claimed in the acrostic, and some of the illegible words could be reconstructed to indicate that the dating is by the Muslim calendar, a clue that would substantiate a later dating. Alan Crown, building on the observations of F. Perez Castro, suggested that the Abisha Scroll was contrived by the fourteenth century C.E. priest Abisha and his son Pinhas. Crown believes that the creation of the scroll was a political move on the part of Pinhas to solidify his priestly status amid two other priestly families.[12]

The discovery of the book of the law by the high priest Hilkiah (2 Kgs 22:8) during the reforms instituted by the Judean King Josiah in the late seventh century B.C.E. offers both a parallel to and an implicit defense against charges of "pious fraud" in the scenarios reconstructed above. In each case, the reformer sought ancient sanction for current change, and in each case there was a history of previous reform, segments of which could legitimately be focused on contemporary issues. Regardless of its origin, the Abisha Scroll did become a revered object, and inspired the production of an unusual number of SPs in its wake.

The original housing of the document is not recorded, but a brass scroll case was made for it by Abisha b. Pinhas b. Abisha b. Pinhas b. Joseph b. Ozzi b. Pinhas b. Eliazar, the High Priest in Nablus (1431–1509).[13] Von Gall speculated that at one point the Abisha Scroll was housed in a scroll case (CW2473) now held in the Special Collections archive at Michigan State University.[14] It is more likely that CW2473 housed the Damascus Scroll, which was given a new scroll case in 1524 (the date CW2473 was crafted). There was a relationship between the priesthoods of Damascus and Nablus, and the question can be left open. This relationship is further evidenced by the fact that a tapestry for the Abisha Scroll was made and

12. Alan Crown, "The Abisha Scroll of the Samaritans," *BJRL* 58 (1975): 63. See F. Perez Castro, *Séfer Abišaʿ: Edición del fragmento antiguo del rollo sagrado del pentateuco hebreo samaritaner de Nablus, estudio, transcripcion, aparato critico y facsimiles* (Textos y estudios del Seminario Filologico Cardenal Cisneros 2; Madrid: Seminario Filológico Cardenal Cisneros, 1959).

13. Crown, *Samaritan Scribes and Manuscripts*, 409.

14. August Freiherr von Gall, ed., *Der Hebraische Pentateuch der Samaritaner* (Giessen: Töpelmann, 1914–1918; repr., Berlin: de Gruyter, 2011), lii.

presented by Jacob b. Abraham b. Isaac of the Metuchia family in Damascus, a person who is not otherwise known.

Historical mention of the Abisha Scroll, particularly by tourists, is recorded periodically. Nathan Schur notes an attempt by John Usgate, a Vicar of West Wycombe, to buy the Abisha Scroll in 1734.[15] In the early twentieth century, the impoverished Samaritan community was encouraged to allow the Abisha Scroll to be photographed as part of a project initiated to help the community raise money to become self-sufficient. The project was undertaken by the American Samaritan Committee, whose initiator, chair, and chief benefactor was E. K. Warren, a wealthy businessman from Three Oaks, Michigan, who had become enamored of the Samaritan community during visits to Palestine in 1901. John Whiting, United States Vice-Counsel in Jerusalem, arranged for the photos to be taken. The deteriorated nature of the manuscript, the poor photos, and the mistaken judgment of a well-respected Old Testament scholar that the photos were not of the Abisha Scroll, rendered the images unsaleable.

While still hidden from the world[16] and so removed from scholarly inspection, the Abisha Scroll maintains a central role in the Samaritan cultus. On the Day of Atonement, the tenth day of the first month, the Abisha Scroll is brought out to confer a special blessing on the congregation.[17] Like the seemingly timeless Melchizedek of old, the Abisha Scroll ushers us into the next millennium.

---

15. Nathan Schur, "The Modern Period (from 1516 A.D.)," in *The Samaritans* (ed. Alan Crown; Tübingen: Mohr Siebeck, 1989), 117.

16. Tourists are shown a different scroll. The Samaritans would not even show the actual Abisha scroll to the eminent Samaritan scholar Alan Crown in his visits to Nablus.

17. Reinhard Pummer, "Samaritan Rituals and Customs," in Crown, *The Samaritans*, 687.

8
The Samaritan Pentateuch and the Beginnings of Textual Criticism

A century before any Samaritan manuscript arrived in Europe, the Reformation had fueled both Roman Catholic and Protestant biblical research, with scholars attempting to support their respective positions in the new sectarian conflict. Roman Catholics favored the Koine Greek LXX version of the Old Testament, while Protestants sanctioned the Hebrew MT. Biblical languages became a serious focus of study, and an avid interest in old biblical manuscripts developed. An arbitrator between these two texts—Greek and Hebrew, Roman Catholic and Protestant—was sought by both sides.

The first European scholar to anticipate that the SP might play such a mediating role was Joseph Justus Scaliger (1540–1609), a French scholar with linguistic skills and travel experience who focused his attention on both classical and religious texts. Though born Roman Catholic, Scaliger became a Protestant. Aware of the Samaritan community and their unique Pentateuch, Scaliger wrote to the Samaritans in Palestine, inquiring about their rituals and their writings. Two letters in reply, one from a Samaritan in Gaza and another from a Samaritan in Egypt, answered some of his questions. The Samaritan correspondents also sent to Scaliger a copy of the Samaritan *Book of Joshua* (quite different from the biblical book), but no SP arrived in Europe during his lifetime. Still, Scaliger's efforts reflect the fact that the early text-critical history of the SP in Europe was dominated by an internecine debate between Roman Catholic and Protestant biblical scholars. The context for that debate is surveyed below.

LXX: The Roman Catholic Bible

The LXX was originally translated from Hebrew sometime during the third and second centuries B.C.E. in Alexandria. The translation was produced by Jewish scribes for the sake of the many Hellenized Jews in Palestine and, particularly, the Diaspora. These dispersed Jewish communities came to speak the indigenous Greek of their new homelands and no longer read Hebrew. The Greek-speaking early church naturally adopted this text as their version of the Old Testament,[1] and the rapid growth of Christianity facilitated the duplication and availability of thousands of copies of the LXX. By the time the SP first arrived in Europe in the seventeenth century, several editions of the LXX were already readily available to scholars. Taking advantage of the printing press (invented in the late 1430s), Cardinal Francisco Jiménez (Ximenes) de Cisneros of Spain financed the *Complutensian Polyglot Bible* in 1514–1515. The four volumes of this work dedicated to the Old Testament present, in parallel columns, the MT, the Latin Vulgate, and the LXX. In the Pentateuch, the *Targum Onkelos* is found at the bottom of the page with a Latin translation. The publishers had access to seemingly early manuscripts of the LXX from the Vatican library, the library of St. Mark's in Venice, and Jiménez's personal library, assuring a text based on early readings.

In 1518, a few years after the publication of the *Complutensian Polyglot Bible*, the Aldine edition of the LXX was printed in Venice. It takes its name from Aldus Manutius, the leading publisher and printer of the Venetian High Renaissance. The texts for the various biblical books in this edition are not uniform, but they are all closer to the Greek of Codex Vaticanus than to the *Complutensian Polyglot Bible*. Codex Vaticanus (B) is very early (mid-fourth century C.E.), and scholars agree that it was likely the best text of the Bible currently available. The Dutch humanist Erasmus (1469?–1536), became aware of Vaticanus through correspondence with the Vatican, and portions were collated by various contemporary scholars, but the many errors in the transcriptions were not fully realized until a full transcription was made available in the nineteenth century. It is clear that the Aldine text is closer to Codex Vaticanus than is the *Complutensian*,

1. Understanding of the extent of that use may require revision as the pluriformity of the early scriptural tradition, including the precursor of a Greek SP, becomes better understood.

and the editor of the Aldine edition says that he collated many ancient manuscripts, but unfortunately none of them are named.

Later in the sixteenth century, the *Antwerp Septuagint* (1571–1580), a text based on the *Complutensian Septuagint*, was printed at the expense of Philip II of Spain by the famous printer Christophe Plantin (8 vols., folio, 1569–1572). Benedictus Arias Montanus led the publication effort, aided by an international team of Spanish, Belgian, and French scholars. The most valuable edition of the LXX to arrive in Europe, in time to contribute to the great conflict over the antiquity of the various versions, was the Roman or "Sixtine" edition. Published in 1586, it was important both because it reproduced Codex Vaticanus "almost exclusively" and because it was produced under the direction of Cardinal Caraffa by the authority of Pope Sixtus V (1521–1590). It was specifically designed to assist the Catholic scholars who were preparing the new edition of the Latin Vulgate ordered by the Council of Trent in the mid-sixteenth century.

MT: The Protestant Bible

The MT was copied, edited, and distributed by a group of Jewish scholars known as the "Masoretes" between the seventh and tenth centuries C.E. The oldest extant copy, the Leningrad Codex, dates from the end of that period (ca. 1009 C.E.) and was copied in Cairo. The MT is the product of Jewish scholars who wished to establish a standard text from the many copies of the Hebrew Scriptures that were in continual production and circulation. In creating this uniform standard, the scribes added helpful marks to indicate vowels, accents, and intonations as Hebrew ceased to be a spoken language. Though the consonantal text differs little from the text generally accepted by the Jews in the early second century C.E. (and also differs little from the even older proto-MT group of Qumran texts), it has numerous differences of both greater and lesser significance when compared to extant fourth-century manuscripts of the LXX.

In contrast to the Roman Catholics, who believed the LXX to be the best version of the Old Testament, the Protestants followed Martin Luther in favoring the Jewish Masoretic Hebrew text. Luther's own translation of the Bible was based on the edition by Gershom ben Moses Soncino, published in Brascia in northern Italy in 1494. This text was typical of manuscripts that were part of the developing standard MT. It was also used by the Protestant translators of the King James Version of 1611. The specific Hebrew Masoretic manuscripts used by Christian scholars in the seventeenth century are unfortunately not identified. Many copies of the MT were available to translators, and these copies show very little variation. The Oratory, the work site of Jean Morin, a principle figure in the religious debates over texts worked, had three volumes of this rather standard MT dating to about 1210.[2]

The Samaritan Pentateuch Arrives in Europe

Europeans had their first glimpse of the SP in 1623, when a copy, much later labeled "Codex B" by August von Gall, arrived in France.[3] This manuscript was produced by a Samaritan scribe in Damascus in 1345 or 1346.[4] A persecution of Samaritans had followed an insurrection in Nablus at the foot of Mount Gerizim in 1316, causing the Samaritans to flee in search of security and peace elsewhere. A favorite city of exile was Damascus, and here many copies of the SP were produced in the first half of the fourteenth century. In addition to Damascus, Samaritan communities formed what eventually became three additional major centers of scribal production in Egypt, Shechem, and Zarephath.

The three most prominent Samaritan families in Damascus were the Ikkara, Pigma, and Segiana families. The scribe of the manuscript that arrived in Paris identified himself as Abraham, son of Jakob, son of Tabia, son of Se`ada, son of Abraham, of the second of those prominent families, Pigma. He indicated in the manuscript's colophon that this was the sixth manuscript he had copied. Two other manuscripts copied by Abraham also exist, including von Gall's Codex V (1339/1340), his fifth manuscript, and Codex A, his seventh manuscript, written sometime in the same year. Abraham's brother Natanael (Mattana) was the scribe of von Gall's P (1434/1435), his first, and H, a manuscript that followed in 1436/1437. Codex B is currently housed in the Bibliothèque Nationale in Paris.

---

2. Jean Morin, *Exercitiones Ecclesiasticae in Utrumque Samaritanorum Pentateuchum* (Paris: Antonius Vitray, 1631), 9.

3. Von Gall, *Hebräische Pentateuch der Samaritaner*. Codex B becomes the base for von Gall's text. In the early twentieth century, von Gall organized all of the SPs and fragments available to him and described them, their *tasqils*, and bills of sale. He also created a critical apparatus for the text that allowed him to collate the variant readings of the texts he used.

4. The uncertainty concerning the specific year of production arises from the fact that the manuscript is internally dated on the basis of the Muslim lunar calendar, whose years overlap the Gregorian solar calendar unevenly.

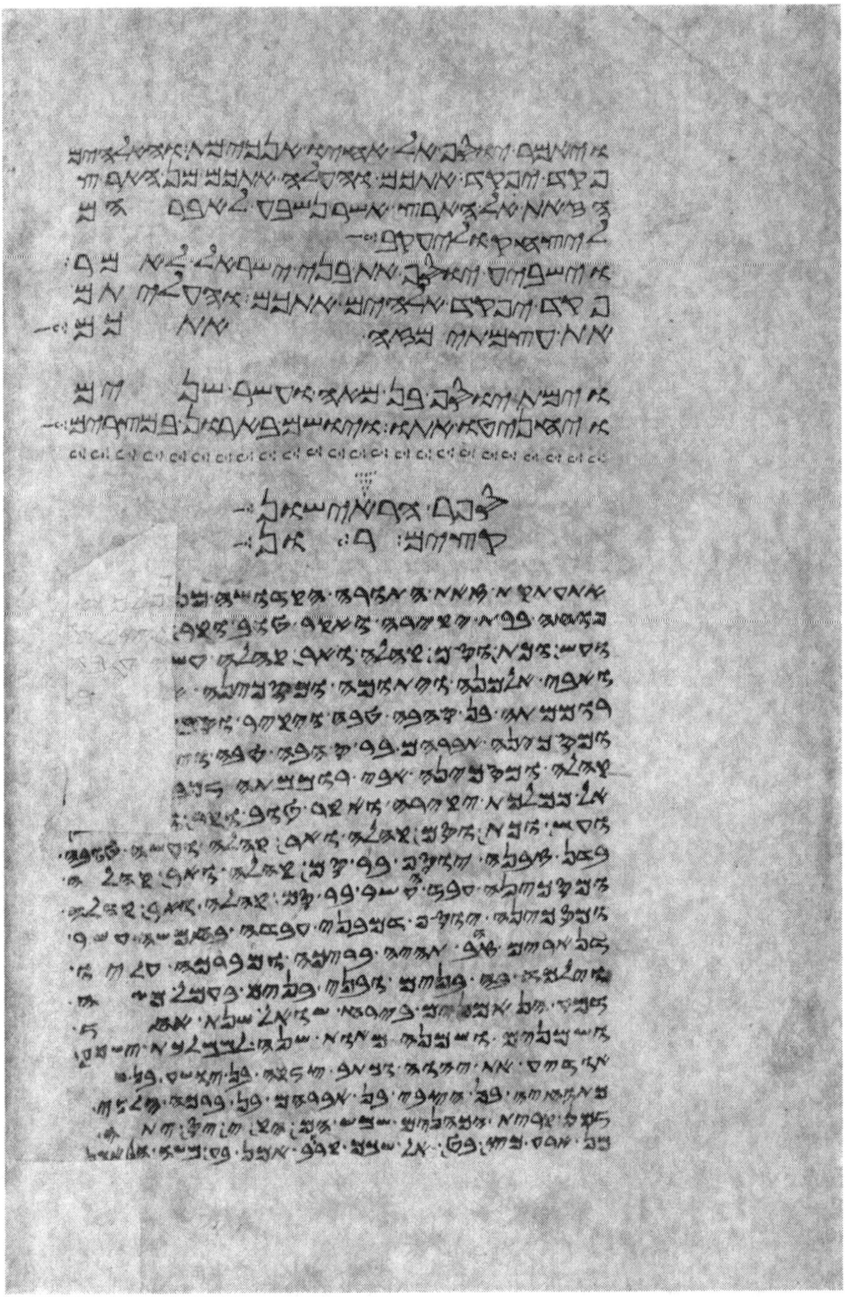

Bill of sale at the end of the Book of Genesis in CW 2484. Courtesy of Special Collections, Michigan State Universities Libraries.

In a computer sorting of manuscripts by selected textual items such as plene readings (indication of vowel lengths), exchange of gutturals, omission of the definite article, substitution of י for ה as a suffix, it becomes clear that Codex B shares a number of characteristics common to a group of manuscripts that includes von Gall's A, D, F, and G. Each of these manuscripts, except D, also dates from the mid-fourteenth century, a period of high production for surviving SPs. Parts of Codex D date from the twelfth and thirteenth centuries,[5] perhaps suggesting that this earlier manuscript may have been a model for Codex B and the other members of the group.[6] There are 272 parchment leaves in this manuscript.

Codex B is an attractive manuscript, typical of the SPs from this period. Each page is about 32 centimeters high and 25 centimeters wide, somewhat smaller than the average size during this period, and contains thirty lines of text in carefully written majuscule letters. A page written on the hair side of the animal skin has a shiny look and has taken on a yellowish tint. The flesh side of the skin has a flat or matte white look. The text reads from right to left and both margins are justified. The left side is justified by placing the last two letters at the margin even if this means leaving space between the letters of the last word. As noted in chapter 6, many SP manuscripts include an acrostic, usually woven into the text in Deuteronomy, in which the scribe records biographical data. The acrostic of Codex B reads:

> I am the poor servant dependent on the grace of God, Abraham, son of Jakob, son of Tobia, son of Seadah, son of Abraham of the Pigma family, and I wrote this Holy Torah in the year 746 (1345/1346 C.E.) of the rule of the Ishmaelites (Muslims). It is the sixth Torah [I have written]. I thank Yahweh and ask him in the faith of the son of Aram (Moses) that he be a witness upon the writing of it. Amen. And let it be a blessing upon all the congregation of Israel. Amen. Amen.

Here Abraham does not say where he wrote the manuscript, but in his acrostic in Codex A and other manuscripts he identifies Damascus as the location of his labors.

---

5. Ibid., vi.

6. Robert T. Anderson, "Clustering Samaritan Hebrew Pentateuchal Manuscripts," in *Études samaritaines: Pentateuque et targum, exégèse et philology, chroniques* (ed. Jean-Pierre Rothschild and Guy Dominique Sixdenier; Leuven: Peeters, 1988), 57–66.

An Acrostic from CW 2484 in Deuteronomy identifying the scribe. Courtesy of Special Collections, Michigan State Universities Libraries.

Codex B was the first Samaritan source available to European scholars, and as such it played a central role in the controversies over the true text of the Bible that were about to begin in the seventeenth century. In many respects, it was fortuitous that Codex B would serve as the sole representative of the SP text. While there was not as much diversity among SPs as among copies of the LXX, there was more diversity than was displayed among existing copies of the MT, and it was fortunate that Codex B was such a good text.

Jean Morin

The nexus for bringing these Hebrew, Greek, and Samaritan sources together in Europe was Jean Morin (in Latin, Johannes Morinus; 1591–1659). Much of Morin's professional life was spent editing biblical manuscripts, particularly the SP, for the *Paris Polyglot Bible* that appeared in 1645. To study Morin is to study the origins of modern textual criticism and to observe the dynamics of the discipline—and its occasional lapses from objectivity.

Morin was born in Blois, France, of Protestant parents. He learned Latin and Greek at Rochelle, and continued his studies in Leiden before moving on to Paris. He converted to Roman Catholicism and joined the congregation of the Oratory in Paris in 1618. After ordination Morin traveled in England and Rome (at the invitation of Pope Urban VIII) before settling down at the Oratory to focus on biblical texts, particularly the SP and Targum (a free paraphrase of the Pentateuch in Aramaic). Morin's chief fame rests on his biblical and critical work set forth prominently in *Exercitiones Ecclesiasticae in Utrumque Samaritanorum Pentateuch* (1631), (*Ecclesiastical Discussion of the Samaritan Pentateuch*). In his defense of the superiority of the Roman Catholic endorsed LXX text, Morin became enamored of the SP and very critical of the Hebrew MT. When Codex B arrived in Paris in 1623 C.E., it was appropriately delivered into Morin's hands in the Oratory. Armed with copies of the MT and the LXX (though citing neither the Aldine Edition nor Codex Alexandrinus), Morin used the SP to support his thesis that the LXX was superior to the MT preferred by Protestants.

Assuming that the SP supported the readings of the LXX rather than the MT, Morin first sought to establish that the SP text was older and, therefore, presumably closer to the original *Urtext* than the MT. Because the written characters (the paleo-Hebrew script) used in copies of the SP were older than the Hebrew characters, it seemed to him logical that the SP must predate the MT. On this point, he cited the Babylonian Talmud and several rabbinic commentaries, notably Samuel Iaphe and Solomon Iarki, in support of the antiquity of the Samaritan characters.

No one questions the fact that the characters used by the Samaritan scribes are older than the script typically used in copies of the MT, so on that point Morin seemed to display an accurate pre-judgment. Unfortunately, Morin did not fully examine whether the use of an older script necessitated an earlier date of composition. The Samaritans could have preserved, and in fact did intentionally preserve a more archaic script. Nevertheless, working from the assumption that an older style of script meant an older date of composition, Morin went on to argue for the basic reliability of the SP.

Many of his examples of this reliability are taken from the church fathers, particularly Jerome. Morin noted that the SP sometimes supplies a word or phrase that completes part of a sentence or story. For example, thanks to Jerome, Morin noted that in Gen 4:8 the Hebrew text omits נלכה השדה ("let us go to the field"), leaving the phrase, "And Cain said to Abel, his brother…" with no object.[7] The Samaritan text, the earlier witness in Morin's view, supplies the missing phrase, as do the LXX, the Vulgate, and, as Morin learned from his colleague Gabriel Sionetes, the Syriac.

That textual omission in Gen 4 could be unintentional, but Morin suspected that some omissions in the MT were driven by ulterior motives.[8] For example, Morin believed that the MT intentionally left out a word in Deut 27:26. Jerome had already picked up a clue to the missing word from Paul who, citing the verse in Gal 3:10, adds the word *pas*: "Cursed be everyone who does not stand by *all* that is written in the book of law and do it." Appropriately, in Morin's thinking, the LXX likewise reads "*all* the words in the law" in the Deuteronomy passage. Whether or not the LXX preserves the original text, it seems likely to most scholars today that Paul quotes from the LXX in Gal 3. Some scholars suggest that the Samaritan textual tradition may have played an active role in the New Testament community, and that citations usually attributed to the LXX may well be Greek translations of the SP in the many instances at which the LXX and SP read the same. As we have seen, there is very little evidence of interest

7. Morin, *Exercitiones*, 219–21.

8. Ibid., 221.

in the Samaritans in the writings attributed to Paul. Although Samaritans were a major missionary interest for many Christians in the early church, Paul's efforts were focused elsewhere. In any case, while much of Morin's work on the SP has not stood the test of subsequent scholarly validation, he helpfully alerted scholars to the possibility of Samaritan readings behind some New Testament citations.

As another example of the accuracy of the SP, Morin noted the consistency of the SP version of Num 32, which mentions the half tribe of Manasseh with the Gadites and the Reubenites each time the latter two are mentioned.[9] In the MT, the half tribe of Manasseh appears, inexplicably, only with the final mention of Gad and Reuben in verse 33. In Num 24:7, the Samaritan text reads מגוג ("Magog his king shall be high"), in agreement with several other manuscripts, including the LXX, rather than מאגג ("his king shall be higher than Agag") as in the MT.

Morin used Exod 32:18 in the SP to correct both the MT and the LXX, thereby affirming, at least in this instance, the SP's superiority. The MT available to Morin appears to have omitted a word:

> It is not the sound of the cry of might, nor is it the sound of [omitted word] I hear.

The LXX supplies οινος ("wine") as the missing word. Most of the SP manuscripts, including Codex B, read ענות ("sins").[10] Morin accepted the SP reading as the resolution of the problem.[11] Morin similarly contended that the SP correctly supplies three verses missing in the MT after Num 10:10.[12] In point of fact, the SP here adds verses taken from Deut 1:6–8 to produce a more consistent reading, reflecting a harmonistic editorial practice characteristic of the SP. Contemporary scholars see most of these differences as examples of later intentional insertions smoothing difficult readings, against Morin's contention that the original pristine text had been corrupted in the MT.

In Morin's opinion, the basic soundness of the SP is further attested by the fact that several improvements on the MT conjectured by the church

9. Ibid., 222.

10. This is also the reading in the MT published as *Exodus and Leviticus* (fasc. 2 of *BHS*; ed. Gottfried Quell; Stuttgart Deutsche Bibelgesellschaft, 1977).

11. Morin, *Exercitiones*, 223.

12. Ibid., 225–26.

fathers are actually found in the SP.[13] For example, although both the SP and MT read למוקש at Exod 10:7 when Pharaoh's servants ask, "How long shall this man be a מוקש (*snare*) to us?", the Greek church fathers preferred "pain" or "hurt," a reading sanctioned by the SP and translated into Greek as εις ἄτας.[14]

Morin highlighted the strengths of the SP text but also, conversely, the weakness of the MT. These judgments are not purely textual, for there appear to be anti-Semitic overtones in Morin's criticisms of the MT. The Jewish community in France was banned from many provinces, and new bans were issued in Morin's time. Morin claimed that the Jews intentionally altered the LXX to suit their doctrines. Perhaps most notably, Morin argued that the Masoretes purposefully changed an earlier reading of Isaiah 6 from "virgin" to "young woman" to undermine the expectation that the Messiah would be born of a virgin.

In chapter 8 of *Exercitiones*, Morin described the extent of error in the Hebrew texts that have been recognized by the Jews themselves. He listed these recognized errors as corrections of the scribes and differences of readings between Ben Naphtali and Ben Asher. Ben Naphtali and Ben Asher were tenth-century C.E. scribes, representing two schools of Masoretic scholars known by the same names that had differences of opinion on how the Hebrew text should be read. Morin also noted differences between Eastern and Western Jews on vowels and accents, differences among Western texts themselves, and frequent contradictions between the Talmud and Hebrew biblical texts. Morin also cited a Spanish text (which he did not identify) that offered readings different from those in the MT.[15] For example, in Gen 19:13, the MT reads את הזה המקום ("this place" with sign of the direct object) rather than אל המקום הזה ("to this place") as in the unnamed Spanish text. Further, Morin pointed out that the MT is self-contradictory. One example he cited is the tendency to waver between the spelling variations: אהלה (Gen 9:21; 12:8; 13:3) and אהלו (Gen 26:25).[16] Morin continued his argument with the MT by citing what he calls "stupid" grammatical errors. As an example, he cited the use

13. Ibid., 30–238.
14. Ibid., 231.
15. Ibid., 350.
16. Ibid., 352.

of דיצה rather than ציד in Gen 27: 3 and pointed to the whole Qere-Kethib apparatus as a witness to careless mistakes.[17]

Morin co-opted the third chapter of the Spanish Rabbi Yehuda Halevi's *Kuzari* (book of the Khazars) completed in 1140 as a Jewish witness supporting his contention that there were a number of misreadings in the Hebrew Bible.[18] Halevi's volume revolved around the Khazars, a semi-nomadic Turkic people who established an empire between the seventh and tenth centuries, comprising much of modern-day European Russia, western Kazakhstan, eastern Ukraine, Azerbaijan, large portions of the northern Caucasus (Circassia, Dagestan), parts of Georgia, the Crimea, and northeastern Turkey. Many of the Khazars converted to Judaism during the reign of King Bulan between the mid-700s and the mid-800s. In Halevi's narrative, a Greek philosopher, a Christian missionary, a Muslim mullah, and a Jewish sage each engage King Bulan in conversation. The king is most intrigued by the rabbi and finally concedes that Judaism is the true and correct religion. In the third chapter of Halevi's work, the rabbi asks the king, "Now what would you say if you were to find in Scripture a letter that conflicts with common sense, for instance זדו where you would expect זרו (confusion between ד and ר, in Lam 4:18) or נפשי ("my soul") where you would rather have נפשו ("his soul," in Ps 24:4) and many others like it?" The king replies, "Once you leave the decision about such cases to common sense, you are liable to have the entire Bible changed; first letters, then words, then whole sentences, vowels, accents, and then the entire manuscript will be altered. How numerous are the verses which would assume the opposite meaning of what they say now if merely a single one of these oppositions were changed, not to speak of wholesale emendations."[19] Both questioner and king imply that there are innumerable letters, words, and sentences in the Hebrew version that defy common sense.

Generally speaking, Morin's critique can be divided into attacks on the accuracy of the MT and a review of kabbalistic preoccupations that he felt were responsible for a number of errors in the MT. Morin concluded that the Jewish "scribes introduced an infinite number of errors into the text."[20]

17. Since the scribes were reluctant to change the sacred text even when they suspected it was in error, the Qere ("read")-Kethib ("written") tradition grew to acknowledge and suggest correction to those errors.

18. Ibid., 355.

19. Ibid., 58.

20. Ibid., 311.

Historically, kabbalistic interpretations emerged out of earlier forms of Jewish mysticism in twelfth- and thirteenth-century southern France and Spain, and enjoyed a renaissance originating in Palestine in the sixteenth century. Adherents found meaningful mysteries behind names, numbers, visions, and other phenomena in the scriptural text. Morin argued that these interpretations led to intentional distortions of the text. Letters were sometimes reversed, as in Ps 21:2, where ישמח מלך ("the king rejoices") is transformed into משיח מלך ("the Messiah is king"), and Isa 40:26 (Morin erroneously identified it as 46:26), where מי ברא אלה ("who created these?") becomes אלהים ברא ("God created"). Morin cites a long list of kabbalistic play with the six letters of the first word of Gen 1:1. The usual reading is בראשית ("in the beginning"):[21]

בית ראש, "high house (or sanctuary)" (see Jer 17:12)
אבתשרי, "God created in the month of Tishri"
בראשתי, "he created two laws, written and oral"
בריתיש, "in visions there are"
ירא שבת, "revere the Sabbath"

The Kabbalists and some of the Talmudists were also engaged in gematria, assigning numerical values to letters, words, and phrases to give them a coded meaning. This practice, in Morin's opinion, amounted to another source of textual distortion. For example, the alphabet was sometimes used backward so that the first letter became the last letter or words were reversed or divided in unique ways. Such procedures facilitated some, at least, of the Hebrew textual corruptions that Morin felt could be corrected by the SP.

A similar tone of extreme deprecation of the Masoretic Hebrew text, colored by polemical bias against Protestantism (and perhaps a tinge of anti-Semitism), characterizes Morin's greatest work, the posthumous *Exercitationes biblicae de hebraeici graecique textus sinceritate* (*Discussion of the Soundness of the Hebrew and Greek Texts of the Bible*), published in 1660. In this volume, Morin brought what he considered to be irrefutable arguments against the then current theory of the absolute integrity of the Hebrew text and the antiquity of the vowel points.

21. Ibid., 165–66.

Protestant Responses to Morin

Apprehension among Protestants that the SP would challenge the MT was evident even before Morin published his work. William Eyres of Emmanuel College (Cambridge), and one of the translators of the King James Version, wrote to Archbishop Ussher arguing for the authenticity of the MT against the LXX and the SP a full fifteen years before the SP became available in Europe. In a later letter, Ralph Skynner, curate at the Parish Church of St. Nicholas, Sutton, Surrey, alerted Ussher to the work of Claudius Duret, a French lawyer who claimed that Moses gave each tribe a copy of the law in Samaritan characters. Eyres and Skynner anticipated the polemical preoccupation of scholars with the SP text, providing a larger intellectual context for Morin's work. Many Protestants rose to Morin's challenge, and the series of responses lasted more than twenty-five years.

In June 1632, Archbishop Ussher referred to Morin's work in a letter to Ludovicio Capellus of the Reformed Saumere Seminary.[22] Ussher was well aware of the Catholic-Protestant polemics surrounding the SP, but Ussher's own interest in the SP was more focused on his well-known preoccupation with biblical chronology. By 1624, Ussher already had his own copy of the SP, obtained through the agency of Thomas Davis, a merchant in Aleppo. During the 1620s and 1630s Ussher acquired a total of six SPs, including Gall's N, a 1362/1363 C.E. manuscript presently housed in the British Museum. Ussher willingly shared his manuscripts with other savants in the British Isles. John Selden (1584–1654), an English jurist and scholar, sent a letter to Ussher thanking him for information from the latter's SP.[23] The French scholar and manuscript dealer Nicholas Peiresc (1580–1637) became aware of Ussher's manuscripts five years later through the mediation of Selden.[24] For reasons that are still unclear, it would be another four years before Morin became aware of Ussher's "Irish copy" of the SP through the efforts of Thomas Comberes. Ussher and Selden apparently did not respond to Morin's comments on the SP, the former probably because of other preoccupations, the latter from a lack of language tools.

---

22. Richard Parr, *The Life of the Most Reverend Father in God, James Usher, Late Lord Arch-Bishop of Armagh, Primate and Metropolitan of All Ireland* (London: printed for Nathaniel Ranew, St. Paul's Churchyard, 1686), 461.

23. Samuel Weller Singer, ed., *The Table Talk of John Seldon* (Edinburgh: Ballantyne, 1890), xx.

24. Ibid., 121.

But in 1631 a Protestant counterattack was unleashed against Morin's arguments. In that year, Simon de Muis published his *Assertio Veritas Hebraicae Prima* (*An Assertion of the Superiority of the Hebrew Text*), and soon followed this study with *Assertio Altera* (*Another Assertion*, 1634) and *Castigato Anima Adversionem Morini* (*Criticism of the Observations of Morin*).

There is not much biographical data available on de Muis, but one curious anecdote reported by the eighteenth century dramatist, Thomas Dibdin, implies that de Muis was not always motivated by purely scholarly interests.[25] Dibdin claims that Cardinal Richelieu became enamored of the thought that the Paris Polyglot, which took seventeen years to produce, should be called the "Richelieu Polyglot." To this end, the cardinal sought to ingratiate himself with the general editor of the project, Guy Michel Le Jay. Noting Le Jay's contempt for the editor of the Arabic and Syriac texts, Richelieu had that editor thrown into prison. When funds were needed for the project, Richelieu donated generously. In the end, however, Le Jay refused to attach the cardinal's name to the work, and a furious Richelieu hired de Muis to write a 500-page book criticizing the polyglot and pointing out its errors and flaws. Dibdin comments that, had the other side hired him, de Muis would have explained the errors as truths. Whether or not Dibdin's characterization is completely fair, de Muis' work is consistently supportive of the Hebrew MT against the SP and the LXX.

The works of Morin and de Muis were joined by several publications written by Johannes Buxtorf, professor of Old Testament at Basle, who argued that the Hebrew vowel points and characters were at least as old as Ezra.[26] In 1644, Johannes Henricus Hottengerus (1620–1667) of Zurich University continued the attack on Morin with his *Excertationes Anti-Morinionae de Pentateucho Samaritans* (*Anti-Morinian Discussions concerning the Samaritan Pentateuch*), followed a decade later by Arnold Boates's *Vindiciae Veritate Hebraicae Contra J. Morinum et L. Capellum*[27](*Defense for the Hebraic Accuracy Against J. Morinum and L. Capellum*).

25. Thomas Dibdin, *The Reminiscences of Thomas Dibdin* (London: H. Colburn, 1827), 18–19.

26. See for example Johannes Buxtorf, *Tiberias, sive Commentarius Masoreticus* (Basil: Rauracorum, 1620).

27. Johannes Henricus Hottengerus, *Excertationes Anti-Morinionae de Penta-*

That most of these attacks on Morin were motivated by religious presuppositions is apparent from the fact that the opposition to Morin was exclusively Protestant and very passionate in its defense of the infallibility of the inspired word of God. In a letter to Ussher in the late 1630s, Francis Taylor referred to Morin as the "false catholic and Dositheean."[28] Twenty years later Ussher received a letter from Boates in which he chided Morin and his "adulterine Samaritan Pentateuch."[29]

Some Protestants and Jews did question the overstated claims for the infallible integrity of the MT, although few dared express their reservations in print. One notable exception was the French Huguenot Ludivicio Capellus (1585–1658), who held the chair in Hebrew at Saumere. He assumed correctly that the Samaritan characters were more ancient than the Hebrew and that vowel points were a late addition to the Hebrew. During his research, Capellus was in communication with both Ussher and Morin, the two major scholarly figures who actually possessed copies of the SP. Despite his boldness, Capellus had great difficulty publishing his work, since he was not a Catholic and held an unorthodox (although ultimately correct) Protestant position regarding the MT. Finally, in 1645, he was able to have published *Diatriba de veris et antiquis Ebræorum literis* (*Discourse on the Validity and Antiquity of the Hebrew Letters*), and in 1650, with the help of a son who had converted to Catholicism, *Critica Sacra* (*Biblical Text Criticism*) was published.

During this extended sectarian squabble, both Catholics and Protestants generally looked for places where the SP supported their argument and ignored the rest of the text. Despite all that was being written about the SP, and the claims and counterclaims made by each side of the debate, no thorough systematic examination and comparison of the text was published. Morin assumed that the extensive agreement between the LXX and the SP constituted a vote for the authenticity of each, while Ussher, Eyres, and especially de Muis were equally convinced of the primacy and purity of the MT.

Perhaps in a fashion faithful to its true text history, the SP was no help in resolving the chronological and genealogical discrepancies in Gen 4 and 5 that were of such pressing interest to Ussher and others in the

---

teucho Samaritans. (Zurich: Johannes Jacobi Bodmeri, 1644); Arnold Boates, *Vindiciae Veritate Hebraicae Contra J. Morinum et L. Capellum* (Paris: 1653).

28. Parr, *Life of James Usher*, 475–76.

29. Ibid., 589.

mid-seventeenth century. The SP presents a completely different set of ages for the deaths of the biblical figures, agreeing with neither the MT nor the LXX. Ussher, who was preoccupied with chronology and found the Genesis problem particularly perplexing, decided simply to ignore the SP at this point, as he had ignored the LXX. A more recent resolution to the genealogy problem suggests that the SP followed the tradition of the MT halfway through the genealogies and then switched to the tradition found in the LXX, suggesting that both the SP and the LXX are probably adaptations of the MT. In the end, Ussher may have taken the easy route in coming to the right conclusion. At one point Morin visited England, but there is no evidence that he saw any of Ussher's SPs.

In 1649, Peiresc sent three SPs to Morin, but they are not identified and may be copies of manuscripts already on the continent, albeit not yet seen by Morin. As late as 1679, Peiresc presented another SP to Cardinal Barbarini. The last SP to arrive in Europe in the seventeenth century was a copy received by Bishop Huntington while traveling in Shechem and given as a gift to Archbishop Narcissus Marsh. It is now known as von Gall's Gothic A, housed in the Bodleian Library at Oxford.

Brian Walton's *Polyglot Bible* (1654 and 1657) steered a rather moderate course between the positions marked out by the Protestant Buxtorf and the Catholic Morin, suggesting that the conflict was at last receding. But, quite to the contrary, the Catholic/Protestant quarrel regarding the value of the SP was only experiencing a lull, to be revived again beginning in the middle of the eighteenth century. Christian Ravius (1613–1677), a German Orientalist based primarily in Uppsala, Sweden, and a sometime professor at Utrecht and Frankfurt, made a new presentation of the Protestant support of the MT.[30] Awhile later, Charles Frances Houbigant (1686–1783), a priest of the Paris Oratory, reasserted Morin's anti-MT position with a similar passion.[31] The Benedictine Poncot came to Houbingant's defense, and was in turn challenged by the Protestant Johann David Michaelis.[32]

30. For an example of his work on grammar, see Christian [Ravius] Rau, *A General Grammer [sic] for the Ready Attaining of the Hebrew, Samaritan, Calde, Syriac, Arabic and Ethiopic Languages* (London: Wilson, 1650).

31. Charles François Houbigant, *Biblia Hebraica cum notis criticis et versione Latina ad notas criticas facta; accedunt libri graeci, qui Deutero-Canonici vocantur in tres classes distribute* (4 vols.; Lutetiae-Parisiorum: Apud A. C. Briasson & L. Durand, 1753).

32. Maurice Poncet, "Orient. und exeg. Bibliothek," xxi., 177–89; Johann David Michaelis, *Noveaux exlaircissements sur l'orgine et la Pentateuque des Samaritains*

In an interesting conclusion to these exchanges, Johann Hassencamp of Rintelm responded to Oluf (Olaus) Gerhard Tychsenby by claiming that Codex Alexandrinus (a version of the LXX often cited by both Catholics and Protestants) was, in fact, a translation from an early SP![33]

The Samaritan Pentateuch and Modern Textual Criticism

The sectarian debates of the seventeenth and eighteenth centuries were finally transcended by Heinrich Friedrich Wilhelm Gesenius (1786–1842), who brought the discussion of the text-critical value of the SP into an objective arena. Gesenius shaped a number of major advances in the textual criticism of biblical texts, and his influence on SP studies extended through the next 150 years. A student of Tychsen at Göttingen, Gesenius arguably became the leading Old Testament scholar of the nineteenth century. Among his many achievements was the publication of *De pentateuchi samaritani origine, indole et auctoritate commentatio philologico-critic* (*On the Origin, Nature, and Authority of the Samaritan Pentateuch: A Philological-Critical Commentary*).

Gesenius's conclusion that the MT is superior to the SP has dominated textual criticism well into the twentieth century. As noted earlier in chapter 5, Gesenius identified approximately six thousand textual variants between the MT and the SP and divided them into eight classes, creating a helpful model for systematic text-critical analysis with a plethora of examples. Contemporary scholarship has refined Gesenius's analysis in a manner portended by a somewhat later contemporary of Gesenius. As noted by the anonymous author of an article published in 1853 in *The Journal of Sacred Literature*, many of the differences between the SP and MT noted by Gesenius are actually only copyist errors or alternate ways of saying the same word.[34]

(1760), cited in John W. Nutt, *Fragments of a Samaritan Targum: Edited from a Bodleian Ms., with an Introduction, Containing a Sketch of Samaritan History, Dogma and Literature* (London: Trübner, 1874), 89.

33. Johann Matthaeus Hassencamp, *Der entdeckte wahre Ursprung der alten Bibelübersetzungs* (Minden: Koerber, 1775). See also Oluf Gerhard Tychsen, "Disputio historico," in *Numorum hebraeo-samaritanorum vindiciae* (ed. Francisco Perez Bayer et al.; Valentiae Edetanorum: Montfort, 1790). Tychsen (1734–1815) is known today primarily as one of the founding fathers of Islamic numismatics.

34. *Journal of Sacred Literature* 4 (July 1853): 298–327.

Gesenius's relatively low estimation of the SP was balanced by the conclusions of Paul Ernst Kahle (1875–1964). A German scholar of the Middle East, Kahle ended up in Oxford after 1939, presumably in part because of his friendship with Jews in Nazi Germany. Kahle returned to Germany after the conclusion of World War 2. Kahle evened the battle of the texts by emphasizing the antiquity of the SP on the basis of its form and older readings. In some important ways, Kahle presaged the modern discussion of the SP and provided a needed balance to Gesenius. Kahle identified a "pre-Samaritan text" based on similarities between the SP and several noncanonical books, including Jubilees, 1 Enoch, and the Assumption of Moses. He noted the many late modifications of both the LXX and the MT and demonstrated that the LXX also shows a textual development, being derived from a number of translations that had been standardized relatively late by the Christian church. Likewise, the Masoretic school of scholars had substantially edited the manuscripts that were available to them. Kahle's work has favorably influenced attitudes of modern scholarship toward the text of the SP and has found considerable verification in recent analysis of the texts from Qumran.[35] Bruce Waltke, among others, has revived the discussion of the textual value of the SP in recent times, deducing that the LXX and SP often reflect the same Palestinian recension of the text (following the Cross local text paradigm).[36] Yet, Waltke asserts, the SP need not predate the MT, and is in fact often dependent upon it.[37] A systematic comparison would likely show the SP to be in agreement with the MT more often than the LXX.

In some important ways, Waltke is another case of a conservative Protestant arriving at the conclusion that the Catholic Morin was wrong. At the beginning of the twenty-first century, the presuppositional tension in biblical studies runs less along denominational lines and is more a quarrel between religious liberals and conservatives or competing text-critical paradigms. Just as the improving quality of the debate in the seventeenth century began to realign the issues on scholarly grounds, so the increasing presence of solid scholarship, from a variety of perspectives in professional journals and societies today, modifies and redefines current scholarly positions in helpful ways.

35. VanderKam and Peter Flint, *Meaning of the Dead Sea Scrolls*, 93.

36. Waltke, "Prolegomena to the Samaritan Pentateuch."

37. Waltke, "Samaritan Pentateuch and the Text of the Old Testament," 234.

For example, in a 1970 article Waltke summarized the contributions of the SP by noting:

> The Samaritan Pentateuch (SP) has two primary values for the literary critic of the Old Testament: (1) it points up the relative purity of the Masoretic Text (MT); and (2) when used in conjunction with the Septuagint (LXX) it can be a useful, though limited, tool in the hand of the critic as he seeks to restore the original text. In the field of higher criticism, the SP helps to establish the antiquity of the Pentateuch.[38]

Although Waltke's relatively negative conclusions were based on his own investigation, his views align with the earlier academic consensus that the SP differs from the MT in 6000 details and agrees with the LXX against the MT 1600 times. That consensus has faltered with the full publication of the texts from Qumran, which has led to recognition of the pluriformity of scriptural texts in the Second Temple period. The changing tenor of conversation is illustrated by a 1994 article by Kyung-Rae Kim. After collating the textual variants once again, Kim concluded:

> According to my own data, in 964 cases the Samaritan Pentateuch agrees with the Septuagint against the Masoretic Text. Of these, in 471 instances the readings are possibly irrelevant (independent), leaving only 493 cases in which the Septuagint almost certainly reflects a reading which is also found in the Samaritan Pentateuch. Of the 493 agreements, according to my calculations 328 cases reflect common harmonizations. Many such harmonizations could have occurred independently, since these textual alterations were made under the influence of the context or a parallel text.... The Septuagint contains many more harmonizations than the Samaritan Pentateuch. Therefore, the 493 (or possibly 964) agreements do not prove any close relationship between the two texts.[39]

Kim's conclusion means that the SP could be recognized as a separate witness, while the agreement with the Greek texts can be understood as evidence of a common exegetical style dependent upon a shared base text. Today, the SP no longer plays only a supporting role in text-critical study of the Bible, but has taken its rightful place as a leading character within the drama.

---

38. Ibid., 212.
39. Kim, "Studies in the Relationship," 1–2.

At the same time, in the wake of the many complex readings of the Bible in the second period of textual transmission, the SP has been further reevaluated. The discovery and publication of Qumran texts that show characteristics similar to the SP but without the sectarian additions, the "pre-Samaritan group," has renewed scholarly interest in this area. As noted in chapter 2, the works of Judith Sanderson on 4QpaleoExod^{m} and Nathan Jastram on 4QNum^{b} have further refined our understanding of the pre-Samaritan group in relation to the texts of Exodus and Numbers. Esther Eshel and Hanan Eshel, labeling this group as "harmonistic texts," divided the Qumran material that tends to show this harmonizing tendency into two groups:

> In our opinion, this distinction had a crucial impact upon the issue of the Samaritan Pentateuch's chronological development. The scrolls pertaining to the second group reflect a more comprehensive harmonistic editing than the SP, and were written in either late Hasmonean or Herodian script. On the other hand, scrolls featuring harmonistic editing, with the same additions and scope as the SP, were dated to the end of the second century B.C.E. or the beginning of the first century B.C.E.[40]

The texts from Qumran have made a tremendous impact on the analysis of the text history of the scriptural documents, providing new light for understanding the relationship between the Samaritan text and other scriptural textual traditions in the late Second Temple period. Ayala Lowenstamm notes that whenever there is a smoothing or simplification of a text it is the Samaritan tradition that abandons the more difficult readings. And Lowenstamm adds that the distinctive and strongly supported Samaritan pronunciation of the Pentateuch shows close connection to the pronunciation of the Qumran scrolls. For example, the Masoretic suffixes *-kem* and *-tem* appear as *-kemmah* and *-temmah* in the Qumran Scrolls; in the SP, they are spelled in the Masoretic fashion but always pronounced

40. Eshel and Eshel, "Dating the Samaritan Pentateuch's Compilation," 237–38. They conclude: "That harmonistic editing reflected in 4QPaleoExod^{m}, 8QPhyl, XQPhyl 3, 4QNum^{b}, 4QTest, 4Q364, and 4QPhyl J—has the same scope as that of the SP and most of the harmonistic changes documented in these scrolls also exist in the SP. However 4QDeut^{n}, 4QDeut^{j}, 4QDeut^{kl}, 4Q158, the Nash Papyrus, 8QPhyl, 4QMez A, 4QPhyl G, and 8QMez have a more comprehensive editing than what is documented in the SP."

like the longer forms found in the Scrolls.[41] The peculiarities of the SP do not reflect a special dialect of any northern tribe, but represent the common Hebrew prevalent in Palestine between about the second century B.C.E. and the third century C.E.

Overall, the Samaritan, Masoretic, and LXX textual traditions have a long and complex relationship that reflects, at the very least, mutual influence, borrowing, sectarian presuppositions, differing cultural contexts, and errors of various kinds. Textual criticism has worked intensively to unravel those relationships, providing a richer appreciation for the vibrant literary origin of the scriptural text. At the beginning of the twenty-first century, the SP's contribution to this discussion is growing.

41. Ayala Loewenstamm, "Samaritan Pentateuch," *EncJud* 15:753–54.

9
The Samaritan Pentateuch in Translation

The SP has been carried across eras of political upheaval and changing cultures by translation into several major languages as new cultures defined the common language of the time and place. Samaritans claim, and all evidence confirms, that the SP, like the MT, was originally composed in Hebrew. The new languages usually arrived in the entourage of invading armies, but sometimes were utilized by Samaritans fleeing to other parts of the Mediterranean world.

We will see that the trail of translations of the SP intersects with several phenomena related to the Samaritan community: the development of Targums; the Samaritan diaspora reflected in literature and archaeology; the relationship between the formation of the SP and the LXX; focus on the unique items in the SP, relationships among Samaritans, Jews, and Muslims; and the first presence of Samaritans in Europe.

There is no evidence of any SP translations into other languages at the time of the Assyrian annexation of Samaria following the eighth-century B.C.E. invasion of the northern kingdom of Israel, or during the Babylonian and Persian periods that followed.[1] Consequently, the earliest translation of the SP from Hebrew begins with the Targum tradition.

Aramaic Targums

Aramaic emerged as the major language of the ancient Near East during the Neo-Assyrian (934–608 B.C.E.) and Neo-Babylonian (626–539 B.C.E.) periods. The language originated in Aram in Syria, moved into the entire northern Tigris-Euphrates valley, and finally became the lingua franca of

1. Research on more colloquial interpretations (Targums) may reveal an Aramaic usage in one of these latter periods.

western Asia and Egypt. It is evidenced in the biblical books of Daniel and Ezra and was the language of Jesus and early Jewish writings like the Talmud and many of the early Samaritan writings. In the course of that long period of development, and with the involvement of so many subcultures within its vast expanse, Aramaic evolved with many dialects and regional differences. It influenced, and was in turn influenced by, the cultures it absorbed. It was natural that the biblical traditions of both Jews and Samaritans would find expression in the daily language (Aramaic, Greek, and Arabic) of their respective communities.

Targums (explanations and interpretations of Torah) were created as a response to the needs of the laity for scriptural interpretation in every day, up to date, colloquial language. The word *targum*, the earliest known word for "translation," is from the Akkadian language, perhaps migrating from an Indo-European language, possibly Hittite. Originally, Targums in the Levant were oral interpretations or explanations of the biblical text.[2] For example, a rabbi may have recited a biblical text in Hebrew from either a text or memory, and he or a translator would translate or interpret the Hebrew into Aramaic. As with any translation, Targums varied in how literally they translated the biblical text and how much interpretive expansion was added. For example, they often gave names to scripturally anonymous places and persons, and clarified or gave explanations of scriptural passages that did not make sense. The Targums were not written because any given community was judged more naïve or less educated (though that too could be a motivation), but because language evolves and the texts of one generation can lose much of their meaning for a later generation.

Scholars have tended to ignore Targums in textual criticism because the Targums, unlike the LXX, intentionally did *not* attempt to reproduce the literal equivalent of the original text. But the once firm divide between composition and exegesis is proving to be a permeable boundary, and the previously negative judgment about the text-critical value of the Targums is being reconsidered. It is more appropriate to say that the Targums moved further away from literal equivalence in translation. The move from literal translation to paraphrase and interpretation is a very slippery slope. All translations are paraphrases of sorts, attempting to capture in the new language the meanings expressed within the culture of the old language.

---

2. Roger Le Déaut, *The Message of the New Testament and the Aramaic Targum* (Rome: Biblical Institute Press, 1982), 5.

Sometimes this is done with a very literal rendition of words and ideas (a static translation). Sometimes a more dynamic translation, not bound to the phraseology of the original, is helpful to explain ideas that are lost in the transition of time or cultural context.[3]

Translation implies respect for the content of the original text and a desire to reproduce its meaning as closely as possible in a new linguistic context. Word-for-word "lexical" replacement of the original text can be inadequate, however, for a number of reasons. The meaning of words in the original text can change over time, and literal equivalency of what the word meant in the past may not capture what the word has come to mean in the present. Some references in the original text—for example, references to particular places or persons—may have become obscure and require explanation. Biblical passages are often brief and omit details that were assumed by the original writer to be common knowledge. Sometimes the context of the original text needs to be explained. In addition, the cultural meaning of an idea may change over time. Ideas in the original text may be offensive to the translating community, and that community may wish to use alternative language to communicate a proximate idea (seen earlier regarding the birth of Joseph's grandchildren in Gen 50:23, rendered differently by the MT and the SP). Anthropomorphic references to God are a common problem in the Targums of both Jews and Samaritans and illustrate this changing cultural place of an idea. In addition, ideas in the original text may spark an explanatory sermon. The book of Hebrews in the New Testament, for example, seems to be just such a midrash, or explanatory sermon, on Ps 110:1. Such homilies do occur in Jewish Targums, but are not characteristic of Samaritan ones.

If the original text is in a classical or formal manner of speech, a translation may prefer colloquial speech, as evident from the many "modern language" or "daily language" English versions of the Bible. One aim of the Targums was to put the Scriptures into vernacular form. The lines between translation, paraphrase, explication, and editing are complicated and far from clear cut. In addition to these ambiguities, as we search for Jewish or Samaritan pentateuchal quotes in the New Testament, we need to be sensitive to the likelihood that the text of the Hebrew Scripture was often transmitted to the New Testament community through a Targum, either

3. The many subtleties of the problem of translation are thoroughly explored in David Bellos, *Is That a Fish in Your Ear?* (New York: Faber & Faber, 2011).

Jewish or Samaritan, whose ambiguous status between biblical text and Targum may not have been as pronounced as it is now.

Traditions of Jewish Targums are more prevalent and easier to trace than Samaritan Targums. Jewish Targums evolved during the Second Temple period and continued through the end of the first millennium C.E. The Babylonian Targum is the best known and most influential Jewish Targum and is associated with Onkelos (ca. 35–120 C.E.), a Roman convert to Judaism, who is said to have produced this Targum about 110 C.E. The other major Jewish Targums were created in Palestine, and so are called "Palestinian Targums."

It is impossible to know at what point Onkelos (or any translator) was aware that he was moving from literal equivalents to interpretive expansions. Even in a Targum that tries to be literal, Onkelos obviously could not resist the temptation to avoid anthropomorphisms for God, and to seek analogies or to allegorize in difficult passages. As translations, the Jewish Targums largely reflect midrashic pedagogical interpretations of the Scripture from the time of their production. The Samaritan Targums, by comparison, are considerably less focused on pedagogy.

An example that involves the SP may be taken from the Palestinian Targum translation of Gen 4:8. Rimon Kasher cites a Genizah Targum that fleshes out the conversation between Cain and Abel at Gen 4:8, a conversation that begs to be presented.[4] The SP also includes such a conversation. Is that conversation the product of a later Samaritan Targum or a proper retention of the text before the conversation was lost in the Masoretic version? In other words, has the SP incorporated an interpretive expansion of the "original" reading, or was the MT text garbled at some point by a scribe?

Although not as extensive as the Jewish Targumim, a Samaritan Targum tradition did develop. A traceable Samaritan diaspora emerged in the Hellenistic period parallel to the Jewish diaspora. This situation necessitated a translation of the SP into the local language, which because of the limited scope of the Samaritan diaspora was Aramaic. Specific evidence of the Samaritan Targum does not emerge until the third or fourth century C.E. The oldest layer of Samaritan Aramaic, and the first main period of development, is represented by manuscript MS Or. 7562, located

4. Rimon Kasher, "The Palestinian Targums to Gen 4:8: A New Approach to an Old Controversy," in *Biblical Interpretation in Judaism and Christianity* (ed. Isaac Kalimi and Peter J. Haas; London: T&T Clark, 2006).

in the British Museum, a Samaritan Targum produced "at the beginning of their independent literary activity."[5] This manuscript shares features in common with Targum Onkelos and the Dead Sea Scrolls, providing some indication of its relative date. A second main period of Samaritan Targum production began in the fourth century C.E. and is represented by manuscript MS 6, housed in the Shechem synagogue. MS 6 represents a stage of Aramaic parallel to the Aramaic of the Jewish Talmud. The third and last main period in the development of the Samaritan Targum is represented by manuscript MS 3, also housed in the Shechem synagogue. MS 3 is a revision made by Samaritan priests, probably Arabic speaking, who sometimes did not fully understand the contents of the Targum and consequently made many errors. For example, although intended to be composed in Aramaic, the MS 3 editors actually included the use of words that are really Arabic, Hebrew, Greek, Latin or corruptions of one of those languages.[6]

European scholars were introduced to the Samaritan Targum by Jean Morin, the same scholar who had introduced them to the SP (see discussion in ch. 8). While Morin was fortunate enough to have a very good text of the Pentateuch (Codex B), the only text of the Targum available to him was a 1514 manuscript of very uneven quality. The first twenty-six chapters were from a text of type A, which includes many errors and later linguistic usages. The remainder was based on a type J text, the oldest layer of Samaritan Targums.[7] Faced with this strange amalgam, scholars were inclined to think that Morin's Targum included vestiges of some early Cuthean language, building on Josephus's characterization of the Samaritans as "Cutheans." That term is derived from a city northeast of Babylon mentioned in 2 Kgs 17:24 as the origin of the peoples the Assyrians had brought in to replace the exiled northern tribes. Although Josephus's reconstruction was tenuous at best, it carried considerable weight in seventeenth-century biblical criticism. In the nineteenth century, the German scholar and rabbi Samuel Kohn (1841–1912) unraveled the linguistic confusion of the Targum, noting that the various portions of the text represented the evolution of Aramaic, the change of languages in the Middle East, and the theological presuppositions of the scribes. Such

5. Abraham Tal, "Samaritan Literature," in Crown, *The Samaritans*, 448.

6. Ibid., 444–49.

7. Abraham Tal, "Targum," in *A Companion to Samaritan Studies* (ed. Alan Crown et al.; Tübingen: Mohr Siebeck, 1993), 226–28.

changes are a consistent problem in translations.[8] Nevertheless, Aramaic Targums played a significant role for the religious understanding of the Samaritans, and were frequently presented as a parallel column to Samaritan Hebrew in many copies of the SP.

Greek Versions

Given the Hellenism prevalent in Palestine and the cities of the Samaritan Diaspora, it is not surprising that the Samaritans made use of at least parts of the Pentateuch in Greek. Samaritans were clearly aware of the LXX, influenced it, and were influenced by it. Persistent questions remain as to whether the Samaritans shared a common recension with the Jews or had developed a distinctive Greek translation of their own. The three most influential sources of information on this question are a selection of manuscripts found among the Dead Sea Scrolls at Qumran, inscriptions from the Samaritan diaspora, and the *Samariteikon* found in Origen's Hexapla.

Evidence from Qumran

The Dead Sea materials found at Qumran are likely the earliest place to look for evidence of a Greek translation of the SP. As with the available texts of the LXX, texts similar to later copies of the Greek SP have been identified as pre-Samaritan, though they do not include the distinctive Samaritan additions, particularly to the Decalogue. Some of the relevant Qumran Greek manuscripts evidence a more comprehensive editing than what is documented in available SPs dating from a much later period.[9] But the harmonistic editing reflected in some of these Qumran manuscripts demonstrates the same scribal sensitivities (concerned with the same passages and harmonized in the same fashion) as the later SPs.[10] This leaves us

---

8. This is convincingly demonstrated in Robert Hiebert, ed., "*Translation Is Required*": *The Septuagint in Retrospect and Prospect* (SBLSCS 56; Atlanta: Society of Biblical Literature, 2010).

9. 4QDeut^{n}, 4QDeut^{j}, 4QDeut^{kl}, 4Q158, the Nash Papyrus, 8QPhyl (8Q3), 4QMez A (4Q149), 4QPhyl G (4Q134), and 8QMez (8Q4).

10. 4QpaleoExod^{m}, 8QPhyl (8Q3), XQPhyl 3 (XQ3), 4QNum^{b}, 4QTest (4Q175), 4Q364, and 4QPhyl J (4Q137). See Eshel and Eshel, "Dating the Samaritan Pentateuch's Compilation," 237–38. The works of Sanderson (*An Exodus Scroll from Qumran*) and of Jastram ("Text of 4QNum^{b}") are relevant here as well.

with a possibility, but not clear evidence, that the Samaritans were involved in the production of a Greek Pentateuch. More definitive judgments concerning the Qumran materials must await further analysis.

Samaritan Inscriptions in Greek

Further evidence for a Greek SP may be drawn from early Samaritan inscriptions. There were Hellenistic Samaritan communities in Palestine in the first century, just as there were Hellenistic Jewish communities. These Hellenistic Samaritan communities produced Greek dedicatory and honorary inscriptions for their synagogues, but whether these were drawn from a complete Greek translation of the SP remains unclear. [11] In addition to communities that had become Hellenized by choice, there were also Samaritan communities that became Greek-speaking as the result of flight from their homelands to other parts of the Roman Empire during times of oppression. The most notable sites of this Samaritan Diaspora were Delos, Thessalonica, Thasos, Rhodes, Athens, Piraeus, Rome, Syracuse, Ostia, Puteoli, Sicily, and Constantinople.[12] Archaeological and literary evidence provide glimpses into the Samaritan communities located in some of these sites.

Delos, Syracuse, Thessalonica, and Ostia provide the most explicit archaeological evidence of Samaritan use of the Greek language. Delos is in the center of a group of islands known as the Cyclades southeast of the Greek mainland. Because of its significant associations with Greek history and mythology, it has been heavily excavated. In 1912, a team of archaeologists led by André Plassart of the Ecole française d'Athènes discovered the remains of a building on Delos dating before 88 B.C.E. Plassart believes the building had early use as a synagogue for several reasons: the site includes a reservoir that Bruneau argues was used for ritual bathing; an inscription associates the building with "God Most High," a common Jewish epithet for the divine used also by Samaritans; and another inscription associated with the building uses the term proseuchê, the most common Greek word for a synagogue.[13] In the early 1980s, two Samaritan synagogue inscrip-

11. Pieter van der Horst, *Japheth in the Tents of Shem: Studies on Jewish Hellenism in Antiquity* (Leuven: Peeters, 2002), 17.

12. Alan D. Crown, "The Samaritan Diaspora," in Crown, *The Samaritans*, 210–12.

13. Phillipe Bruneau, "Les Israelites de Delos et la Juiverie delienne," *BCH* 106 (1982): 465–504.

tions in Greek were found 90 meters north of the building uncovered by Plassart. The conclusion seems sound that, whatever its previous use, it was at one time used by Samaritans. Since then, other honorific and dedicatory inscriptions related to the synagogue and the Samaritans have been found.[14] Mention of Mount Gerizim in some of the inscriptions confirms the Samaritan identity of the building's occupants.[15] The archaeological remains and inscriptions at Delos give ample testimony that the Samaritans were there and that they did use Greek. Yet none of the recovered inscriptions are scriptural, so the evidence from Delos neither supports nor denies the likelihood of a Samaritan Greek Pentateuch.

In our search for evidence of a Greek Samaritan Pentateuch, a Samaritan inscription found in Thessalonica is more helpful. This text includes a portion of Scripture in Greek and thus demonstrates that the Diaspora Samaritans did use a Greek Pentateuch (or at least translated portions of the sacred text into Greek). A Greek archaeologist, Stratis Pelekidis, made the Thessalonica inscription known in the early 1950s, and it was more widely published in 1968 by B. Lifshitz and J. Schibly.[16] The biblical text cited, Num 6:22–27 (a favorite Samaritan text often inscribed for use at religious sites or on religious artifacts), is contained in seventeen lines of Greek. An accompanying dedication in Samaritan Hebrew includes mention of Nablus. Significantly, the Greek text inscribed on the stone follows the Samaritan text of Numbers rather than the LXX, including the order of versification—in the LXX, Num 6:27 appears between verses 23 and 24.[17] While it can be fairly concluded that the Thessalonica inscription does not reflect text taken from the LXX, whether or not the inscription reflects a uniquely Samaritan Greek translation of the SP is not so clear. Since the inscription was not recovered *in situ*, it is best dated by paleography. James Purvis has studied the orthography of Samaritan characters in the portion of the inscription that is written in Samaritan Hebrew, and concludes that they reflect letter forms from many periods. He suggests that the Samar-

---

14. A. Thomas Kraabel, "New Evidence of the Samaritan Diaspora Has Been Found on Delos," *BA* 47 (1984): 44–46; Donald D. Binder, "Delos" [cited 21 October 2011]; online: http://www.pohick.org/sts/delos.html.

15. Anders Runesson et al., *The Ancient Synagogue from Its Origins to 200 C.E.* (Leiden: Brill, 2008), 126.

16. B. Lifshitz and J. Schiby, "Une synagogue samaritaine à Thessalonique," *RB* 75 (1968): 368.

17. Serfio Noja, "The Samareitikon," in Crown, *The Samaritans*, 410.

itan community at Thessalonica used Greek and was dependent on old inscriptions and manuscripts for its knowledge of written Samaritan, and that the inscription most likely dates from between the fourth and sixth centuries C.E.[18]

Pope Gregory the Great (ca. 540–604 C.E.) provides the major literary evidence pertaining to the Samaritan community in Sicily (*Epist* 6:33; 8:21). Gregory makes several comments that express concern over Samaritan slave holdings, thus revealing that the Sicilian Samaritans were merchants and farmers wealthy enough to own slaves. Pietro Orsi discovered two Samaritan inscriptions in Syracuse, Sicily in August, 1913.[19] The texts appear inside two inscribed circles on a marble column 56 centimeters high and 27 centimeters in diameter. The first reads קומה יהוה, and the second ויפצו אביך, representing a portion of Num 10:35 ("Rise up, YHWH"; "May your enemies be destroyed"), a passage that also appears on sixteenth-century Samaritan scroll cases (see the discussion in ch. 7). There is some indication that the Samaritans at Syracuse were not really familiar with Samaritan Hebrew. The craftsman who produced the inscriptions discovered by Orsi aligns the letters to the left margin, as in Latin, rather than the right margin, as in Semitic languages. Also, the shape of the Samaritan characters is idiosyncratic, perhaps reflecting, like those in Thessalonica, copying forms from an eclectic group of manuscripts. While these observations imply that the Samaritans of Syracuse could not meaningfully read Samaritan Hebrew, there is no evidence of the use of a Greek or Latin Targum or translation.

Samaritans settled in other places, but apart from inscriptions from these just mentioned locations there are no additional clues suggesting the form of the SP used by these diaspora Samaritan communities. Samaritans in Ostia and Delos were merchants and involved in shipping. As in Delos, a synagogue was discovered at Ostia in 1961, outside the city fortifications near the ancient coastline.[20] It is considered the oldest synagogue of the diaspora, but although there is explicit evidence of Jewish use (a menorah

18. James Purvis, "The Paleography of the Samaritan Inscription from Thessalonica," *BASOR* 221 (1976): 123.

19. Vittorio Morabito, "The Samaritans in Sicily," in Crown and Davey, *New Samaritan Studies*, 237–55.

20. L. Michael White, "Synagogue and Society in Imperial Ostia: Archaeological and Epigraphic Evidence," in *Judaism and Christianity in First Century Rome* (ed. Karl P. Donfried and Peter Richardson; Grand Rapids: Eerdmans, 1998), 64; and "Syn-

relief), there is no evidence of specific Samaritan use of the building. This lack of specificity illustrates a problem frequently encountered in Samaritan studies: it is often difficult to establish a distinction between Samaritans and Samarians—that is, inhabitants of the province of Samaria, regardless of their religious affiliation. Caution is required in evaluating the archaeological and inscriptional remains recovered from throughout the Mediterranean world, for it is frequently impossible to distinguish between Jews and Samaritans. Some who are called Samaritans are really undistinguishable Samarians and some who are called Jews may well be Samaritans.

Summary of the Evidence from Inscriptions

With more or less clarity, we can establish that there were Samaritan communities in cities throughout the Roman and Greek world, including Puteoli, Rome, Athens, Thasos, Rhodes and Piraeus. Samaritans were likely residents in Constantinople, where their great leader, Babba Rabbah, spent the last years of his life. Since Greek was the primary language in all of these places, it is quite possible that some Samaritans, at least, had access to their Pentateuch in Greek translation or paraphrase. But as yet, there is no conclusive evidence confirming this possibility.

It is possible that the Samaritans, throughout their diaspora, simply made use of a modified LXX. As mentioned in chapter 5 and earlier in this chapter, there is evidence of a close relationship between the SP and the LXX and a likely mutual influence between the two. It seems likely that the Samaritans made use of the LXX in the same way that they used the Jewish Targums. It is also possible that the text of the LXX, Targums, and any translated SP was quite fluid in both the Jewish and Samaritan communities, with influence traveling in both directions. Alan Crown has described several ways in which the SP and Codex Alexandrinus (of the LXX) show evidence of a relationship.[21] For example, a stylistic influence is evident in the way the scribes of both Alexandrinus and the SP weave letters into the similar crosshatch patterns used to decorate the ends of biblical books. Crown believes it is more likely that the SP copied the idea from Codex Alexandrinus.[22] On the other hand, colemetry, the intentional

agogue and Society in Imperial Ostia: Archaeological and Epigraphic Evidence," *HTR* 90 (1997): 23–58.

21. Crown, *Samaritan Scribes and Manuscripts*, 3, 12, 56, 57, 510, 511, 515.

22. Ibid., 509

use of columns as punctuation, decoration, and text marking, appears in the earlier Samaritan Hebrew manuscripts and was likely borrowed by the scribes of Alexandrinus from the SP.[23] In the MT, the columnization of the verse structure of Gen 10:26 follows no evident logic, and often breaks descriptive sense of the text, suggesting that the structure may have come from the SP, where both text and structure make sense.[24] While it is admittedly difficult to attribute cause and effect or the direction of the influence, some relationship is evidenced by these scribal characteristics that appear in both the SP and the LXX.

Structural characteristics are a better indication of relationship between the SP and the LXX than textual content, which tends to be more ambiguous. The two texts have been collated by various scholars. Kyung-Rae Kim cited 964 cases where the SP and the LXX agree against the reading in the MT, but only 493 of those instances are unquestionably the same reading. Even in those 493 cases, the similarity could reflect harmonizations arrived at independently in the two traditions, and there are many harmonizations in the LXX that are not shared by the SP. Kim concluded that the text alone cannot prove a relationship between the two traditions.[25]

Origen's *Samareitikon*

Origen (184/185–253/254 C.E.), perhaps most famous for popularizing the allegorical method of biblical interpretation, was a significant Christian theologian and biblical scholar who lived and worked in Alexandria. One of his works was the *Hexapla*, in which he published six different versions of the Pentateuch, the only section of the Hebrew Bible that the Samaritans accept, in parallel columns. In his comments, Origen makes reference to about fifty alternate readings in Greek that he attributes to the *Samareitikon*, presumably the Bible of the Samaritans. The *Samareitikon* is one of the lasting enigmas within Samaritan studies. Origen's comments suggest that he knew and had access to a unique Samaritan Greek translation. If this is true, it remains to be discovered whether that translation was based on the Hebrew version or an Aramaic Targum.

At the end of the nineteenth century, Samuel Kohn suggested that Origen had a complete Samaritan Targum in Greek translated for Samari-

23. Ibid., 510.

24. Ibid., 508.

25. Kim, "*Studies in the Relationship*," 1–2, 7–8.

tans of the diaspora.[26] Many felt that the few differences between the proposed *Samareitikon* and the LXX could be easily resolved without assuming two separate documents. In 1911, Paul Glaue and Alfred Rahlfs published parchment fragments of Deut 24:1–29:26 that refer to Mount Gerizim rather than the Masoretic reading of Mount Ebal.[27] Reinhard Pummer has warned against using a "Mount Gerizim" reading in Deut 27:4 as the criteria for identifying a unique Samaritan reading, and a stronger argument is emerging that suggests that the *Samareitikon* represents a version of a distinctive Samaritan Hebrew text composed by translators familiar with the LXX.[28]

Latin and Arabic Versions

Surprisingly, there is no evidence for the existence of the SP in Latin. At the same time, it should also be noted that the Old Latin version of Deut 27:4 reads, in agreement with the SP, that after crossing the Jordan the Israelites are to set up stones on Mount Gerizim rather than on Mount Ebal.

Islam swept over the Near East in the seventh century (634 C.E. for Palestine and Syria; 643 for Egypt), and Arabic quickly replaced Latin as the lingua franca. For Jews, Christians, and Samaritans the relatively sudden ascendency of Arabic and Islamic culture presented an urgent need to translate their Scripture into Arabic. It is not surprising that the Jews and Samaritans were both moving toward Arabic translations of their Scriptures in the same time period and were likely conscious of each other's efforts. Best known is the tenth-century work of Rabbi Saadia ben Joseph ("Gaon," his official title as head of an Academy), who was born circa 882 in Fayyum, Egypt (hence sometimes called "al-Fayyumi") and died in 942 in Baghdad. His translation, called *al-Tafsir* ("interpretation") used the Arabic language written in Hebrew characters. There is some drama in identifying the scribe

26. Samuel Kohn, "Samareitikon und Septuaginta," *MGWJ* 38 (1894): 1–7, 49–67.

27. Paul Glaue and Alfred Rahlfs, *Fragmente einer griechischen Übersetzung des samaritanischen Pentateuchs* (Berlin: Weidmann, 1911), 167–200, 433 pl. 1.

28. See Crown, *Samaritan Scribes and Manuscripts*, 412; and the fragment published by Charlesworth, "What Is a Variant?" Also see Jacob Wasserstein, "Samareitikon," in *A Companion to Samaritan Studies* (ed. Alan Crown et al.; Tübingen: Mohr Siebeck, 1993), 210. Nodet (*Search for the Origins of Judaism*, 184) writes, "In contrast, it must be concluded that the *Samaritikon* of Origen is not another Greek translation, but really a Hebrew text, although it does not exactly coincided with the present editions of SP, but rather with an Aramaic version."

of the first Arabic SP. One was used in Nablus in the eleventh and twelfth centuries and in Egypt somewhere near the end of the thirteenth century. Four Arabic SPs survive from that time period, dating to 1204, 1215, 1219/1220 and 1226/1227 C.E. respectively. Some Samaritans believe that the earliest manuscript was produced by Abu al Hasan as Suri. This attribution cannot be proved, and it was strongly rejected by the scribe of Arabe 6 in the Bibliothèque Nationale. That scribe (Abu Said?) sees his own work, Arabe 6, as a major correction to an earlier, corrupt version. He denies that this earlier version was produced by Abu al Hasan because it includes terms that a Samaritan obviously would not use.[29] The scribe attributes the earlier version to the Jew al-Fayyumi (Saadia ben Joseph). A colophon repeated in many subsequent copies of Abu Said's text reflects the drama:

> He Who Follows the Example of Righteousness Finds the Way. The servant who needs the mercy of the sublime God, Abu Sa'id b. abi al-Husain b. abi Sa'id, may God grant him a good fate at the end of his days, said: verily [when] I saw the translation of the Noble Book which is in the hands of our fellow worshipers, may God increase their number and restore them, which is corrupt both in form and meaning, because of their ignorance of the Arabic language, whilst some of them claim it is a translation of the eminent scholar Abu al-Hasan as-Suri, may God have mercy upon him; but it is not his and it is not permissible to utter it, especially the rendering [in Samaritan characters] "When thou goest to return to Egypt" [Exod 4:21–22], which is within the realm of pure heresy, and so are other similar passages. It is rather a translation of al-Fayyumi, a scholar of the Jews, may God requite him. Accordingly, the advantage of the matter forced me to translate this copy, the previous ones and what I might write later, God willing, in a proper and eloquent language. Thus, copies will be produced out of it in order to refute the falsehood which al-Fayyumi relied on and those who are satisfied with his translation, and for the purpose of having a good reputation with God and with the adherents of righteousness amongst His people, if the sublime God so wills.
>
> The marginal notes attached to the version are all mine[30] and are the result of my diligence. Most of them are unusual notions, praise be to God for His benefaction. In a case of finding a trustworthy authority in the science of the Arabic language, then he can ask anyone to write in

29. Crown, *Samaritan Scribes and Manuscripts*, 495, 502.

30. Here Sa'id clarifies that he is making his own notes, not simply using the notations of Saadia Gaon.

> his own handwriting as I did. If that writer has followed the given conditions, at that moment God will be the Judge between both of us, and God is the best protector.

The Arabic Pentateuchs used by the Samaritans can be clustered into five basic groups.[31] The Samaritans initially took over the Saadia Gaon Arabic Pentateuch discussed above. It is easily identifiable because, remarkably, it follows the Jewish readings when they differ from the Samaritan text. This Pentateuch is the Arabic text in the triglot manuscript BL Or. 7562 housed in the British Library. Incidentally, the Samaritan Hebrew in this triglot manuscript is possibly the oldest identifiable distinctive Samaritan text type. This Samaritan Hebrew text is likely from the time of the fourth century Samaritan renaissance under Baba Rabbah. The Arabic text is from the tenth century. A second Arabic type text emerged when, according to Samaritan oral tradition, Abu'l Hassan, alarmed that the Samaritans were using an Arabic translation of an obviously Jewish text, set out to amend the situation. Some, including the Abu Sa'id described in the extended colophon above, doubt that the author of this text is Abu'l Hassan. It is represented by manuscript Shechem 6 and is generally known as the Old Arabic translation of the SP. It likely dates from the eleventh century and was composed in Syria. It is usually found with the Arabic written in Samaritan characters, in columns parallel with the Samaritan Hebrew text. In the thirteenth century, Abu Sa'id, unconvinced that the Old Arabic text was not another version of Saadia Gaon's *Tafsir*, set about to create a third type of Arabic SP designed to function as an improvement in several ways. Abu Sa'id purged the text of distinctively Jewish idioms and ideas, improved the quality of the Arabic, and added appropriate Samaritan notes to replace the notes composed by Saadia Gaon.

Beside these three main Arabic versions of the SP, two other minor Arabic Pentateuchs are used by Samaritans. In addition, there are Arabic SPs that are simply various combinations of the three main Arabic SP versions, and there is a version that is essentially a slight modification of Christian Arabic translations now in use.

Eventually, Arabic translations of the SP made their way to Europe. Nicholas Peiresc had a hand in the acquisition of most of the SPs that arrived in France. In 1628, the year that Morin published his first remarks

---

31. These groups form the basic outline of Hasheeb Shehadeh's "The Arabic Translation of the Samaritan Pentateuch" (Ph.D. diss., Hebrew University, 1977).

on the SP, Peiresc was in Damascus, where he acquired two more SPs, one of which (von Gall's C) contained an anomalous leaf in both Hebrew and Arabic. The other (von Gall's M) was a genuine triglot incorporating Aramaic, Arabic, and Hebrew. These were presented to Cardinal Barbarini and promptly took their place in the sectarian squabbling that dominated European understanding of the SP in the seventeenth century. Peiresc took a unique interest in the Arabic SPs and sought to obtain more copies and, in doing so, to interest more scholars in the value of the texts. In 1632, Peiresc was informed that an Arabic text with chapter headings in Samaritan was on its way to Europe, and a letter from Peiresc to a friend in January of 1633 celebrates its eventual arrival.[32]

According to the colophons in at least two Arabic SPs produced in 1685, each was copied from a text brought to Paris from Marseille in 1684. Each manuscript bears a note from the respective scribes, Schelema ibn Jakob for CW 10262 (at Michigan State University) and Yuhanna ibn Girgis ibn Qatta for Arabe 3 (in the Bibliothèque Nationale). Also included in each are copies of notes from their textual model. These notes make clear that both were copied from a text bearing a colophon, now preserved in each copy, witnessing that the model was brought to Paris by Capuchin "rabbis" in 1684. This model manuscript does not appear in any catalogue, but if it was in Paris in 1684, the individual who copied it must also have been in Paris. Without additional information, we are left with the curious choice of either a Parisian Samaritan scribe or an elusive explanation complicated by the fact that one of the 1685 copied manuscripts found its way back to Palestine at the turn of the century. J. P. Rothschild assumes that Yuhanna worked in Paris and produced a number of manuscripts.[33] Yuhanna says he made three copies of Arabe 6, a Samaritan Targum belonging to Peiresc, in 1681. One of these manuscripts, the Rouen BM 1477 (now identified as Arabe 7), was probably copied from the same model. Among other works, Yuhanna had previously copied Arabe 116 (1677), a Melkite calendar, and Arabe 3137 (1680), and later copied Arabe 3 (1685). This prolific production in Paris begs the question, for whom?

Were there Samaritans living in Europe in the seventeenth century? The SP came to Europe during the heyday of theories about "the lost tribes

32. Philippe Tamizey De Larroque, *Lettres de Peiresc aux frères Dupuy, Janvier 1629–Decembre 1633* (Paris: Imprimerie Nationale, 1890), 409–10.

33. Jean-Pierre Rothschild, *Catalogue des manuscrits samaritains* (Paris: Bibliothèque Nationale, 1985), 15.

of Israel" migrating to Europe in general and England in particular. The Anglo-Israelite theory aided the resettlement of Jews in England during the seventeenth century. Strictly speaking, Jews (descendants of the tribe of Judah) would not literally be included among the "lost" ten northern tribes, but this subtlety apparently did not register with the adherents of the theory. Samaritans living in Palestine heard of the "lost tribe" theory and, knowing that they, rather than the Jews, were the descendants of the lost tribes (or at least had equal claim), took new hope in the face of a current community crisis. In 1623, the high priest of the Samaritan community in Nablus died with no appropriate heir to take the office. Hearing rumors that there were Samaritans in England, the Samaritan community was hopeful when churchman and orientalist Robert Huntington (1637–1701) visited Nablus in 1671. They questioned him extensively about Samaritans living in England and, for whatever reason, Huntington led them to believe that many "Israelites" (a term the Samaritans used for themselves) did indeed reside there. It is unclear whether Huntington misunderstood their question, or did not want to disappoint the Samaritans, or hoped he could play upon their ignorance in order to acquire artifacts. In any case, the Samaritans believed him. The next year they publically acknowledged the failure of the succession to the priesthood, and in 1675 they sent a letter to Europe praying that European Samaritans could send someone to resume their priesthood. If Yuhanna was living in Paris, it is surprising that he did not have contact with Samaritans in the Middle East. Or perhaps he did have contact, and he too encouraged the illusion that there were Samaritans in Europe.

Since the SP appeared so often in Arabic, whether in a column beside the Samaritan Hebrew or on its own, it spurred interest in the Arabic versions of the Bible as significant texts for comparison alongside of the Hebrew, Syriac, Greek, and Latin. Study of Arabic ultimately led to interpretations on the basis of cognate languages, and opened new doors of conjectural criticism, for both good and ill.[34]

In 1616, the same year that della Valle acquired the first SP brought to Europe, Thomas van Erpen (1584–1624) published an Arabic Pentateuch.[35] It was the work, according to Heinrich Hävernick (1805–1845), of an Afri-

34. Goshen-Gottstein, "Textual Criticism," 373.

35. Thomas van Erpen, *Pentateuchus Mosis, Arabice, Lugduni Batavor. ex typographia Erpeniana linguarum orientalium* (1622), 4.

can Jew living in the thirteenth century.[36] Peiresc noted this publication and was subsequently excited to find a page of Arabic text in the aforementioned SP, von Gall C, which he bought in Damascus in 1628. Presumably, later on the same trip he had the good fortune to find a complete Samaritan Arabic SP, part of the triglot manuscript, von Gall M. By 1632, the same year that Ussher was also speaking about an Arabic manuscript, Peiresc was delighted to hear that an Arabic Pentateuch was on its way from the Levant and expressed his hope that it would solve some problems in the text he had before him, presumably the triglot (von Gall M). By 1634 he had grown impatient with how little work was being done on the Arabic text (only a few pages had been studied) and urged Morinus to include the Arabic in the proposed Paris Polyglot, where it was eventually published. The presence of Arabic copies of the SP furthered textual studies using cognate languages to inform difficult Hebrew readings, a method that served as a model for the later use of Ugaritic, Akkadian, and Eblaite materials. In 1649 Peiresc sent three SPs to Morin, one of which contained the Arabic text. As far as we know, this last transaction with Morin concluded Peiresc's traffic in Arabic Bibles.

The eighteenth century marked the beginning of serious European interest in the Arabic SP, largely due to the work of Antoine Isaac, Baron Silvestre De Sacy (1758–1838), a French linguist and orientalist. His classic work on the Samaritan-Arabic Pentateuch, *Mémoire sur la version arabe des livres de Moïse à l'usage des Samaritains*, is still in print.[37] De Sacy correctly deduced that there was no Arabic SP before the tenth century and that the highly valued Barberini Triglot Arabic Pentateuch, used by Jean Morin, is a good place to begin a discussion of the Arabic Pentateuch. Most of the manuscript dates from 1227, but as De Sacy was aware, the manuscript is eclectic, and the last portion dates from centuries later. In addition to the Barberini Triglot, De Sacy commented extensively on two other Arabic Pentateuchs, Arabe 2 and 4, both from the Bodleian Library at Oxford. De Sacy was careful and detailed in his descriptions of the manuscripts but, in the larger course of SP studies, has had limited influence.

36. Ibid. See also De Larroque, *Lettres*, 383.

37. Antoine Isaac Silvestre De Sacy, *Mémoire sur la version arabe des livres de Moïse à l'usage des Samaritains et sur les manuscrits de cette version* (Paris: Duverger, 1808).

Modern Language Translations

Translation of the SP into modern languages has been slow in coming for several reasons. The subsidiary role into which the SP was cast by European biblical scholarship and the somewhat unflattering assessment made by rival scholars about the SP undoubtedly resulted in a lack of interest beyond the small circle of text critics attracted to the SP only for text critical purposes. In addition, the often marginal role in which the Samaritan community was cast produced the same consequence for the literature of the community, particularly the Samaritan Chronicles, the Samaritan Joshua, and the SP.

That overly negative assessment is changing. The Qumran scrolls have demonstrated beyond doubt that the SP and its predecessors were major participants in the Second Temple scriptural tradition. The writers of the New Testament and, more broadly, the early Christian community of Judea and Samaria were influenced by and in dialogue with the Samaritan community and its literature. Modern interest in the SP is growing, and growing beyond the limited circle of text critics. The appendix of this book describes recent publications of the SP, societies dedicated to Samaritan studies, efforts to digitize and make freely available significant manuscripts of the SP, and the first English translation of the SP. After nearly four hundred years of access to the scholarly biblical community, the SP is coming into its own.

Postscript: A Reintroduction

Given the resurgence in SP studies and the great amount of work yet to be done, a conclusion seems premature and inappropriate here. Rather, a look forward seems the best way to end this book.

In recent years, the Samaritan community has expanded, growing numerically and becoming much more visible to an international community. The Samaritan population has grown from fewer than two hundred to more than six hundred. Extensive building has been done on Mount Gerizim, and the community has essentially moved there from neighborhoods closer to Tel Aviv. An enhanced sense of communal identity has led members of the Samaritan community to envision new roles for themselves and Mount Gerizim. Among the more ambitious is the establishment of a peace center on Mount Gerizim. This effort, even if local in design and somewhat meager in scope, is a laudatory attempt to bring together conflicting elements of Israeli and Palestinian societies. Samaritans are participating in various kinds of international meetings considering various social, cultural, and religious themes. The community itself and scholarship about its culture is becoming increasingly visible. New communication technologies, including websites and blogs, are giving the Samaritan community and Samaritan studies an enhanced presence on the world stage, representing a gift benefiting both biblical scholars and the Samaritan community.

Just as the Samaritan community has become more visible in recent years, so, too, Samaritan scholarship has intensified in recent decades. While much has been accomplished, there is still much to do. As SP studies proceeds through the beginning of the twenty-first century, several emphases seem to be emerging. Foremost among these emphases are new efforts to make SP manuscripts, presently located in libraries and museums scattered around the world, available to the global scholarly community through digital images accessible on internet websites. Often the images produced can be manipulated in high resolutions that not only make plain the script but can also reveal erasures and corrections not clearly visible to the naked eye. Greater access to these manuscripts will provide the opportunity for comparative textual investigation as never before. When one considers the errors and abuses to which the SP was subjected in the history of European scholarship of the seventeenth and eighteenth centuries, contributed to by the paucity of manuscript evidence and fed by religious rivalry, we can only imagine what discoveries are in store as a result of greater manuscript accessibility!

The exploration of comparative textual investigation has also been reinvigorated, sometimes enhanced by computer assisted comparisons and statistical studies, and certainly motivated in part by the wealth of material made available from the full publication of the Qumran scrolls. As a result, the SP and its predecessors are assuming their rightful place in the textual history of the late Second Temple period, helping to fill out our understanding of textual pluriformity and ancient scribal practices in this formative period of scriptural text tradition. The support role earlier played by the SP in predominantly MT and LXX textual investigations is fast fading as changes in fundamental text-critical paradigms have begun to move the SP center stage.

As the SP assumes its proper role in the constellation of textual studies at the turn of the eras, the influence of the SP and its adherents is also being noticed in New Testament studies. What was previously considered to be evidence of the LXX in New Testament literature must now be reassessed in a much more nuanced fashion, understanding the fluidity of the textual tradition and the vibrant interplay between exegesis and composition evident in scribal practices during the first two centuries C.E. Research into the hitherto elusive *Samariteikon* will undoubtedly result in additional and perhaps surprising understandings of the text traditions used in the New Testament. The Samaritan influence on, and use of the SP by, the early Christian community remains a largely unexplored yet promising field of research.

Finally, scholarly attention is being drawn to the importance of oral tradition in the development and preservation of the SP. Efforts to reflect that oral tradition in printed versions of the SP are now present, and will almost certainly improve, perhaps providing useful insight into additional trajectories of Second Temple textual transmission. Performance criticism, a developing discipline focused largely on the texts of the MT and the New Testament, will certainly benefit by the preserved Samaritan oral tradition.

At the beginning of the twentieth century a leading SP scholar characterized the SP as esoteric, of limited interest only to a small group of textual scholars. Perhaps now, a new judgment can be rendered. The SP is a living textual tradition, sacred to an ancient yet vibrant religious community, and a vital component of the text history resulting in the Hebrew Bible and New Testament. In the years to come, we may discover that the SP has an irrefutable contribution to make to our understanding of the history and literature of the Second Temple period and of the early Christian community and its literature.

For Further Reference: Modern Tools and Translations

Readers interested in further examination of the SP will find a number of tools to assist in research. This appendix describes some of the more important tools and resources available for examination of the SP.

August Freiherr von Gall produced a five-volume critical edition of the SP in 1918, *Der Hebräische Pentateuch der Samaritaner.* Despite its limitations, it remains the standard critical edition of the SP.[1] This text is an eclectic reconstruction incorporating many but not all of the manuscripts available at the beginning of the twentieth century. The text is accompanied by a critical apparatus listing variant readings. Von Gall's SP has been criticized for an uneven reconstruction that often favors readings identical to the MT. Nevertheless, the repeated reprinting of von Gall's work attests to the continued usefulness of this critical edition and the current lack of more comprehensive critical editions.

Between 1961–1965, Avraham and Ratson Sadaqa published *Jewish and Samaritan Version of the Pentateuch.*[2] The text is a parallel version, with the pointed MT on the right side of the page and the unpointed SP on the left. According to the editors, "an old Samaritan manuscript from the eleventh century" is used to represent the SP in Genesis through Numbers, while the Abisha Scroll is used for Deuteronomy. Large bold print is used to identify variations in words and phrases in both parallel versions. Ellipses signify material that is missing in one of the versions but present in the other. This publication is hard to find. Although it arguably pro-

1. A much more modest presentation was prepared by William Scott Watson (*Samaritan Pentateuch Manuscripts: Two First-Hand Accounts* [Analecta Gorgiana 79; Piscataway, N.J.: Gorgias, 2008]).

2. Avraham Sadaqa and Ratson Sadaqa, eds., *Jewish and Samaritan Version of the Pentateuch* (Tel Aviv: Reuven Mas, 1961–1965).

vided the model for later publications, it has in many important ways been replaced by more recent parallel versions.

One of the most important developments facilitating the scholarly investigation of the SP occurred in 1985, with the formation of the Société d'Études Samaritaines, an international organization of scholars formed for the investigation of the origin, history, literature, religion, and culture of the Samaritan community. The society, with approximately 70 members, sponsors international congresses for the delivery and discussion of papers on a variety of topics relevant to the Samaritans and their literature. Several important volumes of papers presented at the occasional congresses of the society have greatly contributed to the modern investigation of the SP.

Abraham Tal released *The Samaritan Pentateuch: Edited according to MS 6 (C) of the Shekem Synagogue* in 1994.[3] MS 6 (C), a manuscript produced in 1204 C.E. and now housed in the Shechem Synagogue, is used as the representative text for the SP. This presentation of the SP is not an eclectic reconstruction, as with von Gall, and so filled a gap in SP studies by presenting a single respected text. Text missing from MS 6 (C) is replaced by bracketed text.

In 2010, Tal improved on his 1994 publication and partnered with Moshe Florentin to produce *The Pentateuch: The Samaritan Version and the Masoretic Version*, which seeks chiefly to identify differences between the SP and the MT. The SP and MT are presented on facing pages, the differences between the two parallel versions indicated by gray background, blank spacing, and omission signs. The SP is again represented by MS 6 (C), and the MT appears to be taken from the Leningrad Codex, although the editors do not identify it.[4] An extensive introduction provides a taxonomy and description of the SP "changes" (perhaps better seen as differences), with examples.[5] As noted by Tov in his 2011 review, Tal and Florentin's description of the variations between the SP and the MT as "intentional/unintentional" is problematic and assumes the priority of the proto-MT. At the same time, Tal and Florentin achieved a major advance by representing the oral tradition of the Samaritans in an extensive appendix. The reading tradition of the Samaritans is at times at odds with the

3. Abraham Tal, ed., *The Samaritan Pentateuch: Edited according to MS 6(C) of the Shekem Synagogue* (Tel Aviv: Tel Aviv University Press, 1994).

4. See Tov, review of Tal and Florentin, 386–87.

5. Tal and Florentin, *Pentateuch*, 25.

consonantal SP and should not be ignored, as Tal and Florentin remind the reader in the introduction.[6] Although aware of the pre-Samaritan group from Qumran, Tal and Florentin do not incorporate this group of texts into their comparisons or textual notes. This decision reflects their conclusion that the SP, especially in its oral rendition, was fixed in the Middle Ages.[7]

Ze'ev Ben-Hayyim has been called the "master of Samaritan studies" and "the greatest scholar of Samaritan studies in our times" for his work on Samaritan linguistics.[8] Of his many publications, perhaps the most significant for SP studies is *The Literary and Oral Tradition of Hebrew and Aramaic among the Samaritans*.[9] Volume 5 of this series, translated into English under the title *A Grammar of Samaritan Hebrew*, remains the standard Samaritan grammar in English. In the English preface to the original Hebrew edition, Ben-Hayyim indicates that the description given in the grammar is based upon what he "heard and learned," indicating that the oral tradition of the Samaritans is also considered.[10]

In 2008, Mark Shoulson published a parallel version of the Jewish and Samaritan texts of the Torah entitled *The Torah: Jewish and Samaritan Versions Compared*.[11] A computerized transcription of the Leningrad Codex is used to represent the MT, and a transcription of the Shekhem Synagogue MS 6 (C) published by Abraham Tal in 1994 represents the SP on the opposing page. The MT is pointed while the SP is not. Variations between the two texts are noted, with minor variations appearing in boldface type slightly larger than the ordinary text and major variations appearing in even larger boldface type. Material not appearing in one or the other texts, usually not in the MT, is signified by ellipses.

The Chamberlain-Warren collection of Samaritan Manuscripts and Artifacts, housed in the Special Collections of the Michigan State University, has become the subject of a project to produce digital images of manuscripts for use by various "stakeholder communities." The project, under the direction of Jim Ridolfo, William Hart-Davidson, and Michael McLeod, began in 2007 and has enjoyed the financial support of the U.S.

6. Ibid., 45–46.

7. Ibid., 23.

8. Tov, review of Tal and Florentin, 391; Tsedaka, "Different Pronunciations," 217.

9. Ben-Hayyim, *Literary and Oral Tradition*.

10. Ben-Hayyim, *A Grammar of Samaritan Hebrew*, xvii.

11. Shoulson, *Torah*.

National Endowment for the Humanities Office of Digital Humanities.[12] By producing digital, online images of the Samaritan Chamberlain-Warren Collection, the directors of the project are intent on serving a diverse group of interested individuals, including scholars whose interests are academic and investigative, as well as the Samaritan community itself. Accessibility to the collection seems to be the chief goal of the project, and if successful it will certainly assist comparative SP studies, and will perhaps serve as a model for similar initiatives involving additional collections of manuscripts scattered in libraries and museums around the globe.

The Oxford Reference Online is a massive reference tool that continually updates bibliography. It includes a section entitled "Samaritans/Samaria." The most extensive print copy of a bibliography on the Samaritans was initiated by Alan Crown and entitled *A Bibliography of the Samaritans*. The bibliography is now in its third edition.[13]

Benjamin Tsedaka and Sharon Sullivan released a parallel English translation of the SP and MT in 2012, *The Israelite Version of the Torah: First English Translation Compared with the Masoretic Version*.[14] Like other parallel versions, a translation of the SP and the MT appear on opposing columns. Differences between the two are signified by text in bold print and capital letters. When text is missing in one or the other versions, the missing sections are represented by ellipses. The translation of the SP represents aspects of the Samaritan oral tradition in the transliteration of personal names (including the Divine Name) that often appears unfamiliar or awkward to the English reader. Occasional marginal notes provide short commentary on the SP text or information about Samaritan religion and ritual. An introductory article by James Charlesworth prefaces the English translation.

---

12. Jim Ridolfo et al., "Archive 2.0: Imagining the Michigan State University Israelite Samaritan Scroll Collection as the Foundation for a Thriving Social Network," *The Journal of Community Informatics*; online: http://ci-journal.net/index.php/ciej/article/view/754/757.

13. Alan Crown and Reinhard Pummer, eds., *A Bibliography of the Samaritans* (3rd ed.; Lanham, Md.: Scarecrow, 2005).

14. Benyamin Tsedaka and Sharon Sullivan, *The Israelite Version of the Torah: First English Translation Compared with the Masoretic Version* (Grand Rapids: Eerdmans, forthcoming).

Works Cited

Albertz, Rainer. *Religionsgeschichte Israels in alttestamentlicher Zeit*. GAT 8. Göttingen: Vandenhoeck & Ruprecht, 1992.

Albrektson, Bertil. "Reflections on the Emergence of a Standard Text of the Hebrew Bible." Pages 49–65 in *Congress Volume: Göttingen 1977*. Edited by J. A. Emerton. VTSup 29. Leiden: Brill, 1978.

———. "Masoretic or Mixed: On Choosing a Textual Basis for Translation of the Hebrew Bible." *Textus* 23 (2007): 33–49.

Albright, William F. "New Light on Early Recensions of the Hebrew Bible." *BASOR* 140 (1955): 27–33.

Albright, William F., and C. S. Mann. "Stephen's Samaritan Background." Pages 285–300 in Johannes Munck, *The Acts of the Apostles*. AB 31; Garden City, N.Y.: Doubleday, 1967.

Anderson, Robert T. "Clustering Samaritan Hebrew Pentateuchal Manuscripts." Pages 57–66 in *Études samaritaines: Pentateuque et targum, exégèse et philology, chroniques*. Edited by Jean-Pierre Rothschild and Guy Dominique Sixdenier. Louvain: Peeters, 1988.

———. "The Elusive Samaritan Temple." *BA* 54 (1991): 104–7.

———. "Hebrew Sources of Stephen's Speech." Pages 205–15 in *Uncovering Ancient Stones: Essays in Memory of H. Neil Richardson*. Edited by Lewis M. Hopfe. Winona Lake, Ind.: Eisenbrauns, 1994.

———. *Studies in Samaritan Manuscripts and Artifacts: The Chamberlain-Warren Collection*. Cambridge: American Schools of Oriental Research, 1978.

Anderson, Robert, and Terry Giles. *The Keepers: An Introduction to the History and Culture of the Samaritans*. Peabody, Mass.: Hendrickson, 2002.

———. *Tradition Kept: The Literature of the Samaritans*. Peabody, Mass.: Hendrickson, 2005.

Barton, John. "The Significance of a Fixed Canon of the Hebrew Bible," Pages 67–83 in vol. 1.1 of *Hebrew Bible/Old Testament: The History of Its Interpretation*. Edited by Magne Saebø. Göttingen: Vandenhoeck & Ruprecht, 1996.

Becking, Bob. "Do the Earliest Samaritan Inscriptions Already Indicate a Parting of the Ways?" Pages 213–22 in *Judah and the Judeans in the Fourth Century B.C.E.* Edited by Oded Lipschits, Gary Knoppers, and Rainer Albertz. Winona Lake, Ind.: Eisenbrauns, 2007.

Beckwith, Roger. *The Old Testament Canon of the New Testament Church.* Grand Rapids: Eerdmans, 1985.

Beentjes, Pancratius. "Israel's Earlier History as Presented in the Book of Chronicles" Pages 57–75 in *Deuterocanonical and Cognate Literature Yearbook 2006: History and Identity: How Israel's Later Authors Viewed Its Earlier History.* Edited by Nuria Calduch-Benages and Jan Liesen. Berlin: de Gruyter, 2006.

Bellos, David. *Is That a Fish in Your Ear?* New York: Faber & Faber, 2011.

Ben-Hayyim, Ze'ev. *A Grammar of Samaritan Hebrew.* Jerusalem: Hebrew University Magnes Press, 2000.

———. *The Literary and Oral Tradition of Hebrew and Aramaic among the Samaritans.* 5 vols. Jerusalem: Hebrew University Magnes Press, 1957–77.

———. "The Tenth Commandment in the Samaritan Pentateuch," Pages 487–91 in *New Samaritan Studies of the Sociétè d'Études Samaritans III and IV: Essays in Honour of G. D. Sixdenier.* Edited by Alan Crown and Lucy Davey. Studies in Judaica 5. Sydney: Mandelbaum, 1995.

Ben Zvi, Ehud. *History, Literature, and Theology in the Book of Chronicles.* London: Equinox, 2006.

———. "Who Knew What? The Construction of the Monarchic Past in Chronicles and Implications for the Intellectual Setting of Chronicles." Pages 349–60 in *Judah and the Judeans in the Fourth Century B.C.E.* Edited by Oded Lipschits, Gary Knoppers, and Rainer Albertz. Winona Lake, Ind.: Eisenbrauns, 2007.

Binder, Donald D. "Delos." Cited 21 October 2011. Online: http://www.pohick.org/sts/delos.html.

Blenkinsopp, Joseph. "The Development of Jewish Sectarianism from Nehemiah to the Hasidim." Pages 385–404 in *Judah and the Judeans in the Fourth Century B.C.E.* Edited by Oded Lipschits, Gary Knoppers, and Rainer Albertz. Winona Lake, Ind.: Eisenbrauns, 2007.

Blumenkranz, Bernard. *Die Judenpredigt Augustins: Ein Beitrag zur Geschichte der Jüdisch-Christlichen Beziehungen in den ersten Jahrhunderten.* Basel: Brepols, 1946.

Boates, Arnold. *Vindiciae Veritate Hebraicae Contra J.Morinum et L. Capellum.* Paris: 1653.

Bowley, James, and John Reeves. "Rethinking the Concept of 'Bible': Some Theses and Proposals," *Hen* 25 (2003): 3–18.

Bowman, John. *Samaritan Documents Relating to Their History, Religion, and Life.* POTTS 2. Pittsburgh: Pickwick, 1977.

———. *The Samaritan Problem: Studies in the Relationship of Samaritanism, Judaism, and Early Christianity.* Translated by A. Johnson Jr. Pittsburgh: Pickwick, 1975.

———. "Samaritan Studies I: The Fourth Gospel and the Samaritans." *BJRL* 40 (1958): 298–308.

Bright, John. *A History of Israel.* 3rd ed. Philadelphia: Westminster, 1981.

Brooke, George. "The Rewritten Law, Prophets, and Psalms: Issues for Understanding the Text of the Bible." Pages in 31–40 in *The Bible as Book: The Hebrew Bible and the Judaean Desert Discoveries.* Edited by Edward Herbert and Emanuel Tov. London: British Library, 2002.

Bruneau, Phillipe. "Les Israelites de Delos et la Juiverie delienne." *BCH* 106 (1982): 465–504.

Buchanan, George W. "The Samaritan Origin of the Gospel of John." Pages 149–175 in *Religions in Antiquity: Essays in Memory of Erwin Ramsdell Goodenough*. Edited by Jacob Neusner. Leiden: Brill, 1968.

Buxtorf, Johannes. *Tiberias, sive Commentarius Masoreticus*. Basil: Rauracorum, 1620.

Carlson, Stephen C. *Gospel Hoax: Morton Smith's Invention of Secret Mark*. Waco, Tex.: Baylor University Press, 2005.

Chancey, Mark A. *Greco-Roman Culture and the Galilee of Jesus*. SNTSMS 134. Cambridge: Cambridge University Press, 2009.

———. *The Myth of Gentile Galilee*. Cambridge: Cambridge University Press, 2002.

Charlesworth, James. "What Is a Variant? Announcing a Dead Sea Scrolls Fragment of Deuteronomy." Cited 14 Feb 2011. Online: www.IJCO.org/?categoryId=46960.

Chiesa, Bruno. "Textual History and Textual Criticism of the Hebrew Old Testament." Pages 1:257–72 in *The Madrid Qumran Congress: Proceedings of the International Congress on the Dead Sea Scrolls, Madrid 18–21 March, 1991*. 2 vols. Edited by Julio Trebolle Barrera and Luis Vegas Montaner. Leiden: Brill, 1992.

Coggins, Richard J. *Samaritans and Jews: The Origins of Samaritanism Reconsidered*. Oxford: Basil Blackwell, 1975.

Cohen, Shaye, J. D. *Josephus in Galilee and Rome: His Vita and Development as a Historian*. Leiden: Brill, 1979.

Collins, John. *An Introduction to the Hebrew Bible*. Minneapolis: Fortress, 2004.

Coogan , Michael. *The Old Testament: A Historical and Literary Introduction to the Hebrew Scriptures*. New York: Oxford University Press, 2006.

Crane, Oliver Trumbull, trans. *The Samaritan Chronicle or Book of Joshua, the Son of Nun, Translated from the Arabic with Notes*. New York: John B. Alden, 1890.

Crawford, Sidnie White. "4QDeut^{n}." Pages 127–40 in *Deuteronomy, Joshua, Judges, Kings*. Vol. 9 of *Qumran Cave 4*. Edited by Eugene Ulrich, Frank Moore Cross, Sidnie White Crawford, Julie Ann Duncan, Patrick Skehan, Emanuel Tov, and Julio Trebolle Barrera. DSD 14; Oxford: Clarendon Press, 1995.

———. *Rewriting Scripture in Second Temple Times*. Grand Rapids: Eerdmans, 2008.

———. "The 'Rewritten' Bible at Qumran: A Look at Three Texts." Pages 1–8 in *Eretz-Israel*. Archaeological, Historical, and Geographical Studies 26. Edited by Baruch Levine, Philip King, Joseph Naveh, and Ephraim Stern. Jerusalem: Israel Exploration Society, 1999.

———. "The Rewritten Bible at Qumran: A Look at Three Texts." Pages 131–47 in *Scripture and the Scrolls*. Vol. 1 of *The Bible and the Dead Sea Scrolls*. Edited by James Charlesworth. Waco, Tex.: Baylor University Press, 2006.

Cross, Frank Moore. "4QExod-Levf." Pages 133–44 in *Qumran Cave 4.VII: Genesis to Numbers*. Edited by Eugene Ulrich. DJD 12. Oxford: Clarendon, 1994.

———. "Aspects of Samaritan and Jewish History in the Late Persian and Hellenistic Times." *HTR* 59 (1966): 201–11.

———. "The Biblical Scrolls from Qumran and the Canonical Text." Pages 67–75 in *Scripture and the Scrolls*. Vol. 1 of *The Bible and the Dead Sea Scrolls*. Edited by James Charlesworth. Waco, Tex.: Baylor University Press, 2006.

———. "The Contribution of the Qumran Discoveries to the Study of the Biblical Text." Pages 278–92 in *Qumran and the History of the Biblical Text*. Edited by Frank Moore Cross and Shemaryahu Talmon. Cambridge: Harvard University Press, 1975.

———. *From Epic to Canon: History and Literature in Ancient Israel.* Baltimore: Johns Hopkins University Press, 1998.

———. "The History of the Biblical Text in Light of Discoveries in the Judean Desert." Pages 177–95 in *Qumran and the History of the Biblical Text*. Edited by Frank Moore Cross and Shemaryahu Talmon. Cambridge: Harvard University Press, 1975.

Crossan, John Dominic. "Parable and Example in the Teaching of Jesus." *NTS* 18 (1971–72): 285–307.

Crown, Alan David. "The Abisha Scroll of the Samaritans." *BJRL* 58 (1975): 36–65.

———. "Qumran or the Samaritans: Which Has the Closer Relationship to Early Christianity?" Pages 221–28 in *Proceedings of the Tenth World Congress of Jewish Studies.* Jerusalem: World Union of Jewish Studies, 1990.

———. "Redating the Schism between the Judeans and the Samaritans," *JQR* 82 (1991): 17–50.

———, ed. *The Samaritans*. Tübingen: Mohr Siebeck, 1989.

———. "Samaritan Scribal Habits with Reference to the Masorah and the Dead Sea Scrolls." Pages 159–77 in *Emanuel: Studies in Hebrew Bible, Septuagint, and Dead Sea Scrolls in Honor of Emanuel Tov.* Edited by Shalom Paul, Robert Kraft, Lawrence A. Schiffman, and Weston Fields. VTSup 94. Leiden: Brill, 2003.

———. *Samaritan Scribes and Manuscripts*. TSAJ 80. Tübingen: Mohr Siebeck, 2001.

———. "Studies in Samaritan Scribal Practices and Manuscript History: The Rate of Writing Samaritan Manuscripts and Scribal Output." *BJRL* 66 (1983–1984): 97–123.

Alan Crown and Reinhard Pummer, eds. *A Bibliography of the Samaritans.* 3rd ed. Lanham, Md.: Scarecrow, 2005.

Crown, Alan, and Lucy Davey, eds. *New Samaritan Studies of the Sociétè d'Études Samaritans III and IV: Essays in Honour of G. D. Sixdenier*. Studies in Judaica 5. Sydney: Mandelbaum, 1995.

Crown, Alan, Reinhard Pummer, and Abraham Tal, eds. *A Companion to Samaritan Studies.* Tübingen: Mohr Siebeck, 1993.

Davies, Phillip. *Scribes and Schools: The Canonization of the Hebrew Scriptures.* Louisville: Westminster John Knox, 1998.

De Larroque, Philippe Tamizey, ed. *Lettres de Peiresc aux frères Dupuy, Janvier 1629–Decembre 1633*. Paris: Imprimerie Nationale, 1890.

De Sacy, Antoine Isaac Silvestre. *Mémoire sur la version arabe des livres de Moïse à l'usage des Samaritains et sur les manuscrits de cette version*. Paris: E. Duverger, 1808.

De Troyer, Kristin. "When Did the Pentateuch Come into Existence?" Pages 269–86 in *Die Septuaginta—Texte, Kontexte, Lebenswelten.* Edited by Martin Karrer and Wolfgang Kraus. WUNT 219. Tübingen: Mohr Siebeck, 2008.

Dexinger, Ferdinand. "Samaritan Origins and the Qumran Texts." In *Methods of Investigation of the Dead Sea Scrolls and the Khirbet Qumran Site: Present Realities and Future Prospects*. Edited by Michael Wise, Norman Golb, John Collins, and Dennis Pardee. ANYAS 722. New York: New York Academy of Sciences, 1994.

Dibdin, Thomas. *The Reminiscences of Thomas Dibdin*. London: H. Colburn, 1827.

Doresse, Jean. *The Secret Books of the Egyptian Gnostics: An Introduction to the Gnostic Coptic Manuscripts at Chenoboskian*. London: Hollis & Carter, 1960.

Duncan, Julie Ann. "4QDeut^{j}." Pages 75–91 in *Qumran Cave 4.IX: Deuteronomy, Joshua, Judges, Kings*. Edited by Eugene Ulrich, Frank Moore Cross, Sidnie White Crawford, Julie Ann Duncan, Patrick Skehan, Emanuel Tov, and Julio Trebolle Barrera. DJD 14. Oxford: Clarendon, 1995.

Eccles, Robert S. "Hellenistic Patterns in the Epistle to the Hebrews." Pages 207–26 in *Religions in Antiquity*. Edited by Jacob Neusner. Leiden: Brill, 2001.

Egger, Rita. "Josephus Flavius and the Samaritans." Pages 109–14 in *Proceedings of the First International Congress of the Sociétè d'Études Samaritaines*. Edited by Abraham Tal and Moshe Florentin. Tel Aviv: Chaim Rosenberg School for Jewish Studies, 1991.

Elledge, Casey. "Rewriting the Sacred: Some Problems of Textual Authority in Light of the Rewritten Scriptures from Qumran." Pages 87–103 in *Jewish and Christian Scriptures: The Function of "Canonical" and "Non-canonical" Religious Texts*. Edited by James Charlesworth and Lee M. McDonald. London: T&T Clark, 2010.

Erpen, Thomas van. *Pentateuchus Mosis, Arabice, Lugduni Batavor. ex typographia Erpeniana linguarum orientalium* (1622).

Eshel, Esther. "4QDeut^{n}: A Text That Has Undergone Harmonistic Editing." *HUCA* 62 (1991): 117–54.

Eshel, Esther, and Hanan Eshel. "Dating the Samaritan Pentateuch's Compilation in Light of the Qumran Biblical Scrolls." Pages 215–40 in *Emanuel: Studies in Hebrew Bible, Septuagint, and Dead Sea Scrolls in Honor of Emanuel Tov*. Edited by Shalom M. Paul, Robert Kraft, Lawrence A. Schiffman, and Weston W. Fields. VTSup 94. Leiden: Brill, 2003.

Eshel, Hanan. "The Samaritan Temple at Mount Gerizim and Historical Research." *Beit Mikra* 39 (1994): 141–55.

Feldman, Louis H. *Studies in Hellenistic Judaism*. Leiden: Brill, 1996.

Feldman, Louis H., and Gohei Hata, eds. *Josephus, the Bible, and History*. Detroit: Wayne State University Press, 1989.

———, eds. *Josephus, Judaism, and Christianity*. Leiden: Brill, 1987.

Fossum, Jarl. "Sects and Movements." Pages 293–389 in *The Samaritans*. Edited by Alan D. Crown. Tübingen: Mohr Siebeck, 1989.

———. "Social and Institutional Conditions for Early Jewish and Christian Interpretation of the Hebrew Bible with Special Regard to Religious Groups and Sects." Pages 239–55 in vol. 1.1 of *Hebrew Bible/Old Testament: The History of Its Interpretation*. Edited by Magne Saebø. 2 vols. Göttingen: Vandenhoeck & Ruprecht, 1996–2008.

Freed, Edwin. "Samaritan Influence in the Gospel of John." *CBQ* 30 (1968): 580–87.

Frykholm, Amy. "Caught in a Revolution: Tripoli Priest Sedky Daoud Hamdy." *The Christian Century* 128:22 (November 1, 2011): 10–11.

Gall, August Freiherr von. *Der Hebräische Pentateuch der Samaritaner.* Giessen: Töpelmann, 1914–1918. Repr., Berlin: de Gruyter, 2011.

Gaster, Moses. *The Samaritans, Their History, Doctrines, and Literature.* London: Oxford University Press, 1925.

Geiger, Abraham. "Einleitung in die biblischen Schriften 11: Der samaritanische Pentateuch." Pages 54–67 in vol. 4 of *Abraham Geiger's Nachgelassene Schriften.* 5 vols. Edited by Ludwig Giger. Berlin: Gerschel, 1877.

Gesenius, H. F. W. *De Pentateuchi Samaritani Origine, Indole et Auctoritate: Commentatio Philologico-Critica.* Halle: Rengerianae, 1815.

Giles, Terry. "The Chamberlain-Warren Samaritan Inscription CW 2472." *JBL* 114 (1995): 111–16.

Giles, Terry, and William J. Doan. *Twice Used Songs: Performance Criticism of the Songs of Ancient Israel.* Peabody, Mass.: Hendrickson, 2009.

Glaue, Paul, and Alfred Rahlfs. *Fragmente einer griechischen Übersetzung des samaritanischen Pentateuchs.* Berlin: Weidmann, 1911.

Goedendorp, Pieter F. "If You Are the Standing One, I Also Will Worship You." Pages 61–78 in *Proceedings of the First International Congress of the Sociêtê d'Etudes Samaritaines.* Edited by Abraham Tal and Moshe Florentin. Tel Aviv: Chaim Rosenberg School for Jewish Studies, 1991.

Goshen-Gottstein, Moshe H. "The Textual Criticism of the Old Testament: Rise, Decline, and Rebirth." *JBL* 102 (1983): 365–99.

Grabbe, Lester. "'Many Nations Will Be Joined to YHWH in That Day': The Question of YHWH Outside Judah." Pages 175–87 in *Religious Diversity in Ancient Israel and Judah.* Edited by Francesca Stavrakopoulou and John Barton. London: T&T Clark, 2010.

———. "Pinholes or Pinheads in the Camera Obscura? The Task of Writing a History of Persian Period Yahud." Pages 157–82 in *Recenti tendenze nella ricostruzione della storia antica d'Israele: convegno internazionale; Rome, 6–7 marzo 2003.* Rome: Accademia nazionale dei Lincei, 2005.

Grant, Robert. *Gnosticism and Early Christianity.* New York: Columbia University Press, 1959.

Greenberg, Moshe. "The Stabilization of the Hebrew Bible, Reviewed in the Light of the Biblical Materials from the Judean Desert." *JAOS* 76 (1956): 157–67.

Haacker, Klaus. "Samaritan, Samaria." *NIDNTT* 3:449–67.

Haelewyck, Jean-Claude. "Les origins du Judaisme. A propos de l'essai de E. Nodet." *RTL* 23 (1992): 472–81.

Haenchen. Ernst. *The Act of the Apostles: A Commentary.* Philadelphia: Westminster, 1971.

Hall, Robert G. "The *Ascension of Isaiah*: Community, Situation, Date, and Place in Early Christianity." *JBL* 109 (1990): 289–303.

Hammer, Heinrich. *Traktat vom Samaritanermessias: Studien zur Frage der Existenz und Abstammung Jesu.* Bonn: Carl Georgi, 1913.

Haran, Menachem. "The Song of the Precepts of Aaron ben Manir: A Samaritan Hymn for the Day of Atonement on the 613 Precepts as Listed by Maimonides" [Hebrew]. *Proceedings of the Israel Academy of Sciences and Humanities* 5.7 (1974): 1–36.

Harris, Steven. *Understanding the Bible*. Mountain View, Calif.: Mayfield, 2000.

Hassencamp, Johann Matthaeus. *Der entdeckte wahre Ursprung der alten Bibelübersetzungs*. Minden: Koerber, 1775.

Hendel, Ronald. "The Text of the Torah after Qumran: Prospects and Retrospects." Pages 8–11 in *The Dead Sea Scrolls Fifty Years after Their Discovery (1947–1997)*. Edited by Lawrence A. Schiffman, Emanuel Tov, James VanderKam, and Galen Marquis. Jerusalem: Israel Exploration Society, 2000.

Hiebert, Robert, ed. *"Translation Is Required": The Septuagint in Retrospect and Prospect*. SBLSCS 56. Atlanta: Society of Biblical Literature, 2010.

Hjelm, Ingrid. *Jerusalem's Rise to Sovereignty: Zion and Gerizim in Competition*. JSOTSup 404. London: T&T Clark, 2004.

———. "Mount Gerizim and Samaritans in Recent Research." Pages 25–41 in *Samaritans: Past and Present*. Edited by Menachem Mor and Friedrich Reiterer in collaboration with Waltraud Winkler. Studia Samaritana 5. Berlin: de Gruyter, 2010.

———. "Samaria, Samaritans, and the Composition of the Hebrew Bible." Pages 91–103 in *Samaritans: Past and Present*. Edited by Menachem Mor and Friedrich Reiterer in collaboration with Waltraud Winkler. Studia Samaritana 5. Berlin: de Gruyter, 2010.

———. *The Samaritans and Early Judaism: A Literary Analysis*. JSOTSup 303. Sheffield: Sheffield Academic Press, 2000.

———. "Samaritans: History and Tradition in Relationship to Jews, Christians, and Muslims: Problems in Writing a Monograph." Pages 173–84 in *Samaria, Samarians, Samaritans: Studies on Bible, History, and Linguistics*. Edited by József Zsengellér. Berlin: de Gruyter, 2011.

Horst, Pieter van der. *De Samaritanen: Geschiedenis en godsdienst van een vergeten groepering*. Serie Wegwijs. Kampen: Kok, 2004.

———. *Japheth in the Tents of Shem: Studies on Jewish Hellenism in Antiquity*. Leuven: Peeters, 2002.

Hottengerus, Johannes Henricus. *Excertationes Anti-Morinionae de Pentateucho Samaritans*. Zurich: Johannes Jacobi Bodmeri, 1644.

Houbigant, Charles François. *Biblia Hebrica cum notis criticis et versione Latina ad notas criticas facta: accedunt libri graeci, qui Deutero-Canonici vocantur, in tres classes distribute*. 4 vols. Lutetiae-Parisiorum: Apud A. C. Briasson & L. Durand, 1753.

Isser, Stanley J. *The Dositheans: A Samaritan Sect in Late Antiquity*. SJLA 17. Leiden: Brill, 1976.

Jastram, Nathan. "4QNum[b]." Pages 205–67 in *Qumran Cave 4.VII: Genesis to Numbers*. Edited by Eugene Ulrich, Frank Moore Cross, James Davila, Nathan Jastram, Judith Sanderson, Emanuel Tov, and John Strugnell. DJD 12. Oxford: Clarendon, 1994.

———. "Text of 4QNum^{b}." Pages 177–98 in *The Madrid Qumran Congress: Proceedings of the International Congress on the Dead Sea Scrolls, Madrid 18–21 March, 1991*. Edited by Julio Trebolle Barrera and Luis Vegas Montaner. Leiden: Brill, 1992.

Kahle, Paul. *The Cairo Geniza*. Schweich Lectures, 1941. London: Milford, 1947.

———. "Untersuchungun zur Geschichte des Pentateuchtextes." *TSK* 88 (1915): 399–439.

Kalimi, Isaac. *The Reshaping of Ancient Israelite History in Chronicles*. Winona Lake, Ind.: Eisenbrauns, 2005.

Kartveit, Magnar. "Josephus on the Samaritans—His *Tendenz* and Purpose." Pages 109–20 in *Samaria, Samarians, Samaritans: Studies on Bible, History, and Linguistics*. Edited by József Zsengellér. Berlin: de Gruyter, 2011.

———. "The Major Expansions in the Samaritan Pentateuch: The Evidence from the 4Q Texts." Pages 117–24 in *Proceedings of the Fifth International Congress of the Sociétè d'Études Samaritaines, Helsinki, August 1–4*, 2000. Edited by Haseeb Shehadeh and Habib Tawa with the collaboration of Reinhard Pummer. Paris: Paul Geuthner, 2005.

———. *The Origin of the Samaritans*. VTSup 128; Leiden: Brill, 2009.

Kasher, Rimon. "The Palestinian Targums to Genesis 4:8: A New Approach to an Old Controversy." Pages 33–43 in *Biblical Interpretation in Judaism and Christianity*. Edited by Isaac Kalimi and Peter J. Haas. London: T&T Clark, 2006.

Kim, Kyung-Rae. "Studies in the Relationship between the Samaritan Pentateuch and the Septuagint." Ph.D. diss. Hebrew University, 1994.

Kippenberg, Hans Gerhard. *Garizim und Synagoge: Traditionsgeschichtliche Untersuchungen zur samaritanischen Religion der aramaischen Periode*. Berlin: de Gruyter, 1971.

Kirk, Alan, and Tom Thatcher. *Memory, Tradition and Text: Uses of the Past in Early Christianity*. Atlanta: Society of Biblical Literature, 2005.

Knoppers, Gary. "Cutheans or Children of Jacob?" Pages 223–39 in *Reflection and Refraction: Studies in Biblical Historiography in Honour of A. Graeme Auld*. Edited by Robert Rezetko, Timothy Lim, and W. Brian Aucker. Leiden: Brill, 2007.

———. "Did Jacob Become Judah? The Configuration of Israel's Restoration in Deutero-Isaiah." Pages 39–67 in *Samaria, Samarians, Samaritans: Studies on Bible, History, and Linguistics*. Edited by József Zsengellér. Berlin: de Gruyter, 2011.

———. "Mount Gerizim and Mount Zion: A Study in the Early History of the Samaritans and Jews." CSBS *Bulletin* 64 (2004): 5–32.

———. "Nehemiah and Sanballat: The Enemy Without or Within?" Pages 305–31 in *Judah and the Judeans in the Fourth Century B.C.E.* Edited by Oded Lipschits, Gary Knoppers, and Rainer Albertz. Winona Lake, Ind.: Eisenbrauns, 2007.

———. "Revisiting the Samarian Question in the Persian Period." Pages 265–89 in *Judah and the Judeans in the Persian Period*. Edited by Oded Lipschits and Manfred Oeming. Winona Lake, Ind.: Eisenbrauns, 2006.

Knox, E. A. "The Samaritans and the Epistle to the Hebrews." *Churchman* 41 (1927): 184–93.

Kohn, Samuel. "Samareitikon und Septuaginta." *MGWJ* 38 (1894): 1–7, 49–67.

Kraabel, A. Thomas. "New Evidence of the Samaritan Diaspora Has Been Found on Delos." *BA* 47 (1984): 44–46.

Lagarde, Paul de. *Anmerkungen zur Griechischen Übersetzung: Der Proverbien*. Leipzig: Brockhaus, 1863.

Lange, Armin. "The Status of the Biblical Texts in the Qumran Corpus and the Canonical Process." Pages 21–30 in *The Bible as Book: The Hebrew Bible and the Judaean Desert Discoveries*. Edited by Edward D. Herbert and Emanuel Tov. London: British Library, 2002.

———. "'They Confirmed the Reading' (y. Ta'an. 4.68a): The Textual Standardization of Jewish Scriptures in the Second Temple Period." Pages 29–80 in *From Qumran to Aleppo: A Discussion with Emanuel Tov about the Textual History of Jewish Scriptures in Honor of His 65th Birthday*. Edited by Armin Lange, Matthias Wiegold, and József Zsengellér. FRLANT 230. Göttingen: Vandenhoeck & Ruprecht, 2009.

Le Déaut, Roger. *The Message of the New Testament and the Aramaic Targum*. Rome: Biblical Institute Press, 1982.

Levinson, Bernard. *Legal Revision and Religious Renewal in Ancient Israel*. Cambridge: Cambridge University Press, 2008.

———. "Textual Criticism, Assyriology, and the History of Interpretation: Deuteronomy 13:7a as a Test Case in Method." *JBL* 120 (2001): 211–43.

Lifshitz, B., and J. Schiby. "Une synagogue samaritaine à Thessalonique." *RB* 75 (1968): 368–78.

Lim, Timothy. "The Qumran Scrolls, Multilingualism, and Biblical Interpretation." Pages 57–73 in *Religion in the Dead Sea Scrolls*. Edited by John Collins and Robert Kugler. Grand Rapids: Eerdmans, 2000.

Lincke, Karl F. *Samaria und seine Propheten*. Tübingen: Mohr Siebeck, 1903.

Loewenstamm Ayala. "Samaritan Pentateuch." *EncJud* 15:753–54.

Lowy, Simeon. *The Principles of Samaritan Bible Exegesis*. StPB 28. Leiden: Brill, 1977.

Macchi, Jean-Daniel. *Les Samaritains: Histoire d'une légende: Israël et la province de Samarie*. MdB 30. Geneva: Labor et Fides, 1994.

MacDonald, John, ed. and trans. *Memar Marqah: The Teaching of Marqah*. Berlin: Töpelmann, 1963.

———. *The Samaritan Chronicle No. II (or: Sepher Ha-Yamim): From Joshua to Nebuchadnezzar*. BZAW 107. Berlin: de Gruyter, 1969.

Magen, Yitzhak. "The Dating of the First Phase of the Samaritan Temple on Mount Gerizim in Light of the Archaeological Evidence." Pages 157–211 in *Judah and the Judeans in the Fourth Century B.C.E.* Edited by Oded Lipschits, Gary Knoppers, and Rainer Albertz. Winona Lake, Ind.: Eisenbrauns, 2007.

———. "Mount Gerizim—A Temple City." *Qadmoniot* 33 (2000): 74–118.

———. "Mount Gerizim and the Samaritans." Pages 91–148 in *Early Christianity in Context: Monuments and Documents*. Edited by Frédéric Manns and Eugenio Alliata. SBFCM 38; Jerusalem: Franciscan Printing, 1993.

Magen, Yitzhak, Haggai Misgav, and Levana Tsfania. *The Aramaic, Hebrew, and Samaritan Inscriptions*. Vol. 1 of *Mount Gerizim Excavations*. Judea and Samaria Publications 2. Jerusalem: Israel Exploration Society, 2004.

Manson, William. *The Epistle to the Hebrews*. London: Hodder & Stoughton, 1966.

Mare, W. H. "Acts 7: Jewish or Samaritan in Character?" *WTJ* 34 (1971): 1–21.

Martin, Thomas W. "Hellenists." *ABD* 3:135–36.

Marxsen, Willi A. *Mark the Evangelist*. Nashville: Abingdon, 1969.

Matthews, Christopher R. *Philip: Apostle and Evangelist—Configurations of a Tradition*. Leiden: Brill, 2002.

Matthews, Shelly. *Perfect Martyr: The Stoning of Stephen and the Construction of Christian Identity*. Oxford: Oxford University Press, 2010.

McDonald, Lee Martin. *Forgotten Scriptures: The Selection and Rejection of Early Religious Writings*. Louisville: Westminster John Knox, 2009.

Meyers, Eric M. "Galilean Regionalism as a Factor in Historical Reconstruction." *BASOR* 221 (1976): 93–101.

Montgomery, James A. *The Samaritans, the Earliest Jewish Sect: Their History, Theology, and Literature*. Philadelphia: John C. Winston, 1907. Repr., New York: Ktav, 1968.

Mor, Menahem. "The Building of the Samaritan Temple and the Samaritan Governors—Again." Pages 89–108 in *Samaria, Samarians, Samaritans: Studies on Bible, History, and Linguistics*. Edited by József Zsengellér. Berlin: de Gruyter, 2011.

———. "Samaritan History: 1. The Persian, Hellenistic and Hamonean Period." Pages 1–18 in *The Samaritans*. Edited by Alan D. Crown. Tübingen: Mohr Siebeck, 1989.

———. "Putting the Puzzle Together: Papyri, Inscriptions, Coins, and Josephus in Relation to Samaritan History in the Persian Period." Pages 41–54 in *Proceedings of the Fifth International Congress of the Sociétè d'Études Samaritaines, Helsinki, August 1–4*, 2000. Edited by Haseeb Shehadeh and Habib Tawa with the collaboration of Reinhard Pummer. Paris: Geuthner, 2005.

Morabito, Vittorio. "The Samaritans in Sicily," Pages 237–58 in *New Samaritan Studies of the Sociétè d'Études Samaritaines III and IV: Essays in Honour of G. D. Sixdenier*. Edited by Alan Crown and Lucy Davey. Studies in Judaica 5. Sydney: Mandelbaum, 1995.

Morin, Jean. *Exercitiones Ecclesiasticae in Utrumque Samaritanorum Pentateuchum*. Paris: Antonius Vitray, 1631.

Munck, Johannes. *The Acts of the Apostles*. AB 31. Garden City, N.Y.: Doubleday, 1967.

Neusner, Jacob, ed. *Religions in Antiquity: Essays in Memory of Erwin Ramsdell Goodenough*. Leiden: Brill, 1968.

Nihan, Christophe. "The Torah between Samaria and Judah." Pages 187–223 in *The Pentateuch as Torah: New Models for Understanding Its Promulgation and Acceptance*. Edited by Gary Knoppers and Bernard Levinson. Winona Lake, Ind.: Eisenbrauns, 2007.

Nodet, Etienne. "Israelites, Samaritans, Temples Jews." Pages 121–71 in *Samaria, Samarians, Samaritans: Studies on Bible, History, and Linguistics*. Edited by József Zsengellér. Berlin: de Gruyter, 2011.

———. *A Search for the Origins of Judaism: From Joshua to the Mishnah*. Translated by Ed Crowley. JSOTSup 248. Sheffield: Sheffield Academic Press, 1997.

Noja, Serfio. "The Samareitikon." Pages 408–12 in *The Samaritans*. Edited by Alan D. Crown. Tübingen: Mohr Siebeck, 1989.

Nutt, John W. *Fragments of a Samaritan Targum: Edited from a Bodleian Ms., with an Introduction, Containing a Sketch of Samaritan History, Dogma and Literature.* London: Trübner, 1874.

Parr, Richard. *The Life of the Most Reverend Father in God, James Usher, Late Lord Arch-Bishop of Armagh, Primate and Metropolitan of All Ireland.* London: printed for Nathaniel Ranew, St. Paul's Churchyard, 1686.

Perez Castro, F. *Séfer Abiša': Edición del fragmento antiguo del rollo sagrado del pentateuco hebreo samaritaner de Nablus, estudio, transcripcion, aparato critico y facsimiles.* Textos y estudios del Seminario Filologico Cardenal Cisneros 2. Madrid: Seminario Filológico Cardenal Cisneros, 1959.

Perrin, Norman. *The New Testament: An Introduction.* New York: Harcourt Brace Jovanovich, 1974.

Pummer, Reinhard. "Samaritan Rituals and Customs." Pages in 650–90 in *The Samaritans.* Edited by Alan D. Crown. Tübingen: Mohr Siebeck, 1989.

———. "Samaritanism—A Jewish Sect or an Independent Form of Yahwism?" Pages 1–24 in *Samaritans: Past and Present.* Edited by Menachem Mor and Friedrich Reiterer in collaboration with Waltraud Winkler. Studia Samaritana 5. Berlin: de Gruyter, 2010.

———. "The Samaritans and Their Pentateuch." Pages 237–69 in *The Pentateuch as Torah: New Models for Understanding Its Promulgation and Acceptance.* Edited by Gary Knoppers and Bernard Levinson. Winona Lake, Ind.: Eisenbrauns, 2007.

Purvis, James. "The Fourth Gospel and the Samaritans." *NovT* 17 (1975): 161–98.

———. "The Paleography of the Samaritan Inscription from Thessalonica." *BASOR* 221 (1976): 123.

———. *The Samaritan Pentateuch and the Origin of the Samaritan Sect.* HSM 2. Cambridge: Harvard University Press, 1968.

———. "The Samaritans and Judaism." Pages 81–98 in *Early Judaism and Its Modern Interpreters.* Edited by Robert Kraft and George Nickelsburg. Atlanta: Scholars Press, 1986.

Quell, Gottfried, ed. *Exodus et Leviticus.* Fasc. 2 of *BHS.* Stuttgart: Deutsche Bibelgesellschaft, 1977.

Raurell, Frederic. "The Notion of History in the Hebrew Bible." Pages 1–20 in *Deuterocanonical and Cognate Literature Yearbook 2006: History and Identity: How Israel's Later Authors Viewed Its Earlier History.* Edited by Nuria Calduch-Benages and Jan Liesen. Berlin: de Gruyter, 2006.

[Ravius] Rau, Christian. *A General Grammer [sic] for the Ready Attaining of the Hebrew, Samaritan, Calde, Syriac, Arabic and Ethiopic Languages.* London: Wilson, 1650.

Richard, Earl. "Acts 7: An Investigation of the Samaritan Evidence." *CBQ* 39 (1977): 190–208.

Ridolfo, Jim, William Hart-Davidson, and Michael McLeod. "Archive 2.0: Imagining the Michigan State University Israelite Samaritan Scroll Collection as the Foundation for a Thriving Social Network." *The Journal of Community Informatics.* Online: http://ci-journal.net/index.php/ciej/article/view/754/757.

Robertson, Edward. *Catalogue of the Samaritan Manuscripts in the John Rylands Library.* 2 vols. Manchester: Manchester University Press, 1938–1962.

Robinson, James M. *The Nag Hamadi Library.* San Francisco: HarperCollins, 1990.

Rofé, Alexander. "Historico-Literary Aspects of the Qumran Biblical Scrolls." Pages 30–39 in *The Dead Sea Scrolls Fifty Years after Their Discovery (1947–1997).* Edited by Lawrence A. Schiffman, Emanuel Tov, James VanderKam, and Galen Marquis. Jerusalem: Israel Exploration Society, 2000.

Rothschild, Jean-Pierre. *Catalogue des manuscrits samaritains.* Paris: Bibliothèque Nationale, 1985.

Rothschild, Jean-Pierre, and Guy Dominque Sixdennier, eds. *Étude samaritaines Pentateuque et Targum, exégèse et philologie, chroniques.* Louvain: Peeters, 1988.

Rowley, Harold Henry. "The Samaritan Schism in Legend and History." Pages 208–22 in *Israel's Prophetic Heritage.* Edited by B. W. Anderson and W. Harrelson. New York: Harper, 1962.

Runesson, Anders, Donald D. Binder, and Birger Olsson. *The Ancient Synagogue from Its Origins to 200 C.E.* Leiden: Brill, 2008.

SAC (Spiro-Albright unpublished correspondence 1964–66) in Special Collections, Michigan State University.

Sadaqa, Avraham, and Ratson Sadaqa, eds. *Jewish and Samaritan Version of the Pentateuch.* Tel Aviv: Reuven Mas, 1961–65.

Sanderson, Judith. *An Exodus Scroll from Qumran: 4QpaleoExod^{m} and the Samaritan Tradition.* Atlanta: Scholars Press, 1986.

Scharlemann, Martin Henry. *Stephen: A Singular Saint.* AnBib 34. Rome: Pontifical Biblical Institute, 1968.

Schiffman, Lawrence A. *Qumran and Jerusalem: Studies in the Dead Sea Scrolls and the History of Judaism.* Grand Rapids: Eerdmans, 2010.

———. *Reclaiming the Dead Sea Scrolls.* New York: Doubleday, 1994.

Schmid, Konrad. "The Late Persian Formation of the Torah: Observations on Deuteronomy 34." Pages 237–51 in *Judah and the Judeans in the Fourth Century B.C.E.* Edited by Oded Lipschits, Gary Knoppers, and Rainer Albertz. Winona Lake, Ind.: Eisenbrauns, 2007.

Schorch, Stefan. "The Reading(s) of the Tora in Qumran." Pages 105–15 in *Proceedings of the Fifth International Congress of the Sociétè d'Études Samaritaines, Helsinki, August 1–4,* 2000. Edited by Haseeb Shehadeh and Habib Tawa with the collaboration of Reinhard Pummer. Paris: S. N. Librairie Orientaliste Paul Geuthner, 2005.

———. "The Samaritan Version of Deuteronomy and the Origin of Deuteronomy." Pages 23–37 in *Samaria, Samarians, Samaritans: Studies on Bible, History, and Linguistics.* Edited by József Zsengellér. Berlin: de Gruyter, 2011.

Schur, Nathan. *History of the Samaritans.* Frankfurt: Lang, 1992.

———. "The Modern Period (from 1516 A.D.)." Pages 113–34 in *The Samaritans.* Edited by Alan D. Crown; Tübingen: Mohr Siebeck, 1989.

Scobie, Charles H. H. "The Origins and Development of Samaritan Christianity." *NTS* 19 (1973): 390–414.

———.The Use of Source Material in the Speeches of Acts III and VII." *NTS* 25 (1979): 399–421.

Scroggs, Robin. "The Earliest Hellenistic Christianity." Pages 176–206 in *Religions in Antiquity*. Edited by Jacob Neusner. Leiden: Brill, 1968.

Segal, Michael. "4QReworked Pentateuch or 4QPentateuch?" Pages 391–99 in *The Dead Sea Scrolls Fifty Years after Their Discovery (1947–1997)*. Edited by Lawrence A. Schiffman, Emanuel Tov, James VanderKam, and Galen Marquis. Jerusalem: Israel Exploration Society, 2000.

———. "Between Bible and Rewritten Bible." Pages 10–28 in *Biblical Interpretation at Qumran*. Edited by Matthias Henze. Grand Rapids: Eerdmans, 2005.

Shachter, Jacob, trans. *The Babylonian Talmud: Seder. Nezikin*. 8 vols. Edited by I. Epstein. London: Soncino Press, 1935. Repr., 1987.

Shehadeh, Haseeb. "The Arabic Translation of the Samaritan Pentateuch." Ph.D. diss., Hebrew University, 1977.

Shoulson, Mark. *The Torah: Jewish and Samaritan Versions Compared*. Westport, Co. Mayo, Ireland: Evertype, 2006–2008.

Singer, Samuel Weller, ed. *The Table Talk of John Seldon*. Edinburgh: Ballantyne, 1890.

Skehan, Patrick. "Exodus in the Samaritan Recension from Qumran," *JBL* 74 (1955): 182–87.

Skehan, Patrick, Eugene Ulrich, and Judith Sanderson, eds. *Qumran Cave 4.IV: Palaeo-Hebrew and Greek Biblical Manuscripts*. DJD 9. Oxford: Clarenden, 1992.

Smith, Morton. *Palestinian Parties and Politics That Shaped the Old Testament*. New York: Columbia University Press, 1971.

———. *The Secret Gospel: The Discovery and Interpretation of the Secret Gospel according to Mark*. London: Victor Gollancz, 1974.

Stenhouse, Paul. *The Kitāb al-Tarīkh of Abū'l Fath, Translated with Notes*. Sidney: Mandelbaum Trust, 1985.

Stern, Ephraim, and Yitzhak Magen. "Archaeological Evidence for the First Stage of the Samaritan Temple on Mount Gerizim." *IEJ* 52 (2002): 49–57.

Strawn, Brent. "Authority: Textual, Traditional, or Functional? A Response to C. D. Elledge." Pages 104–12 in *Jewish and Christian Scriptures: The Function of "Canonical" and "Non-Canonical" Religious Texts*. Edited by James Charlesworth and Lee M. McDonald. London: T&T Clark, 2010.

Strugnell, John. "Quelque inscriptions samaritaines." *RB* 74 (1967): 550–80.

Sylvia, Denis D. "The Meaning and Function of Acts 7:46–50." *JBL* 106 (1987): 261–75.

Tal, Abraham. "Samaritan Literature." Pages 444–49 in *The Samaritans*. Edited by Alan D. Crown. Tübingen: Mohr Siebeck, 1989.

———. *The Samaritan Pentateuch: Edited According to MS 6 (C) of the Shekem Synagogue*. Tel Aviv: Tel Aviv University Press, 1994.

———. "Targum." Pages 226–28 in *A Companion to Samaritan Studies*. Edited by Alan Crown, Reinhard Pummer, and Abraham Tal. Tübingen: Mohr Siebeck, 1993.

Tal, Abraham, and Moshe Florentin, eds. *The Pentateuch: The Samaritan Version and the Masoretic Version*. Tel Aviv: The Haim Rubin Tel Aviv University Press, 2010.

Talmon, Shemaryahu. "The Old Testament Text." Pages 159–99 in *From the Beginnings to Jerome*. Vol. 1 of *The Cambridge History of the Bible*. 3 vols. Edited by Peter Ackroyd and Craig F. Evans. Cambridge: Cambridge University Press, 1970. Reprinted as pages 1–41 in *Qumran and the History of the Biblical Text*. Edited by Frank Moore Cross and Shemaryahu Talmon. Cambridge: Harvard University Press, 1975.

———. "The Textual Study of the Bible—A New Outlook." Pages 321–400 in *Qumran and the History of the Biblical Text*. Edited by Frank Moore Cross and Shemaryahu Talmon. Cambridge: Harvard University Press, 1975.

———. "The Transmission History of the Text of the Hebrew Bible in the Light of Biblical Manuscripts from Qumran and Other Sites in the Judean Desert." Pages 40–50 in *The Dead Sea Scrolls Fifty Years after Their Discovery (1947–1997)*. Edited by Lawrence A. Schiffman, Emanuel Tov, James VanderKam, and Galen Marquis. Jerusalem: Israel Exploration Society, 2000.

Thatcher, Tom. *Why John Wrote a Gospel: Jesus—Memory—History*. Louisville: Westminster John Knox, 2006.

Thomas, D. W. "The Textual Criticism of the Old Testament." Pages in 238–63 in *The Old Testament and Modern Study*. Edited by H. H. Rowley. Oxford: Clarendon, 1951.

Tigay, Jeffrey. "Conflation as a Redactional Technique." Pages 53–96 in *Empirical Models for Biblical Criticism*. Edited by Jeffrey Tigay. Philadelphia: University of Pennsylvania Press, 1985.

———. "An Empirical Basis for the Documentary Hypothesis." *JBL* 94 (1975): 327–42.

Toorn, Karel van der. *Scribal Culture and the Making of the Hebrew Bible*. Cambridge: Harvard University Press, 2007.

Tov, Emanuel. "4QLev^{d}." Pages 193–95 in *Qumran Cave 4.VII: Genesis to Numbers*. Edited by Eugene Ulrich, Frank Moore Cross, James Davila, Nathan Jastram, Judith Sanderson, Emanual Tov, and John Strugnell. DJD 12. Oxford: Clarendon, 1994.

———. "4QReworked Pentateuch: A Synopsis of Its Contents," *RevQ* 16 (1995): 647–53.

———. "Biblical Texts as Reworked in Some Qumran Manuscripts with Special Attention to 4QRP and 4QParaGen-Exod." Pages 111–134 in *The Community of the Renewed Covenant*. Edited by Eugene Ulrich and James VanderKam. Notre Dame: Notre Dame University Press, 1994.

———. *Hebrew Bible, Greek Bible, and Qumran: Collected Essays*. TSAJ 121; Tübingen: Mohr Siebeck, 2008.

———. "Hebrew Biblical Manuscripts from the Judaean Desert: Their Contribution to Textual Criticism." *JJS* 39 (1988): 5–37.

———. "The Many Forms of Hebrew Scripture: Reflections in Light of the LXX and 4QReworked Pentateuch." Pages 11–28 in *From Qumran to Aleppo: A Discussion with Emanuel Tov about the Textual History of Jewish Scriptures in Honor of his 65th Birthday*. Edited by Armin Lange, Matthias Weigold, and József Zsengellér. FRLANT 230. Göttingen: Vandenhoeck & Ruprecht, 2009.

———. "The Nature and Background of Harmonizations in Biblical Manuscripts." *JSOT* 31 (1985): 3–29.

———. "The Proto-Samaritan Texts and the Samaritan Pentateuch." Pages 397–407 in *The Samaritans*. Edited by Alan D. Crown. Tübingen: Mohr Siebeck, 1989.

———. Review of Abraham Tal and Moshe Florentin, *The Pentateuch: The Samaritan and Masoretic Version*. *DSD* 18 (2011): 385–91.

———. *Revised Lists of the Texts from the Judaean Desert*. Leiden: Brill, 2010.

———. "Rewritten Bible Compositions and Biblical Manuscripts, with Special Attention to the Samaritan Pentateuch," *DSD* 5 (1998): 334–54.

———. "The Status of the Masoretic Text in Modern Text Editions of the Hebrew Bible: The Relevance of Canon." Pages 234–63 in *The Canon Debate*. Edited by Lee M. McDonald and James A. Sanders. Peabody, Mass.: Hendrickson, 2002.

———. *The Texts from the Judaean Desert: Indices and an Introduction to the Discoveries in the Judaean Desert Series*. Oxford: Clarendon, 2002.

———. *Textual Criticism of the Hebrew Bible*. Minneapolis: Fortress, 1992.

Trebolle Barrera, Julio. "The Authoritative Functions of Scriptural Works at Qumran" Pages 95–110 in *The Community of the Renewed Covenant*. Edited by Eugene Ulrich and James VanderKam. Notre Dame: University of Notre Dame Press, 1994.

Trotter, Robert J. F. *Did the Samaritans of the Fourth Century Know the Epistle to the Hebrews?* LUOSMS 1. Leeds: Leeds University Oriental Society, 1961.

Tsedaka, Benyamim. "Different Pronunciations of the Same Word in the Torah Reading of the Israelite Samaritans in Comparison to Its Significant Attributes." Pages 217–22 in *Samaria, Samarians, Samaritans: Studies on Bible, History, and Linguistics*. Edited by József Zsengellér. Berlin: de Gruyter, 2011.

Tsedaka, Benyamin, and Sharon Sullivan. *The Israelite Version of the Torah: First English Translation Compared with the Masoretic Version*. Grand Rapids: Eerdmans, 2012.

Tsedaka, Israel. "Mount Gerizim and Jerusalem." Pages 21–26 in *Proceedings of the Fifth International Congress of the Sociétè d'Études Samaritaines, Helsinki, August 1–4*, 2000. Edited by Haseeb Shehadeh and Habib Tawa with the collaboration of Reinhard Pummer. Paris: Geuthner, 2005.

Tychsen, Oluf Gerhard. "Disputio historic," in *Numorum hebraeo-samaritanorum vindiciae*. Edited by Francisco Perez Bayer, J. J. Barthelemy, and Oluf Gerhard Tychsen. Valentiae Edetanorum: Montfort, 1790.

Ulrich, Eugene. "The Bible in the Making: The Scriptures at Qumran." Pages 77–93 in *The Community of the Renewed Covenant*. Edited by Eugene Ulrich and James VanderKam. Notre Dame: Notre Dame University Press, 1994.

———. "The Canonical Process, Textual Criticism, and Latter Stages in the Composition of the Bible." Pages 267–91 in *Sha'arei Talmon: Studies in the Bible, Qumran, and the Ancient Near East Presented to Shemaryahu Talmon*. Edited by Michael Fishbane and Emanuel Tov with Weston W. Fields. Winona Lake, Ind.: Eisenbrauns, 1992.

———. "The Dead Sea Scrolls and the Hebrew Scriptural Texts." Pages 77–99 in *Scripture and the Scrolls*. Vol. 1 of *The Bible and the Dead Sea Scrolls*. Edited by James Charlesworth. Waco, Tex.: Baylor University Press, 2006.

———. *The Dead Sea Scrolls and the Origins of the Bible*. Grand Rapids: Eerdmans, 1999.

———. "Pluriformity in the Biblical Text, Text Groups, and Questions of Canon." Pages 1:23–41 in *The Madrid Qumran Congress: Proceedings of the International Congress on the Dead Sea Scrolls, Madrid 18–21 March, 1991*. 2 vols. Edited by Julio Trebolle Barrera and Luis Vegas Montaner. Leiden: Brill, 1992.

———. "The Qumran Biblical Scrolls: The Scriptures of Late Second Temple Judaism." Pages 53–151 in *The Dead Sea Scrolls in Their Historical Context*. Edited by Timothy Lim. Edinburgh: T&T Clark, 2000.

———. "The Qumran Scrolls and the Biblical Text." Pages 51–59 in *The Dead Sea Scrolls Fifty Years after Their Discovery (1947–1997)*. Edited by Lawrence A. Schiffman, Emanuel Tov, James VanderKam, and Galen Marquis. Jerusalem: Israel Exploration Society, 2000.

Ulrich, Eugene, Frank Moore Cross, James Davila, Nathan Jastram, Judith Sanderson, Emanuel Tov, and John Strugnell, eds. *Qumran Cave 4.VII: Genesis to Numbers*. DJD 12. Oxford: Clarendon, 1994.

Ulrich, Eugene, Frank Moore Cross, Sidnie White Crawford, Julie Ann Duncan, Patrick Skehan, Emanuel Tov, and Julio Trebolle Barrera, eds. *Qumran Cave 4.IX: Deuteronomy, Joshua, Judges, Kings*. DJD 14. Oxford: Clarendon, 1995.

VanderKam, James, and Peter Flint. *The Meaning of the Dead Sea Scrolls. San* Francisco: HarperCollins, 2002.

VanderKam, James C., and Peter Flint. *The Meaning of the Dead Sea Scrolls: Their Significance for Understanding the Bible, Judaism, Jesus, and Christianity*. New York: T&T Clark, 2005.

Vermes, Geza. "Biblical Studies and the Dead Sea Scrolls," *JSOT* 39 (1987): 122–25.

Waltke, Bruce. "How We Got the Hebrew Bible: The Text and Canon of the Old Testament." Pages 27–50 in *The Bible at Qumran: Text, Shape, and Interpretation*. Edited by Peter Flint. Grand Rapids: Eerdmans, 2001.

———. "Prolegomena to the Samaritan Pentateuch." Ph.D. diss, Harvard University, 1965.

———. "Samaritan Pentateuch." *ABD* 5:932–40.

———. "The Samaritan Pentateuch and the Text of the Old Testament." Pages 212–39 in *New Perspectives on the Old Testament*. Edited by J. Barton Payne. Waco, Tex.: Word, 1970.

Walton, John, and Andrew Hill. *Old Testament Today*. Grand Rapids: Zondervan, 2004.

Wasserstein, Jacob. "Samareitikon." Pages 210–11 in *A Companion to Samaritan Studies*. Edited by Alan Crown. Reinhard Pummer, and Abraham Tal. Tübingen: Mohr Siebeck, 1993.

Watson, William Scott. *Samaritan Pentateuch Manuscripts: Two First-Hand Accounts*. Analecta Gorgiana 79. Piscataway, N.J.: Gorgias, 2008.

Watts, James. *Reading Law: The Rhetorical Shaping of the Pentateuch*. Biblical Seminar 59; Sheffield: Sheffield Academic Press, 1999.

Weissenberg, Hanne von. "Canon and Identity at Qumran: An Overview and Challenges for Future Research." Pages 629–40 in *Scripture in Transition: Essays on Septuagint, Hebrew Bible, and Dead Sea Scrolls in Honour of Raija Sollamo*. Edited by Anssi Voitila and Jutta Jokiranta. Leiden: Brill, 2008.

White, L. Michael. "Synagogue and Society in Imperial Ostia: Archaeological and Epigraphic Evidence." Pages 30–69 in *Judaism and Christianity in First Century Rome.* Edited by Karl P. Donfried and Peter Richardson. Grand Rapids: Eerdmans, 1998.

Wise, Michael, Martin Abegg, and Edward Cook, eds. *Dead Sea Scrolls.* San Francisco: Harper Collins, 1996.

Wright, G. Ernest. *Shechem: Biography of a Biblical City.* New York: McGraw-Hill, 1965.

Würthwein, Ernst. *Der Text des Alten Testaments.* Stuttgart: Deutsche Bibelgesellschaft, 1988.

Yamauchi, Edwin M. *Pre-Christian Gnosticism: A Survey of Proposed Evidences.* Grand Rapids: Eerdmans, 1973.

Young, Ian. Review of Hanne von Weissenberg, Juha Pakkala, and Marko Marttila, eds., *Changes in Scripture: Rewriting and Interpreting Authoritative Traditions in the Second Temple Period. RBL.* Online: http://www.bookreviews.org/pdf/8251_9022.pdf.

———. "The Stabilization of the Biblical Text in the Light of Qumran and Masada: A Challenge for Conventional Qumran Chronology?" *DSD* 9 (2002): 364–90.

Zsengellér, József. "Canon and the Samaritans." Pages 161–72 in *Canonization and Decanonization: Papers Presented to the International Conference of the Leiden Institute for the Study of Religions (LISOR), Held at Leiden, 9–10 January 1997.* Edited by H. Kippenberg and E. Lawson. SHR 82. Leiden: Brill, 1998.

———. *Gerizim as Israel: Northern Tradition of the Old Testament and the Early History of the Samaritans.* Utrechtse Theologische Reeks 38. Utrecht: Faculteit der Godgeleerdheid, 1998.

———. "Kutim or Samarites: A History of the Designation of the Samaritans." Pages 87–104 in *Proceedings of the Fifth International Congress of the Sociétè d'Études Samaritaines, Helsinki, August 1–4,* 2000. Edited by Haseeb Shehadeh and Habib Tawa with the collaboration of Reinhard Pummer. Paris: Geuthner, 2005.

———. "Origin or Originality of the Torah? The Historical and Textcritical Value of the Samaritan Pentateuch." Pages 189–202 in *From Qumran to Aleppo: A Discussion with Emanuel Tov about the Textual History of Jewish Scriptures in Honor of His 65th Birthday.* Edited by Armin Lange, Matthias Wiegold, and József Zsengellér. FRLANT 230. Göttingen: Vandenhoeck & Ruprecht, 2009.

———, ed. *Samaria, Samarians, Samaritans: Studies on Bible, History, and Linguistics.* Berlin: de Gruyter, 2011.

Ancient Sources Index

Deuterocanonical Books

Modern Authors Index

Subject Index